Careers in Dance

Practical and Strategic Guidance
From the Field

Ali Duffy, PhD, MFA

HUMAN KINETICS

Library of Congress Cataloging-in-Publication Data

Names: Duffy, Ali, 1979- author.
Title: Careers in dance : practical and strategic guidance from the field / Ali Duffy.
Description: Champaign, IL : Human Kinetics, [2021] | Includes
  bibliographical references and index.
Identifiers: LCCN 2020003392 (print) | LCCN 2020003393 (ebook) | ISBN
  9781492592723 (paperback) | ISBN 9781492592730 (epub) | ISBN
  9781492592747 (pdf)
Subjects: LCSH: Dance--Vocational guidance. | Dance--Study and teaching.
Classification: LCC GV1597 .D84 2021 (print) | LCC GV1597 (ebook) | DDC
  792.8023--dc23
LC record available at https://lccn.loc.gov/2020003392
LC ebook record available at https://lccn.loc.gov/2020003393

ISBN: 978-1-4925-9272-3 (print)

The web addresses cited in this text were current as of February 2020, unless otherwise noted.

Acquisitions Editor: Bethany J. Bentley; **Developmental Editor:** Melissa J. Zavala; **Copyeditor:** Annette Pierce; **Proofreader:** Chernow Editorial Services, Inc.; **Indexer:** Andrea J. Hepner; **Permissions Manager:** Dalene Reeder; **Graphic Designer:** Julie L. Denzer; **Cover Designer:** Keri Evans; **Cover Design Specialist:** Susan Rothermel Allen; **Photograph (cover):** Steve Clarke; **Cover Photo Model:** Katie Quinn; **Photographs (interior):** © Human Kinetics, unless otherwise noted; **Photo Asset Manager:** Jason Allen; **Senior Art Manager:** Kelly Hendren; **Printer:** Versa Press

Printed in the United States of America   10 9 8 7 6 5 4 3 2 1

The paper in this book is certified under a sustainable forestry program.

Human Kinetics
1607 N. Market Street
Champaign, IL 61820
USA

United States and International
Website: **US.HumanKinetics.com**
Email: info@hkusa.com
Phone: 1-800-747-4457
Canada
Website: **Canada.HumanKinetics.com**
Email: info@hkcanada.com   **E7887**

Tell us what you think!
Human Kinetics would love to hear what we can do to improve the customer experience. Use this QR code to take our brief survey.

I dedicate this book to my husband, Carlos, and my son, Noah. You fill my life with beauty and love. You're my favorite dancing partners.

Contents

Preface

Pursuing a career in dance requires self-awareness, organization, entrepreneurial thinking, courage, and, above all else, persistence. Finding a niche for yourself in the dance field and then working to establish a professional network, positive reputation, and expertise necessitates a commitment to learning about your strengths, challenges, uniqueness, and preferences. Although some people assume a career in dance would be unprofitable or even impossible, those who dedicate their professional lives to dance often discover unique paths that lead to fulfilling and profitable careers. The trick is knowing what you have to contribute to the field and then aligning your pursuits with your strengths.

Although the performing arts continue to be financially marginalized in the United States, they nevertheless remain innovative and make a difference in people's lives. For example, the proliferation of private dance studios and schools, increased dance instruction in public elementary through high schools (K-12), an influx of dance in pop culture, including on television and social media, and community engagement from regional nonprofit dance companies illustrate active public engagement with dance. Additionally, leadership opportunities abound in dance. Founding a dance company, organization, or business; publishing scholarly works; presenting choreography; advocating for the field; and teaching all present opportunities for leadership within an ever-changing cultural dynamic. Consider also the COVID-19 pandemic that swept the globe beginning in 2019. While the tragedy gravely impacted artists and threatened the presence of live art, dancers, choreographers, educators, writers, and advocates around the world created innovative ways to continue connecting people through dance.

This book aims to provide you with the tools necessary to develop and thrive in your dance career. Whereas some texts briefly touch on these approaches, this book focuses comprehensively on best practices, advice, and strategies for pursuing a career in dance. Because a dance career demands exhaustive physical, emotional, and mental work, it is important that you prepare for it. Successful career dancers must be ambitious and adaptable, seeking multiple opportunities at once and working toward both long- and short-term goals. This takes organizational skills, keen initiative, and, most of all, the desire to uniquely contribute to the dance field.

Many of the ways to pursue a dance career are examined in this text. As the use of technology expands, making global connections and the ability to share experiences easier and faster, influences both near and far, familiar and unfamiliar, increase the rate at which dance and the dance world change. This rapid change makes it difficult to predict how the field will progress, and many career opportunities will remain hidden until new facets of dance are developed. This sense of uncertainty is promising because it means dancers—as entrepreneurs and innovators—will invent new career paths. Taking on these roles to direct your own career takes commitment and an incredible amount of organization and prioritization. Be proactive and continue to learn and develop as a dance artist, educator, and scholar throughout your career.

This book should be used as a reference and motivational tool to help you identify your interests and abilities in the field and pursue your "best fit" positions in dance. Your interests and abilities will and should evolve and change as you develop physically, mentally, and emotionally, and you should expect that the events of your life will also shape how you participate in the dance field and what will be important to you at any given time in your career. Your career is not static. It is likely that you will change directions at some point in your career to focus on certain areas within dance that you may have less passion for now. The likelihood of experiencing a dynamic, evolving working life is one of the reasons you should return to this book throughout your career to continue reassessing your position in the field. Follow the paths that you are passionate about and those in which you have developed strengths. Don't be afraid to recalibrate.

This text includes six parts, and particular areas of the field are grouped together. Each section includes related career options that typically call for similar abilities and processes. Chapters 1 and 2 paint a portrait of dance professions in the United States, providing context about some of the social and cultural influences that affect how dance students pursue and find success in the field. Next, chapter 3 discusses career opportunities in dance education in K-12 and postsecondary educational institutions. The chapter highlights the major processes potential educators will undertake on the way to their careers, such as state teacher certification, application processes, interviewing, curriculum development, and teaching tips. Chapter 4 focuses on opportunities in dance studios and schools. Major topics covered in chapter 4 include application and interviewing processes, curriculum and class development, and classroom management. The chapter also discusses business ownership and management, including staffing, marketing, budgeting, and leadership strategies. Chapters 5 and 6 cover career opportunities in performance, choreography, and production, including in nonprofit dance companies and organizations (chapter 5) and in the commercial dance field (chapter 6). Both of these chapters discuss auditioning, branding, networking, maintaining an active training regimen, and other topics. Chapter 7 focuses on dance research, analytical writing, and journalism. Chapter 8 delves into the ins and outs of dance administration and advocacy, with particular foci on executive leadership roles in organizations, grant writing, and opportunities in federal and state governments. Chapter 9 offers ideas for pursuing a career in dance sciences, therapies, medicine, and somatic practices. Chapter 10 outlines career paths in private competition companies, within competitive high school and postsecondary institutions, and as part of American spectator sport teams. Chapters 11 and 12 make connections between dance and other disciplines, suggesting career opportunities that may be relevant based on the skills acquired in the study of dance. Interdisciplinary opportunities and those within technology, technical theater, and media are explored. The conclusion includes possibilities for continued education in graduate school programs and approaches to acclimating to life as a working professional.

This book features several unique elements that encourage you to be proactive and self-reflective in building your dance career. Profiles of successful professionals are built into each chapter. These working artists, educators, and administrators offer helpful pointers and tidbits of wisdom they have learned throughout their careers that may prove helpful on your own journey. Reflection exercises with open-ended response prompts are located at the end of each chapter to help you consider your goals, strengths, challenges, and ideas. Reflections are designed to encourage focused, self-reflexive thinking and to organize your thoughts and desires so that you will be prepared to self-direct your job-seeking and career development processes.

The possibilities for a fulfilling and lifelong career in dance abound. This book will guide you through an exploration of the field and help you pinpoint your areas of passion and strength. Committing to dance is a bold decision—one that can lead to rewarding adventures and unexpected connections and pathways. By becoming aware of all the career options available, you will approach the dance field with confidence and will be equipped to forge ahead knowing that you are fully prepared. Congratulations on taking your first steps toward your career in dance!

Acknowledgments

I owe a great deal of gratitude to the many people who have contributed to this book. Thank you to the many dance professionals featured, whose profiles will inspire young dancers to make the leap into the field. Your lives are bold and your perspectives fascinating. Thank you also to my editors, Bethany Bentley and Melissa Zavala, who invested an incredible amount of time, care, and expertise in my research and writing.

I am fortunate to have many supportive colleagues, friends, and mentors to thank for their encouragement. Thank you to my colleagues at Texas Tech University, notably Dr. Tanya Calamoneri, Genevieve Durham DeCesaro, and Dr. Dorothy Chansky, for supporting my work and inspiring me to risk and strive. A special thank you to the colleagues I write with every week in the TTU Women's Faculty Writing Program. Our mutual presence and optimism for each other are so meaningful to me. Thank you to my students, past and present, for cheering me to the finish line of my book. You confirm for me that the future of the dance field looks incredibly bright! Thank you as well to my dance family, Flatlands Dance Theatre, for reminding me that a dance career can take so many forms and that shared vision invites creativity and community.

I extend deep gratitude to the many people whose support and mentorship encouraged me and equipped me in my dance career pursuits: Charis Moses, Christine Brandt, Veronica Bradley Perry, Delia Neil, Dr. Ann Dils, BJ Sullivan, Jan Van Dyke, Dr. Jill Green, Dr. Larry Lavender, and Dr. Linda Caldwell. Thank you.

Finally, I would like to extend my gratitude to my family. Thank you to my parents, Shelton and Ritchie Duffy, who always champion me and never questioned my dream of a dance career. Thank you to my sister, Caitlin Duffy, for coming to *all* the recitals, competitions, and musicals and still loving me anyway. Thank you to my brilliant husband, Dr. Carlos Perez, for your steadfast empathy, love, and encouragement as we wrote our first books together. I loved going on this adventure alongside you. To my son, Noah, who turned three during the writing of this book, thank you for showing me what is most important. I hope I make you proud.

Chapter 1

2 x Standard

Spine 792.
8023

DUF

+ RFID Tag

he Big Picture

to free herself, dance into the wind, create a new language.
And birds fluttered around her, writing 'yes' in the sky."

Monique Duval

e a career in dance, it is important to learn how the United States workforce and to know some of your options. This chapter, therefore, paints a portrait of how dance is positioned within society and how it contributes to the U.S. economy and identifies some of its complex social and cultural dynamics. Chapter 1 also defines the major areas in the field in which jobs are available and touches on education and training options.

DANCE AS AN ECONOMIC AND CULTURAL FORCE IN THE UNITED STATES

The performing arts are critical to the economic prosperity and cultural diversity for which the United States is globally regarded. Dance holds an important role in continuing cultural traditions, marking special occasions, producing entertainment, analyzing the human condition, storytelling, and advocating for social justice and change. According to former President John F. Kennedy, "The life of the arts, far from being an interruption . . . in the life of a nation, is very close to the center of a nation's purpose and is a test of the quality of a nation's civilization" (John F. Kennedy Presidential Library and Museum n.d.). The value of art in American society cannot be overstated. The professional contributions you may make through dance continue an important tradition of the arts in the United States.

Although some people believe that a career in dance is not worth pursuing because of quantitative data that paint a bleak picture of financial support, recent statistical evidence to the contrary identifies dance as vital to the American economy. Further, the varied ways dance contributes innovation and jobs to U.S. communities demonstrate the depth of its impact.

Dr. Jill Green

Retired professor of dance, University of North Carolina at Greensboro, scholar, and master teacher of kinetic awareness somatic practice

Describe some of the greatest lessons you've learned in your dance career.
I learned that you have to believe in yourself. No one will do it for you. I learned not to sweat the small things. There are so many issues and challenges. I learned how to pick my fights. I learned how to let go of the judgments and expectations of other people in the area.

Courtesy of North Carolina at Greensboro.

What is your best advice to those hoping to pursue a career in dance?
I believe it is important to have patience and understand that there will be rejection. So many women have "imposter syndrome." They believe they are fakes and really do not belong in academe due to lack of skills or intelligence. This is not true. You belong in higher education if you managed to get a terminal degree. It helps to realize that many people struggle in higher education. Faculty are pulled in so many directions. It helps to be organized and learn how to say no. Finally, learn how to take care of yourself and find ways to have a life outside of academe. While you have to do the work to succeed, you need to take care of yourself as well.

Looking back, what are the best decisions you have made during your career?
My best decision was to get my PhD. The degree opened many doors. Somatics is often thought of as an area with no rigor. During my doctoral work, I learned how to [do a critical analysis of] somatics while also expanding its reach. I learned how to explain the benefit of somatics while also extending its definition and probing the issues. Another decision was not to let go of the joy of movement, simply because I was a scholar. My movement is much richer and more meaningful to me.

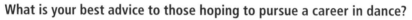

IMPACT OF DANCE ON THE U.S. ECONOMY

According to recent studies presented by the National Endowment for the Arts that detail economic impact, the arts and culture sector contributes $804.2 billion to the nation's gross domestic product, with performing arts companies and independent artists contributing nearly $39.8 billion to the economy (National Endowment for the Arts 2019, 2017). Dance/USA determined that the nonprofit dance sector, which includes professional dance companies and independent dance artists, generates more than $700 million in annual economic activity, including earned income and public and private contributions (Dance/USA 2017). Americans for the Arts reports that the arts and culture sector supports 4.1 million U.S. jobs in that sector (Americans for the Arts 2016). These findings also illustrate that the average annual growth rate of the arts in the U.S. outperforms the growth of the total U.S. economy (National Endowment for the Arts 2019), an encouraging sign for those pursuing arts careers.

How Americans Engage With the Arts

Understanding the ways Americans engage with and contribute to dance is important in considering how dance operates and develops. According to the National Endowment for the Arts Survey of Public Participation in the Arts, 22.8 million adults in the United States (7.4 percent of the population) attended a dance event in 2017 (National Endowment for the Arts 2018). This survey also estimates that 41.5 percent of the U.S. population participated in the creation of an artwork in 2017. In addition to attending shows and participating in art, many Americans receive dance education at some point in their lives, whether through public school dance programs, private dance studios, or community-based programming. According to data collected once per decade by the National Center for Education Statistics, in the 2009-2010 academic year, 12 percent of secondary schools and 4 percent of elementary schools offered instruction designated specifically for dance (National Center for Education Statistics 2012). Of secondary schools, 57 percent required some arts course work for graduation. In the postsecondary education arena, the National Dance Education Organization identified 624 college and university dance programs in 2017 and, of those, 75 programs in 38 states offered dance education curricula. The proliferation of U.S. postsecondary dance programs throughout the twentieth century sparked the need for standards of education. Therefore, the National Association of Schools of Dance was founded in 1981, and this organization facilitates accreditation and implements standard policies and practices for postsecondary dance institutions (National Association of Schools of Dance 2020).

Many families also experience dance through local, privately owned dance studios and community dance classes. Dance studios vary in training approach, genre-specific focus, and artistic and entertainment goals. For example, some studios concentrate on ballet while others focus on hip-hop. Some studios are competitive, emphasizing travel and competition, while others focus on end-of-year recitals and other community productions. Classes at dance studios are typically offered by semester or season or correspond to the academic school year. Community dance classes, by contrast, are offered for a shorter duration, for example, 10 classes during three months in the spring. These classes are usually more affordable than classes offered in a private dance studio, often require minimal or no previous experience for enrollment, and typically require a short-term commitment. Many not-for-profit companies offer classes on a regular or seasonal basis that are often connected to the mission of each organization presenting them. For example, a musical theater company's classes would likely be presented in a musical theater dance genre.

Funding Dance in the United States

Because facilitating a dance company can be costly and because concert dance is often produced by not-for-profit organizations, many dance organizations rely on federal, state, and local funding agencies to support their work. These agencies fund the development, research, production, and archival processes undertaken by dance professionals and the operations of educational and community engagement dance programming across the country. The National Endowment for the Arts (NEA), for instance, funded $3.9 million for dance programming in 2018 and have funded $281 million in dance program grants since 1966 (National Endowment for the Arts 2019). The NEA and other funders provide opportunities for people to engage with the arts and support projects that may celebrate cultural and historical legacy, innovate in interdisciplinarity, or enhance the United States' diplomatic relations through global exchange.

Dance companies and organizations rely on alternative sources of financial support as well. Corporate underwriting is highly coveted by well-established companies and is used to support large-scale projects. Recently, online crowdfunding sources such as Kickstarter, Bonfire, and Indiegogo have provided companies with relatively easy ways to raise modest amounts of money while also promoting themselves online. Individual donors are another important source of income for not-for-profit companies. Many companies offer tiered levels of incentives to individual donors and season ticket holders, such as backstage tours, invitations to special events and celebrations, show tickets, and company apparel. Other possibilities for raising money include silent or online auctions, raffles, apparel sales, and educational and artistic commissions. Another important source of income for not-for-profit companies involves in-kind donations. In-kind donations are services or goods that are donated to the company, such as pro bono attorney or accountant work, donated graphic or website design, or donated food or drink for an event.

Outlook on Arts Employment

Based on data collected from the 2019 U.S. Bureau of Economic Analysis, 5 million people were employed in the arts and culture sector in 2016. Further, while employment rates in the arts declined from 2002 to 2012, these numbers have been sharply rising since 2012 and trending steadily upward. Some experts describe the U.S. recession of 2008 as having a considerable negative impact on the arts. The 2016 National Arts Index report, however, notes that a postrecession recovery period began in 2012 and is ongoing. While this is encouraging, many labor and career experts agree that there are significantly more people interested in pursuing dance careers than there are jobs to fill (U.S. Department of Labor 2019), and competition in dance is fierce. Although the arts could certainly gain from more federal support, cultural diversity, and representation, the enthusiasm for dance and the opportunities for jobs in the field are trending positively and the outlook for expansion in the dance field is good.

Dancers and Choreographers

The not-for-profit arena provides a wonderfully rich field of possibilities for future employment. In its 2017 Snapshot of the Field, Dance/USA determined that almost 16,000 people are employed by not-for-profit dance ensembles in the United States (Dance/USA 2017). The U.S. Bureau of Labor Statistics reports that 21,200 dancers and choreographers worked in 2018, with a median wage of about $18 per hour (U.S. Department of Labor 2019). Further, it conveyed that while the rate of dance industry growth (4 percent) is slower than the national average (between 5 percent and 9 percent) for all occupations, continued interest in dance education and pop culture may indicate higher trends in future job growth (U.S. Department of Labor 2019).

Dance Educators

The job outlook for dance educators in the United States is positive. The U.S. Bureau of Labor and Statistics estimates 12 percent job growth from 2018 to 2028. The median salary in the United States for dance instructors in any kind of school (public K-12, community, or private studio) was $38,720 in 2018. This data set, it should be noted, includes part-time educators' salaries, which skews the perception of full-time educators' salaries. Further, salaries vary considerably depending on factors such as geographical location and level of prior education and experience.

Additional Areas of the Dance Industry

Other areas of the dance industry, such as dance writing and dance sciences do not appear in jobs reports, presumably because few people work in these areas. This should not deter you from seeking opportunities in these professions; they are emerging areas that expand our knowledge of dance and understanding of its purpose, which can increase its impact. Also, because some dance jobs are part time, seasonal, or temporary, data collection agencies may not be as likely to research them because the data vary widely from person to person.

DANCE AS A CULTURAL FORCE IN THE UNITED STATES

Dance is a mainstay of art, entertainment, communication, and social connection in the United States. The cultural heritage and diversity represented through dance in U.S. communities illustrate its importance to citizens' traditions and quality of life.

Dance can also enhance children's educations, providing them important information about history, relationships, body awareness, critical thinking, and health and wellness that can transfer across disciplines. Additionally, the ways dance operates in the daily lives of those who engage in it socially underscore its vitality.

Dance shapes the American identity and creates opportunities for sharing with other countries around the world as well as with fellow U.S. citizens. The companies and organizations that create and teach dance are continuing a long tradition of the arts in the United States. Whereas many careers in dance are centered on concert or entertainment-based genres, it is important to also recognize the many forms of dance that seldom make it to the stage or screen, but are nonetheless invaluable to American culture and history. For example, world dance forms such as Kathakali and dances originating in West Africa hold important value in schools and communities across the country yet are not considered mainstream. However, these areas of the dance discipline, if studied and pursued, can also lead to successful dance careers.

Because dance in the United States is diverse, it is practiced and performed in many ways. Whereas concert forms like ballet and contemporary may be practiced in a dance studio and performed on a stage, social dance forms may be practiced and performed in community centers and at weddings, parties, and in nightclubs. Breakdancing is sometimes practiced and performed on city streets and sidewalks.

Courtesy of Naomi Hill.

Dancers: Molly Roberts, Gabriella Franco, and Amiee Dixon of Flatlands Dance Theatre.

Some world dance traditions are passed down through families and apprenticeships. Some forms, such as Capoeira, are taught alone or in fusion with other genres as modes of fitness or self-protection. However, the representation of some dance forms is subsumed or misrepresented, so that their traditions and lineage are not respected. Sometimes, this is a result of cultural appropriation or ignorance of cultural lineage. Therefore, it is important to many artists, educators, and funders to widen the scope of dance that is financially supported, experienced, and seen across the country. Having knowledge of or skills in non-Western or world dance forms can help you leverage your career into different realms. For example, if you are interested in dance research, studying dance forms originating outside of the United States offers rich possibilities for cultural exchange and education.

EXPANDING NOTIONS OF A CAREER IN DANCE

When considering a career in dance, it is important to recognize and explore all of the areas in your education and experience that could lead to future opportunities. Given how quantitative data about dance jobs is collected and interpreted, it is easy to assume there are few opportunities in the field. However, with a mindset for success and willingness to keep expectations flexible, many people can build a fulfilling and long-term career in dance. By considering the ways dance intersects other disciplines and expanding the definition of "dance career," the many opportunities become clearer and more achievable.

One of the most familiar shapes a dance career can take is a career in performance. Dancers can find multiple opportunities on the concert stage as well as in various entertainment-based companies. This book will guide you through the ins and outs of these and other performance possibilities such as in musicals, on cruise ships, and in film and television. Remember, the more varied your performance experience, the more you can expand your job search to emphasize additional skills you may possess in acting, singing, filmmaking, aerial dance, and storytelling.

Choreography skills can serve you well as you approach a career in dance. Possibilities in companies and for musical productions and dance studios are all paths for pursuing a career in choreography. Additional opportunities are found in the dance competition circuit, K-12 public schools, college residencies, private couple or wedding choreography, gymnastics or ice dancing routines, and choreography for music industry artists. Artistic directors of dance companies choreograph and lead training, branding, and marketing efforts.

Dance education is often referenced for its potential to be lucrative and long term. Opportunities abound for those interested in teaching in private studios, colleges and universities, and, in some states, public K-12 schools. Competition circuits, regional and national festivals, summer intensives, community classes, and company residencies all present additional opportunities for teaching dance. You may also be interested in competition adjudication and dance curriculum design, both of which require a background in dance education.

Developing skills as a writer or researcher could be important as you navigate the field. Universities and private companies and organizations sponsor research, which contributes new knowledge to the field and expands our understanding of how dance operates. Other opportunities for research include serving as performing arts librarians, archivists, dance historians, and research assistants. Dance writing presents many opportunities as well, including performing arts journalism, company marketing, business management and strategic planning, grant writing, and website design and maintenance. Learning to write press releases, media kits, and business plans can prepare you for a variety of positions in the dance field.

Opportunities in administration and advocacy are geared toward professionals passionate about leadership and innovation. Whether you are interested in working as an artistic or executive director of a company, a production manager, a community engagement coordinator, a business owner, an advocate, or a grant writer, analytical and persuasive communication skills are a must. These positions require people who can envision possibilities, recognize and communicate the need for change, and work toward it at the organizational, local, state, or even national level.

Dance science, medicine, and therapies represent more recent additions to the possible areas of study and work in dance. In response to the need for dancer wellness, quality of life, and career longevity, these professions heal or retrain dancers' bodies. Education and training requirements differ in this area depending on which specialty you are interested in pursuing. For example, dance medicine and science specialists hold medical degrees and licenses; dance/movement therapists hold undergraduate and graduate degrees; and somatics practitioners, fitness trainers, and yoga and Pilates instructors obtain certifications in each method or practice.

While you are still deciding which career in dance is right for you, consider how specialized training in areas related to dance may offer additional job prospects and career paths. For instance, supporting the work of performers and choreographers with lighting, costume, sound, and set design could be a lucrative side job. In addition, theater and dance companies hire stage managers, house managers, ushers, videographers, and graphic designers for productions. Further, opportunities for tech-savvy dancers abound in website design, social media, blogging, filmmaking, and film editing. Now is the perfect time to learn more about areas that complement your skills in dance.

Interdisciplinary work—artistic processes, products, and collectives that include more than one discipline—provides ample opportunity to collaborate with others whose ideas excite you. Because many artistic and educational processes in dance organically invite sharing and collaboration, dance's connections to other disciplines are not as far away as they may seem. Dance smoothly intersects with theater, music, and visual art; consider also that the connections between dance and architecture, science, math, medicine, and business could offer chances to explore bridging the arts with other areas.

Now is the time to research and learn about the many professional options available as you pursue a career in dance. Once you expand your notion of what a dance career could be, your approach to your profession becomes open ended, fluid, and full of possibilities.

Trent Williams

Courtesy of Larry Rosalez.

Performer and assistant professor of dance, University of Florida

Describe your career path in dance. What led you to this career and how did you navigate through the various parts of it?

My parents placed me in gymnastics at the Houston Gymnastic Academy in Houston, Texas. This is where I took my first ballet class with Lauren Anderson. She was the first African American principal dancer in the Houston Ballet. I had a lot of other great mentors, such as Nicole Wesley, Darla Johnson, Wayne Smith, Jawole Zollar, and Liz Lerman. They all led me to my dance career. They were very loving and supportive. I believe great mentorship is very important. I can call my mentors anytime and ask them questions about different issues that I have come across throughout my dance career, such as questions about salary, budgeting as an artist, organizing a dance class, writing grant proposals, and so on.

What have been your most significant experiences as a working professional in dance?

Performing alongside Destiny's Child, 112, and Janelle Monáe among others. In 2007, I was invited to dance with Dayton Contemporary Dance Company in world-renowned works by Talley Beatty, Eleo Pomare, Donald Byrd, Rodney A. Brown, William B. McClellan Jr., Debbie Blunden-Diggs, Shonna Hickman-Matlock, and Bill T. Jones, to name a few. In addition, I am currently working on a new project with Liz Lerman and Jawole Zollar called Blood, Muscle, and Bones.

Looking back, what have been the best decisions you have made during your career?

Dancing with Dayton Contemporary Dance Company has helped me as an educator, scholar, dancer, and choreographer. Going back to get my MFA in Dance Performance and Choreography at Florida State University was amazing.

EDUCATION AND TRAINING FOR CAREERS IN DANCE

To create a successful career in dance, you must acquire very specific skills through rigorous training and education. Dance differs from other disciplines in that its training is often front-loaded—that is, it starts from a very young age. Some children begin taking dance classes at age three or four and, if professional performing is their goal, are invested in rigorous daily training by the time they reach high school. Because this book strives to present you with all of the options for a career in dance, though, it is important to remember that, depending on your areas of interest, you may not begin focused education in dance until you reach college.

Training in Private Schools and Studios

Training in privately owned dance studios is a popular way to approach early dance education, and the options to cater your training to your interests and talents can be wide-ranging, depending on your geographical location. Many young dance students start in creative dance or preballet classes as early as age three and then progress up through a predetermined curriculum. These classes often include ballet, jazz, tap, hip-hop, and lyrical, and may also include specialty technique classes, repertory class, and improvisation and choreography. Some studios even implement dance history and dance studies theory into children's studio training because these classes help to prepare them for the rigor of postsecondary dance degree programs and future careers. Finally, some studios center their curricula specifically on world dance forms such as Bhangra or Irish step dance.

Training in a private studio or school offers many benefits. These include multiple opportunities to learn choreography from experienced teachers and artists and to refine performance skills. Most dance studios produce an annual recital or series of performances to highlight the students and demonstrate what they have been learning. Recitals give students a glimpse of performing onstage in front of a live audience and offer a chance for them to develop performance skills. If performing is the goal, students should begin diversifying their educational experience by seeking classes they've never taken before and genres of dance they've never experienced, and begin training in those. Being a well-rounded dancer increases job opportunities later. Another benefit of a private studio is learning to negotiate and work with a team of fellow dancers, which is important because dance often involves face-to-face interaction and the ability to maintain professional, positive relationships.

A downside to private studio training is that it can be expensive and, for some students, cost prohibitive. Many schools offer need-based and merit-based scholarships so children can take advantage of early training no matter their family's background and financial status. Others offer work-study programs, mostly for older students, in which they can work—cleaning the studio or assisting teachers in lower-level classes—in exchange for reduced or free tuition. Finally, some not-for-profit schools and organizations offer scholarships to students through grants that cover tuition costs; these need-based scholarships sometimes limit who is eligible to apply because they are intended to support underserved or underrepresented students.

Competitions and Conventions

Many studios are competition based and include a full season of competition and convention performances and classes. Private companies who administer competitions offer regional and national events in which students from around the country can participate for entrance fees. Competition participants travel to new geographical locations, learn from a variety of teachers outside of their home studio, and can win college scholarships. Additionally, training to refine solo or group performances in a competition setting can teach dancers about responsibility, reliability, punctuality, teamwork, leadership, and preferred learning style.

Summer Intensives and Workshops

Intensives and workshops provide terrific ways to enhance dance training and are typically offered in the summer months when young dancers are not in school. These brief, concentrated experiences are designed to shake up training regimens and expose dancers to different teachers, styles, and locations. Sometimes auditions are required for acceptance into certain, competitive intensive programs, and others are open to anyone. As with studio training, summer intensives can be costly because they often require tuition, transportation, and housing.

Some summer intensive experiences offer students condensed training in a specific technical genre, such as ballet or contemporary. Other programs are geared to students who seek a diverse range of classes and can include several technical genres, choreography, improvisation, and theory. Experiences like these are offered by companies and postsecondary dance programs and may range from one to eight weeks in length. Others offer intensive training to college-level and professional dancers. The American Dance Festival (ADF) Dance Professional Workshop, for example, "offers working artists and educators the opportunity to reinvigorate their practice . . . [by] being mentored and nurtured" (American Dance Festival n.d., para 1) in weeklong summer and winter sessions that include all-day classes and admission to evening performances from companies on ADF's roster. Finally, certification programs, offered year-round, provide specialized instruction that can enhance dance training and offer a variety of career opportunities. Some of these certification programs include Countertechnique Teacher Training, Laban Movement Analysis, Pilates, yoga, and fitness trainer certification systems.

Training in Public K-12 Schools

Dance training in public schools, if properly developed and supported, can offer wonderful instruction to supplement training in a studio. While dance programs in public schools are uncommon, they are well established in a few states. Teachers in these programs typically hold undergraduate degrees in dance or a related area and hold state certifications endorsing them to teach dance in public schools. Some schools benefit from a comprehensive curriculum comprising multiple levels of dance technique and theory classes, while others offer only a few recreational classes in various genres. Still other schools facilitate dance classes connected to physical education programs and may include forms of social dance. The level of program establishment is often connected to funding available in each school.

Another popular way to gain dance experience in public K-12 schools is by joining a dance or drill team. Experience on a dance team may vary widely depending on several factors: the amount of school and district support given to the team, the qualifications of the directors or leadership, and the opportunities afforded to those on the team. For example, some teams are directed by highly qualified educators

The Benefits of Dance in Public K-12 Education

Dance in public education emerged at a time when legislation (Title IX of the Education Amendments of 1972 and the Equal Educational Opportunities Act in 1974) began to encourage coeducational athletics and, at the same time, when dance artists entering the first postsecondary dance degree programs were being encouraged to seek degrees in dance teaching (National Dance Education Organization n.d.; Bonbright 2007). While, at first, the dance discipline was relegated to the realm of physical education, by the 1990s, dance joined forces with music, theater, and visual arts disciplines to support and develop national teaching and learning standards for the arts in public education (Bonbright 2007). Now each state develops its own arts standards and its own dance teacher certification process in order to train and employ dance educators in its public schools.

Not all states include dance curricula, but the benefits of offering dance to children in schools is irrefutable. Of the multiple studies underlining the importance and value of including the arts in every child's education, a recent report compiled by the National Dance Education Organization, the National Endowment for the Arts, and Art Works offered evidence of dance's impact, specifically (National Dance Education Organization 2013). This report notes areas of impact K-12 dance education has on student achievement, teacher satisfaction, and school culture. The impacts of dance education on students include improvement of academic skills in subjects such as reading and math, neurological benefits, lower dropout rates, and overall well-being. The benefits to teachers include higher morale, increased support for integrative and innovative teaching methods, and increased connections to the world beyond the classroom. Benefits related to school culture include improved attendance rates, opportunities for inclusion and accessibility, and promotion of conflict resolution strategies.

or choreographers, while others may be student led. Some dance teams compete in regional and national competitions, while others focus on performances during athletic events and school spirit within the home school. Students pursuing a career in dance should be thoughtful and select rigorous training experiences that will push them as technicians and performers.

Deciding Whether College Is the Right Option for You

Whether or not to attend college is a personal decision and one that should be weighed carefully. Your decision regarding whether or not to train in a college setting will affect how your career will be shaped and what opportunities will be available in the immediate and distant future. Some questions to ask yourself about whether or not you should go to college immediately after high school include (1) Do I need a degree to obtain the immediate position I desire? (2) Am I connected enough to a network, business, or company to secure an immediate position in the dance field, or do I need to build my professional network first? (3) Am I able to manage the financial, personal, and academic responsibilities of being a college student? (4) Am I able to manage the financial, personal, and professional responsibilities of being a working professional? These are questions to consider before making a final decision about your next step after high school.

Other considerations about whether or not to attend college or which school to attend involve financial, academic, and personal circumstances. Many students rely on financial aid, scholarships, and part-time work to offset expenses during postsecondary schooling. Choosing a state school that is close to family or friends may be attractive because of the potential for saving money on tuition and living expenses. Your academic status and progress in high school play a part in determining which colleges will admit you. If college is your goal, either now or in the future, don't assume that your dance skill level will be the only factor important to the faculty and administrators of undergraduate and graduate dance programs. Also, when choosing a college, consider personal factors such as whether you prefer living in rural or urban environments and whether you prefer to start fresh somewhere new or to have friends or family nearby.

Training in Colleges and Universities

Many aspiring dance professionals train in colleges and universities. Dance programs offer students a wide range of specialization and effectively prepare students for careers in all areas of dance. Postsecondary dance programs offer undergraduate and graduate degrees, dance minor programs, and certificate programs. Depending on the institution in which the dance program is located and its mission, dance programs might include interdisciplinary approaches and study across curricula.

One of the most significant benefits in seeking a postsecondary dance education is the degree you receive upon graduation. A dance career takes many shapes and may involve piecing together several part-time or temporary jobs in order to make a living. Having a college degree will create opportunities for you to supplement any part-time or temporary dance work with other positions in and outside the dance industry. Further, you will be presented with more opportunities than you can imagine in a college program, and the contacts you will make in postsecondary dance programs will provide you a foundation of support upon graduation.

Performance careers tend to peak at a young age, so some dancers delay a college education until after they have finished the performance portion of their careers. Dancers who delay the college process may have early career success and have a leg up on developing professional networks; however, one downside to delaying college is that job prospects may be limited, depending on which area of the field a dancer wants to pursue. If, for example, the goal is to teach in a dance studio after high school graduation, a dancer may find that many studios require college degrees of their teaching staff.

Dance Degree Programs

Many dance programs offer both undergraduate and graduate degrees and a dance minor. Within undergraduate degree types, a bachelor of arts (BA) offers a broad range of education in the dance area. Most curricula include elements of performance, composition, history, anatomy, pedagogy, and music. The BA is a generalist degree and, for the most part, is easily combined with a second major or a minor because it requires fewer hours than other degrees in dance. By contrast, a bachelor of fine arts (BFA) requires more hours in technique, performance, and choreography because its focus is on preparing students for these areas of the field. A bachelor of science (BS) degree in dance can support dancers interested in dance sciences and therapies and includes additional course work in kinesiology, anatomy, and science.

Graduate degree programs in dance most often offer a master of arts (MA), master of fine arts (MFA), and doctor of philosophy (PhD). A master of arts degree is useful for deepening your undergraduate study for postsecondary-level jobs in dance education and can also be a stepping-stone toward doctoral study. An MFA, by contrast, is geared to artists interested in deep investigation of performance and choreography, with some emphasis on theory and scholarship as well. Finally, a PhD offers rigorous scholarly training for work in higher education and research. Most graduate degree programs require an undergraduate degree in dance or a related area and professional experience for admission. Some graduate degree programs offer students paid opportunities to serve as teaching or research assistants during their time as students. Teaching and research assistantships provide graduate students experiences that prepare them for the rigors of teaching and researching as faculty members in colleges and universities.

Understanding College and University Cultures

Attending auditions and scheduling campus visits at the schools you are considering is important. Ensure that your interests and future goals align with the mission and values of your chosen program. If an audition is required for admission into a program of interest, make sure you understand all of the audition requirements and processes. Is preregistration required? Should you bring a résumé, headshot, writing sample, or prepared solo? At the audition or visit, introduce yourself to faculty and current students so you can make a personal connection with them and ask questions about the program and university. Pay attention to the movement material you learn while auditioning because this can give you a sense of how technique classes may be taught and which genres of dance are valued at the institution. If an informational session is included in the audition or visit, do not skip this part. It can give you helpful information about the campus; what a typical day is like for dance students; and performance, scholarship, student organization, and extracurricular opportunities the program offers. Also, plan to take a campus tour, even if it is self-guided. Meet with a departmental advisor, if possible. Overall, become acquainted with the schools in which you are interested in attending and choose a school in which you feel at home and in which you will be given ample opportunity for growth and professional leverage after graduation.

Conservatory Settings

Some degree-granting institutions are run as conservatories. Conservatory settings are different from other institutions in that they prioritize training students specifically for careers in professional performance. These institutions are often located in larger metropolitan areas, so there is a good chance for students to establish connections in urban arts hubs and to pursue work without relocating upon graduating. In conservatory settings, it is expected that students will maintain technical progress, develop in their artistry, consistently perform, and, in some cases, explore the arts across disciplines. Many of these programs emphasize technique in ballet or contemporary forms, but also include genres such as hip-hop, modern, African, and jazz.

Summer Study and Intensive Programs

Many colleges and universities offer courses during the summer months, but you may wish to pursue summer study elsewhere. The benefit of going off campus during the summer is that you can expand your training and networks by branching out into a new community or institution. Two well-regarded and historic programs that gear their curricula to college students and professionals are the American Dance Festival Summer Dance Intensive and Jacob's Pillow Dance Festival, associated with the School at Jacob's Pillow.

Extracurricular Opportunities in College

One of the best ways to enhance your collegiate dance experience is to join student organizations and groups on campus. Not only will these groups create an automatic network for you, but they will also increase your marketable skills and offer opportunities for you to demonstrate leadership before graduation. Chi Tau Epsilon (XTE) is the national dance service and honors society, and many universities and colleges have established chapters you can join. Many institutions also sponsor at least one performance-based company or organization as well. Lastly, most institutions will guide you through the process of founding a new organization—a terrific chance to gain leadership skills and envision new ideas.

Collegiate dance teams represent an emerging and important component of many students' postsecondary dance education. Because the goals and purposes of dance teams differ from many collegiate dance programs, experience in these two settings will differ. Collegiate team dancers compete as athletes in regional and national competitions and provide team spirit for sport teams and entertainment for university and community events. One of the benefits of participating on a dance team is that athletic scholarships are sometimes available to team members. Other opportunities that accompany membership on a dance team include expanding your experiences with dance, meeting new people in the community and university, and learning leadership and team development skills that could support your future career.

Leadership, Research, and Community Engagement Opportunities

Many postsecondary dance programs encourage students to develop leadership skills and to become involved with scholarly or creative research and community engagement initiatives. These ideals, usually stemming from larger university or department philosophies, missions, or strategic plans, are meant to broaden the scope of students' educational experiences. For undergraduate students in particular, these educational enhancements are worth pursuing because they expand students' networks, cultivate skills that may not be comprehensively covered in degree program curricula, and provide ways to integrate learning with experiences outside the university setting.

Because studying dance requires active presence, self-motivation, and discipline, many dancers have already attained strong leadership capabilities. An education in any postsecondary dance program will likely continue to develop those skills, depending on how you approach your time as a student there. For example, in many programs, opportunities abound to serve as a leader in student organizations and on departmental committees. Even in individual classes, developing a professional rapport and work ethic with fellow students and professors helps others perceive you as a leader. Some university dance programs emphasize developing leadership skills within their degree requirements. For example, undergraduate dance majors at the University of Maryland are encouraged to take a minor in Arts Leadership (University of Michigan 2020), dance students at Western Michigan University can earn an undergraduate certificate in dance studio management (Western Michigan University 2020), and multiple programs across the country offer arts administration degrees and certifications. Other programs require students to complete an internship during their undergraduate career.

If, during your time in a postsecondary degree program, a faculty member invites you to become involved in a research project, say yes! Working with professors on a scholarly project, a work of choreography, or a production is a wonderful learning opportunity in which you will gain a sense of what it means to be a working professional and, at the same time, gain experience in research. Additionally, many universities offer funding support to students participating in research to attend or present at conferences around the country. This is a great opportunity to deepen relationships with faculty members and gain professional expertise as well.

Depending on the institution in which you study, there may be more or less emphasis on community engagement. In a nutshell, *community engagement*—sometimes called outreach—can connect the university to the community in a mutually beneficial way to meet a need in that community. Community engagement projects may involve teaching, performing, or creating. For example, some college students work with local public school students in after-school programming or integrate dance with other disciplines for not-for-profit performances. The chance to work with faculty members, fellow students, and community members on projects that extend beyond the university will bridge your student and professional work.

SUMMARY

Overall, options for a career in dance are wide ranging and continue to expand as the field does. Because of dance's growth as a discipline of study in K-12 public education and in postsecondary institutions, it continues to provide ample job opportunities in dance education. Its popularity on competition-based television shows and on social media has kept the art form relevant and widely seen. And because dance is expanding its impact in other areas, such as science, writing, and research, career prospects extend beyond the dance studio and stage. The next chapter, which highlights best practices and the qualities of successful dance professionals, asks you to go inward to develop strategies for setting long-term goals and to personalize effective approaches to your career in dance.

Reflections

YOUR DANCE DREAMS

Before thinking about the practicalities, goal setting, and planning of a career in dance, it is important to remember *why* you want to make this your career. Think about the first time the possibility of a career in dance crossed your mind. What were you doing? Who were you with in that moment? What were you dreaming? Write yourself a story of when and how you fell in love with dance and why it sparks such a passion in you. What about dance do you want to continue, amplify, or share with others? What skills could you develop through a lifelong exploration of dance? How will you benefit from a career in dance? Let yourself write freely and let this be your first step toward discovering your purpose as a dance professional.

Chapter 2

Dance as an Entrepreneurial Journey

"Wanderer, your footsteps are the road, and nothing more; wanderer, there is no road, the road is made by walking. By walking one makes the road, and upon glancing behind one sees the path that never will be trod again. Wanderer, there is no road—
Only wakes upon the sea."

Antonio Machado

As dance is an ever changing, expanding field of possibilities, comprehensive preparation for a career in dance requires a proactive, flexible approach. Chapter 1 painted a portrait of how dance is positioned within U.S. society and culture and the career and training opportunities available to you. Chapter 2 now narrows in focus to provide you with tools to position yourself within the field. Whereas the last chapter detailed specific paths you might take in dance, this chapter addresses your mindset and identifies long-term approaches to your career.

Dance is an entrepreneurial journey because it requires you to forge your own path, sometimes in completely original ways. As you learned in chapter 1, the arts, and dance in particular, usually receive little federal funding and the jobs in dance are competitive, are rarely permanent, and aren't always full time. Further, the presence and impact of dance varies by community, city, and state and are constantly in flux based on complex cultural environments and trends. This means that dance is not always well understood or respected. All of these factors equate to a field that demands your ability to think critically and creatively in building a career.

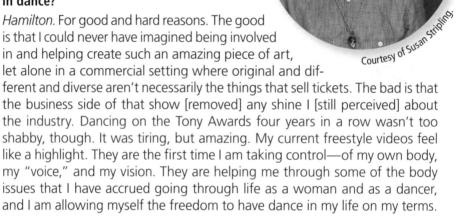

Betsy Struxness

Broadway performer (*Hamilton, Matilda, Leap of Faith, Memphis, Wicked*)

What have been your most significant experiences as a working professional in dance?

Hamilton. For good and hard reasons. The good is that I could never have imagined being involved in and helping create such an amazing piece of art, let alone in a commercial setting where original and different and diverse aren't necessarily the things that sell tickets. The bad is that the business side of that show [removed] any shine I [still perceived] about the industry. Dancing on the Tony Awards four years in a row wasn't too shabby, though. It was tiring, but amazing. My current freestyle videos feel like a highlight. They are the first time I am taking control—of my own body, my "voice," and my vision. They are helping me through some of the body issues that I have accrued going through life as a woman and as a dancer, and I am allowing myself the freedom to have dance in my life on my terms.

What is your best advice to those hoping to pursue a career in dance?

Keep your passion. Dance is hard on your body, and the business is hard on your mind and your emotions. Don't let anyone diminish your passion for it and, if you're miserable, bail. Go find a way to engage with dance that makes your heart full of joy, even if it's a different kind of path than you've found yourself on before.

Courtesy of Susan Stripling.

AN ENTREPRENEURIAL APPROACH TO DANCE CAREERS

Approaching your dance career in the spirit of entrepreneurship may help you identify and direct your energy toward pursuing the most productive professional path. Whereas the term *entrepreneurship* originates from the traditions of business, it applies to careers in dance as well. In general, an entrepreneur identifies a need and then starts a business to fill that gap. While you may indeed start a business during your dance career, it is developing the *qualities* of an entrepreneur you should focus on. Using these qualities will help you more efficiently and effectively establish a dance career.

Successful entrepreneurs, as described by experts in business, exhibit many of the same characteristics that assist them in building their companies and furthering

Describe some of the greatest lessons you've learned in your dance career.

Be 100 percent yourself at all times. You can never guess what someone wants, so always be you and then you'll never be lost. When you stop asking for attention, you'll finally get it. Desperation can be smelled and felt, and it's a complete turnoff to potential employers, creatives, and teachers. Trust yourself. When you're not happy and you're not being treated respectfully, you know it. Trust that and fix it as soon as possible. In this business, happiness and self-care are paramount. Have a side hustle that is creative. There will come a time in your career where there might be a break in consistent work. If you've been developing your own creative voice along the way, it will help you survive when you can't seem to find someone to hire you to execute their vision. Write, photograph, film, sing, take improv comedy lessons, decorate, be a stylist, start your own company. "There were months where I was auditioning for everything I could and getting callbacks, but mainly getting cut from everything. It was grueling, draining, and sometimes demeaning, but, as one learns, if you keep going, it'll pass. And it did. *Hamilton* is the most artistically fulfilling work I have ever had the privilege of making, and it spoiled me. There it was, the dream. Commercial success combined with collaboration and high art."

Looking back, what were the best decisions you made during your career?

Getting a dog. Having a pet made a more serene and loving home life in the midst of a chaotic and harsh career. With the perils and pitfalls of this path, my experiences with my dog have been such a good way to make me enjoy life. Always take vacation. And I mean vacation, not going home to wherever your folks live for a family visit. Travel. Immerse yourself in different cultures, push outside your comfort zone, and explore.

their careers. Successful entrepreneurs are most often described as creative, self-confident, knowledge-seeking, purpose-driven, risk-taking, resilient, and adaptable (Vecco 2019; Duchek 2018; Cardone 2017; Clifton and Badal 2014). Several studies have revealed other top characteristics needed to excel, specifically in the creative economy. These people are tenacious and open. They persevere and possess strong skills in networking, problem-solving, collaboration, and time management and are able to deal with uncertainty (Brandenburg, Roosen, and Veenstra 2016). Many dancers are advantaged at the outset of their careers because they already possess passion for their art form, a strong work ethic, and motivation to succeed. Depending on your specific strengths and challenges related to your degree of introversion or extroversion and overall temperament, you could benefit from approaching your career with special attention to strengthening or enhancing some of these qualities to give yourself a leg up on the competition in the field. While not every dance professional will become a leader or start a business, cultivating the characteristics described as entrepreneurial will surely bolster your position as you negotiate whatever corners of the dance job market you pursue.

ALIGNING STRENGTHS WITH CAREER GOALS

Conducting an analysis of your strengths and experiences will help align your abilities and knowledge with career paths that will lead you to success and satisfaction. This chapter includes reflection questions to consider in your strengths assessment. Throughout this book, you will find descriptions that point to the connections between your strengths and job requirements. Pay close attention to what you like about dance and what you have to offer the field before pursuing a particular area. This important stage of your education will help you market your identity and brand.

Creating a career mission statement is a good place to start narrowing your potential areas of professional pursuit and will help you identify your best qualities and aptitudes. As you continue in a career, your mission statement will shift and evolve to accommodate changes you experience. While it is unlikely that your preferences will change drastically right away, sometimes the more you learn about the field, the more drawn you will be to certain positions in it. At the end of this chapter, you will find reflection prompts to help you craft your own mission statement.

QUALITIES OF A SUCCESSFUL DANCE PROFESSIONAL

While some areas of the field require very particular attributes and interests, many jobs in dance require similar traits. For example, many career opportunities in dance require you to have done your homework, so to speak, before setting foot in an audition or interview or in starting an application process. Preparation is key in this field because, often, the person who is best prepared is the person hired. Being prepared involves researching the opportunity for which you want to aim, knowing whether you are an ideal fit for it, and knowing how to apply or audition. It also involves continuous learning and networking within that particular area of the field so that others will know who you are and what you have to offer.

Self-Motivation

The ability to self-motivate cannot be overstated. A career in dance takes diligence and hard work, and there is rarely a time in a dance career that does not demand your persistent drive toward the next goal or job or promotion. You must be prepared to keep pushing yourself throughout your career because dance requires you to be completely present—and completely you—every day.

Resilience and Self-Care

Most working dance professionals will describe the necessity for resilience and strategies for self-care during their careers because there is a lot of rejection in dance. The jobs are in high demand and the competition is intense. Find a method of calming yourself and a method of retrieving your positivity. You will need these self-care strategies as you move through your career. Bouncing back from rejection and negativity is key to preventing burnout and self-esteem issues, and each person may have a unique way to do this. Reward yourself for your courage and persistence even when you do not secure the job. Find a group of supportive friends to bolster your confidence and remind you of your amazing qualities during difficult periods and transitions in your career. Establishing a cross-training regimen for yourself and creating a list of important medical and therapy practitioners will be helpful too as you navigate your career in a physically and emotionally demanding field.

Professional Demeanor

It is a good idea to present a professional demeanor now with your teachers and your cohort of classmates. This does not mean you have to be inauthentic or overly formal. Rather, it means that people notice when you go the extra mile to say please and thank you, to anticipate the needs of others, and to be polite and friendly in potentially stressful situations. Further, knowing how to compose a professional email message, concisely articulate your talents and goals to others, and persuade others about the value of your ideas will be important as you move through any area of the field.

Networking and Self-Promotion

Your relationships with others in the field will determine a great deal of your success in it. Therefore, thriving dance professionals know how to network and self-promote. For some, these are difficult skills to master because they require significant social interaction, presence, and confidence. If you are more of an introverted person, for example, you may have to work harder to take the risk of meeting new people. Further, publicly announcing your personal accomplishments and strengths to others may feel contrived or prideful. However, you must be willing to let others know who you are and what you can offer in order for them to be willing to hire you.

Not all of the qualities of a successful dance professional are outlined here. Many depend on the area of the field in which you work. In these first two chapters, the most common qualities are highlighted, but also know that additional best practices and traits may be required of you in your career.

Courtesy of Naomi Hill.

Dancer: Kris Olson of Flatlands Dance Theatre.

ROADBLOCKS AND REROUTING

Inevitably, you will encounter unexpected roadblocks, creative ruts, and personal issues that will temporarily stand in the way of your dream career in dance. These happen to everyone. It is important in these moments of potential despair and distraction to regroup, recover, and perhaps even strategically reroute your career. Now, this process sounds easy, but rarely is it. At some point, you may have to let go of parts of your career, or you may choose to let one part subsume the others, or you may feel lost about which direction to turn, which opportunity to take. Again, don't worry, because this happens to most of us in the field at some point in our careers.

The unusual nature of a career in dance is that it does not always direct you in a straight line upward through a hierarchy of promotions and positions. Many dance professionals echo the idea that you should expect some sense of unknowingness as you figure out where you fit. You may try a few different jobs before finding the one that feels right and provides stability. You may have to piece together multiple jobs in order to make a livable wage. And you may find that what you thought you wanted does not align with what you have to offer. Nonetheless, you will discover, sometimes by struggling through difficulties, that you have a place in the dance world—you just have to find your niche and stay the course.

PLANS B, AND C, AND D

Your vision of a future career in dance (Let's call this plan A) may be detailed and include short- and long-term goals. You may have already decided the company in which you will perform, the city in which you will live, who your roommates will be, and how you will continue to train. However, everyone faces unexpected circumstances and disappointments in their careers and personal lives that may lead to a necessity for a career plan B, C, or even D.

Many dancers, throughout the course of their careers, face acute or chronic injuries. Due to the intense physical nature of this profession and the likelihood of making technical errors, overtraining, or falling into unhealthy patterns, injuries may affect your career. Further, as you age, your body will change and you will need to continually recalibrate to make the most of your body's abilities. It is well known that some dance professionals (ballet dancers, in particular) retire from performing careers at a relatively young age. Whereas dancers can expect short careers, choreographers, teachers, writers, and scholars can anticipate very long-term productivity. If you foresee that the beginning of your career will include intense physicality, you would be wise to include training in as many other complementary areas as possible, so you will have options in the future.

Certain gigs in dance don't equate to a livable wage, so you'll need to secure additional part-time or even full-time work to support your work in dance. This is not unusual and, depending on your areas of interest, you may find this situation is the rule and not the exception. Of the many opportunities in dance, few are year-round, full-time positions with benefits and the perks found in other disciplines. The constant pressure to secure the next gig can be frustrating for some and exhilarating for others, so make sure you know what kind of lifestyle you prefer before starting out in any one specialty. If you are someone who enjoys the impermanence of changeable jobs and part-time work, assess the part-time work you are qualified to undertake and that would be flexible enough to support your dance work. For example, some dance company performers work only on weekends with these companies, temporary employees in theme parks work only during certain seasons, such as in the summer months and over the holidays, and dance educators work from September to May, so they have summers open. The amount and intensity of workload in many positions in the dance field ebb and flow. Securing part-time or temporary work may help fill the financial and creative gaps in your résumé.

As you begin working to secure positions in the field, you may find that, although you have trained for years, you are simply not hirable in certain areas. This is not a reflection of a failed dance career or education! This is a chance for you to recalibrate to focus more clearly on the particular niche you can fill. While still in school, obtain skills in as many areas of the dance field as possible. This will allow for more flexibility once you have graduated and are working and have other personal priorities.

Dr. Takiyah Nur Amin

Faculty member at Wooster College, department of Africana studies

What have been your most significant experiences as a working professional in dance?

Today what excites me is that most of the dance scholars whose work I admired are all people who I have worked with or collaborated with in some way. It's also deeply exciting to me when I interact with students nationally and internationally who have read my work to shape their research and who are studying my articles and book chapters in their classes.

What is your best advice to those hoping to pursue a career in dance?

Remember that having a career in dance is so much bigger than being in any given company by whatever arbitrary age you think you should be when meeting that goal. Dance is big. It is a huge field! Many of the people who make happen the performances that students tend to prioritize are folks who you don't necessarily see on stage or on screen. Learn all you can about the field—history, production, movement vocabularies beyond those familiar to you. You truly don't ever know what skills or knowledge will matter to your career. You can make a viable life in dance if you stay focused on the many careers that shape the field.

Describe some of the greatest lessons you've learned in your dance career.

The greatest lesson I've learned is that dance is not just about demonstrating proficiency in Western and historically privileged dance forms. I knew dance long before I ever set foot in a studio or put on a leotard. I have come to value social dance and other vocabularies that show up in informal spaces. They too have rich and valuable histories and are generative and important.

A MINDSET OF LIFELONG LEARNING AND CHANGE

Many professionals in dance sustain long careers because of two very important philosophies that they share: approaching their careers with a zeal for lifelong learning and accepting that a dance career will change over time. As your interests and abilities change, so will your contributions to dance. While it may be difficult to imagine a life in dance other than the one you're currently living or working toward, make a point to envision many possibilities for the future, including possibilities that do not involve physically dancing, and possibilities outside of, but perhaps connected to, the dance field.

Embracing a mindset of continuous learning, unlearning, and relearning will support a long, evolving career. What once existed as a career option in dance may disappear as the field evolves and new options arise. Further, as you continue learning, you will uncover areas of exploration you never imagined in your early career days. Your ability to remain open-minded to new ideas will help ease any transitions you experience.

Dancers should recognize that bodily changes mixed with changes occurring in lifestyle preference, priorities, and emotional and mental states all affect a career in dance and may offer opportunities for change. Taking advantage of rather than resisting these landmark moments can lead to greater fulfillment and longevity. For example, Betsy Struxness, the Broadway performer featured in this chapter, describes how her career goals shifted after she was struck by a car on her way to a rehearsal and was left with a knee injury: "It made me realize that I need to find other ways to earn a living besides using my body . . . someday my body won't be able to keep up. Using dance as my starting point, I've recently been making freestyle dance videos with a heavy lean on fashion and women artists. Through dancing I'm finding out what I want to say and how I want to say it" (Struxness 2019).

While many dancers will not face the emergent changes involved in a sudden accident, they will face bodily changes that come with the aging process. Some of these transformations can be positive: Some dancers report being able to access greater qualitative variety, nuances, and performance presence in their dancing as they get older (Duffy 2020). However, they also report decreased flexibility and strength as they age. Considering now how you might manage the changes you'll experience in the aging process is a smart approach to addressing career longevity.

SUMMARY

Knowing yourself—your preferences, strengths, goals, and challenges—will assist you in designing a purpose for your dance career. Further, understanding how different jobs in the dance field operate—the qualities best attributed to people in these positions, the training and experience you'll need, the people working in these areas, and where these jobs are located—will support a smooth transition from school to the professional world. While you are in the process of developing your skills in different areas, prioritize time to discover the field and all that it can offer you in your career in addition to discovering all that you have to contribute to the field.

Reflections

STRENGTHS ANALYSIS

Conducting an analysis of your strengths and experiences will help align your abilities and knowledge with a career path or paths that will lead you to success and satisfaction. Start by generating a list of your strengths and areas of experience or expertise, both inside and outside of the dance discipline. Then, create separate lists of necessary strengths for each specific career path you are interested in pursuing. Notice the commonalities and discrepancies among your lists. How do these lists inform you about your preparedness and aptitude for each area?

CAREER MISSION STATEMENT

Being clear about *why* you want to pursue a career in dance is perhaps the most meaningful step you can take before forging ahead into it, and creating a career mission statement can help you identify your purpose. Answer the following questions about your career intentions and preferences:

- What kind of work do you envision yourself doing every day? In your dream scenario, do you envision yourself dancing, choreographing, writing, teaching, doing office work, reading, presenting to others?

- With whom do you imagine you want to work? Adults, children, people with disabilities, other artists, elected officials, educators, community partners?

- Where do you picture yourself going to work every day? A studio, a theater, an office, a classroom? Are you outside or inside? Are you in the United States? Are you in a particular city?

- When during each day do you find yourself most engaged and ready to work? Early morning? Late evening? Daytime (school) hours? Would you value temporary work or work that includes traveling?

Look at your responses and condense all of your needs and wants into a brief, impactful mission statement. You can use the following template as a guideline:
I (insert your name here), have a mission to work in the following area or area in dance: (one or more areas) because these areas fulfill my preferences of working with (certain people) during (particular hours of the days and months of the year) and in (certain setting(s)) . These preferences and goals will help me reach my purpose of (purpose) in the dance field.

Chapter 3

Teaching Dance in K-12 Schools and Postsecondary Education

"It is the supreme art of the teacher to awaken joy in creative expression and knowledge."

Albert Einstein

"I believe that we learn by practice. Whether it means to learn to dance by practicing dancing or to learn to live by practicing living, the principles are the same."

Martha Graham

This chapter provides guidance in pursuing a career in elementary school though high school (K-12) or postsecondary dance education. It is important to have an in-depth understanding of the necessary steps undertaken in the process of becoming a secondary dance teacher, such as college degree processes, student teaching, state license testing, applying and interviewing, and classroom management strategies. If teaching in higher education is your goal, it is critical to properly prepare yourself for both undergraduate and graduate schooling, application and interviewing processes, and curricular and classroom challenges. All of these issues will be addressed in addition to commonly cited pros and cons of teaching in each of these sectors. This chapter concludes with a set of reflection prompts to help you identify your goals within the area of dance education.

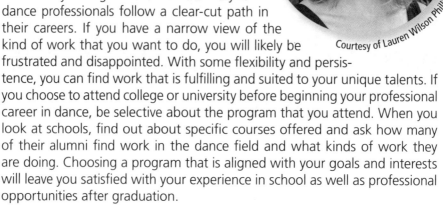

Lauren Wilson Phillis

Public school dance educator, Beaumont Magnet Academy, Knoxville, Tennessee

What is your best advice to those hoping to pursue a career in dance?

Be openminded about the different types of work that you might do in the field. Very few dance professionals follow a clear-cut path in their careers. If you have a narrow view of the kind of work that you want to do, you will likely be frustrated and disappointed. With some flexibility and persistence, you can find work that is fulfilling and suited to your unique talents. If you choose to attend college or university before beginning your professional career in dance, be selective about the program that you attend. When you look at schools, find out about specific courses offered and ask how many of their alumni find work in the dance field and what kinds of work they are doing. Choosing a program that is aligned with your goals and interests will leave you satisfied with your experience in school as well as professional opportunities after graduation.

Courtesy of Lauren Wilson Phillis.

Describe some of the greatest lessons you've learned in your dance career.

The greatest lesson I have learned is to stay humble and not to be afraid to ask for help. When I entered college I was accustomed to being successful in school. I expected to experience the same success as a teacher. I knew it would be hard work, but I thought that I would put in the hard work and immediately become a great teacher. It did not turn out that way. The first time I taught a lesson as part of my dance education course work, I discov-

PLANNING AND TRAINING FOR A CAREER IN DANCE EDUCATION

Teaching dance in secondary and postsecondary schools requires particular approaches and training because educators in these schools are accountable to state, federal, and accrediting organization standards. Additionally, K-12 educators must hold an undergraduate degree (ideally, in dance education or dance) and state-sanctioned teacher licensure. Training for teachers in K-12 and postsecondary schools, therefore, is specifically focused and geared to these accreditation and licensing standards. Qualified dance educators in postsecondary schools hold terminal degrees in dance, which could include a master of fine arts, doctor of philosophy, or doctor of education.

ered that no matter how smart I was and no matter how hard I worked to plan a lesson, delivering that lesson to a roomful of students can be a deeply uncomfortable experience. In order to become a better teacher, I had to fail over and over again in front of students, my classmates, and my professors. Of course, I had successes also, but they were often overshadowed in my mind by self-doubt and fear that I wouldn't be a good teacher. Now, I am much more skilled and confident as a teacher, and I am more aware of my limitations. I am not afraid to ask for help when I am struggling, and I am more forgiving of myself when I make mistakes. I have learned that teaching is a lifelong journey of reflection and self-improvement, always striving to be better and at the same time accepting that I have a lot to offer right now, just the way I am.

Looking back, what are the best decisions you have made during your career?

I think the best decision I made was to follow the degree path of earning a license to teach in public schools. Teaching in public schools has given me stability in my work and afforded me the financial resources necessary to pursue professional development. Although the job requires a great deal of sacrifice, it is also rewarding. I love the collaborative nature of teaching dance in a school setting. I get to work with other arts educators and classroom teachers in my school to give our students a well-rounded education. I also love teaching students who might not otherwise have taken a dance class, either because they did not previously have an interest in dance or because their families could not afford to pay for dance classes at a private studio. Teaching in public schools is not for everyone—it is very different than the studio setting to which most dancers are accustomed—but for me it has been the best possible career path.

K-12 Dance Education

While an undergraduate degree is required for teaching in K-12 public schools across the country, you may have some flexibility in choosing your major or minor or both. Depending on the state, school district, and the saturation of qualified teachers in an area, competitiveness and qualification requirements will vary. For example, some school districts may require a degree specifically in dance education, while other districts may place value on a more general education degree, such as secondary education or early childhood, with specific certifications and licensures in areas of content specialty.

A 2017 National Dance Education Organization study identified 75 dance education degree programs in 38 states (National Dance Education Organization 2017). A bachelor of arts in dance education or dance, a bachelor of fine arts in dance, a

Children in a community dance class creating choreography inspired by various environmental images.

bachelor of science in dance, or a dance minor with an education major would provide a strong foundational education for future teachers. If you prefer a dance major, consider supplementing your dance training with course work in your university's education program by taking a minor or certificate in secondary or early childhood education. This will prepare you for teaching in the dance discipline and will give you a broad overview of issues you will confront as a teacher in K-12 schools overall, such as child development, curriculum design, and relevant legal topics.

A major in dance education will most comprehensively prepare you for teaching dance in secondary schools because all of your course work will be geared toward this specific goal. The content of a dance education degree varies slightly by institution, but according to the National Association of Schools of Dance, accredited curricula must comprise

> studies in dance and dance pedagogy, planned in a developmental progression from foundation to major study . . . should comprise 55–60% of the total program; general academic studies, 25–30%; and professional education, 15–20%. Professional education is defined as those courses normally offered by the education unit that deal with philosophical and social foundations of education, educational psychology, special education, history of education, etc. Student teaching is also counted as professional education." (National Association of Schools of Dance 2019, 84)

Also, future teachers must demonstrate proficiency in at least two forms of technique; must have knowledge of dance history, sciences, music, and production; and must be able to teach a wide range of students, including different ages and levels and in different settings (National Association of Schools of Dance 2019).

If you think you may want to teach content unrelated to dance in K-12 schools at some point, look into your university's education school or program because degrees in those areas may offer a variety of majors with content certifications in certain areas such as special education or core subjects and may offer degree concentrations in specialized areas such as literature, STEM, or early childhood. In this case, you could still include dance as an area of study in college by making dance your minor or a second major. School districts that have a shortage of dance teachers sometimes hire teachers without a dance degree but who have had consistent and rigorous training at the college level. Additionally, some schools that are just beginning a dance program or schools whose dance programs need revitalizing hire teachers with split appointments in dance and a second content area.

Postsecondary Dance Education

To teach full-time at the postsecondary level, you will need an undergraduate degree and a terminal degree, or the highest degree that can be awarded in a specific field. In dance, there are three terminal degrees: master of fine arts (MFA), doctor of philosophy (PhD), and doctor of education (EdD). In addition, most institutions require previous experience in teaching and research and a professional résumé of previous work in the dance field.

The master of fine arts degree in dance is usually offered as a traditional, face-to-face degree that spans two to three years. This practice-oriented degree is geared toward students who want to expand their performance and choreographic ideas and practices. According to the accrediting standards of the National Association of Schools of Dance, a minimum of 65 percent of MFA curricula must be in creative or performance-oriented subjects; at least 15 percent in academic studies such as aesthetics, critical analysis, dance science, history, or pedagogy; and 10 percent in electives related to the dance area (National Association of Schools of Dance 2019). MFA programs require a culminating project or thesis, which may take various creative forms and may include a written component. An MFA prepares students for teaching studio and some theory classes at the postsecondary level.

Doctoral programs, by contrast, require at least three years of full-time graduate course work. These degrees are geared toward dance scholars and may focus on specific content areas such as dance studies, education, pedagogy, or interdisciplinary work. Doctoral studies in dance mostly emphasize reading, writing, and conducting research and less often include performance or movement-based course work. A dissertation illustrating scholarly competence is required for completion of a PhD or EdD. A doctoral degree prepares students for researching and teaching theory courses in higher education settings and for teaching both graduate and undergraduate students.

Teaching dance in K-12 institutions differs from teaching in postsecondary schools because dancers in college programs want to make dance their career and often don't consider dance a hobby or elective as students in K-12 classes might. The goal for dance educators in postsecondary programs is to nurture advanced students toward careers in dance and to, in some cases, train future dance teachers.

Many graduate programs offer teaching assistantships in which graduate students are mentored by faculty members in teaching and may sometimes be assigned their own classes as instructors of record. Typically, these are paid positions and may come with other perks such as tuition assistance and health insurance. Teaching assistantships offer excellent resources for gaining teaching experience and being mentored along the way.

Another of the differences between working in postsecondary schools and K-12 schools is that faculty members in higher education are required to develop research agendas and contribute service to their department, university, and profession in addition to teaching. Research and service in the dance area can be scholarly or creative, and your graduate faculty can help you explore these differences and begin to investigate them during your studies. If you have opportunities to shadow graduate faculty members or participate in research or service in some way, take the chance to learn more about these important areas. Also, if you can become involved in professional dance organizations such as the National Dance Education Organization (NDEO), Dance Studies Association (DSA), International Association for Dance Medicine and Science (IADMS), or American College Dance Association (ACDA), either through governance by serving as a student board representative, by volunteering on a committee, or even just by attending organizations' annual conferences, these experiences will provide wonderful resources for your future job prospects and productivity.

Achievements in teaching, research, and service customarily make up a faculty member's dossier, which demonstrates a commitment to one's university and discipline. The dossier is a tool used by the institution to grant faculty members tenure (or a lifetime appointment). The better acquainted you can become with research and service as a graduate student, the better prepared you will be for faculty work in higher education. Seek opportunities while in school to learn more about these areas by applying for research assistantships, working with graduate faculty members, attending conferences and volunteering with professional organizations, and participating in graduate student service organizations.

STEPS TO A CAREER IN K-12 DANCE EDUCATION

Preparedness for a career in dance education requires an extensive amount of training both in the classroom and the studio. Securing a position in a K-12 school requires that you be prepared for the application and interview processes and the process of establishing yourself as an early-career dance educator.

Student Teaching

Student teaching experience is critical for career preparation in K-12 dance education. Observing and exploring in a classroom setting under the guidance of experienced educators offer an invaluable learning experience. Student teaching assignments are typically one to two semesters long and involve full school days, five days per week. During this time, student teachers shadow a designated dance teacher, learning important information about how she or he manages a classroom; structures daily, weekly, and unit lessons; creates assignments and activities; and how she or he negotiates the various demands of the job, including working with parents and administrators and balancing work with personal needs. Student teachers also may be tasked with creating lesson plans, attending to administrative work, and leading class activities.

Student teachers also discover much about the daily life of a K-12 dance educator. For example, dance teachers often do much more than teach dance classes. Some K-12 dance educators are also directors of drill or dance teams; some teach content both in and outside of the dance discipline; some have administrative duties; and some choreograph concerts, musicals, and competitive routines for school groups. Additionally, some K-12 dance educators supplement their salaries and keep active in other areas by working part-time in dance studios or being involved with community or not-for-profit dance companies. Dance teachers in K-12 schools, in order to maintain licensure, must also seek continuing education credits, which may require attending conferences or other out-of-school events.

During your time as a student teacher, ask questions and conduct yourself professionally. Use student teaching experiences to discover what you love about teaching and how you want to lead your own classroom in the future.

Teacher Certification

K-12 teacher certification in dance is different in each state. In Texas, for example, only certification for grades 6-12 is available. Thirteen states require no credentialing to teach dance (National Dance Education Organization 2017). Five states and Washington, D.C., have state-approved dance certification processes, but do not have university dance education programs. The standards for teaching dance and the way teacher certification tests are structured also differ in each state. Some states place value on the social and cultural aspects of dance, and emphasize these in their curricular requirements, while others prioritize performance and technique in codified forms such as ballet and jazz. Some states require written tests about dance, while others require standardized tests in reading, math, and writing or in the physical education area rather than in dance.

Check in consistently with faculty and an advisor in your undergraduate institution to make sure you understand your state's requirements (or the state to which you wish to relocate) and the process of preparing for and taking certification tests. Finally, make sure you study for these tests. They are often expensive and are quite rigorous because they are intended to assess your competence and readiness for professional work with children in K-12 schools.

Applying and Interviewing

Dance education positions can be found by searching on job and school district websites and through word of mouth. Job postings require applicants to submit a résumé, references, and sometimes a teaching philosophy statement. Seek help from a mentor or undergraduate faculty member for writing and refining these documents. Also, secure at least three professional references who would be willing to speak very highly of you and your abilities related to the positions to which you'll apply. Your undergraduate professors are an excellent resource for this, as are previous supervisors for positions you have held in dance studios or community programs. Your references should be able to speak about your strengths in dance education as well as attributes such as reliability, professionalism, collegiality, responsibility, and work ethic.

You will interview with the principal or vice principal of the school to which you are applying and perhaps also with the head of the dance program. Interviews for K-12 positions are facilitated much like those in other industries. You will be asked a series of questions about why the position interests you and how you envision yourself successfully fulfilling its requirements. It is important that you dress professionally, speak confidently and clearly about your strengths, and show enthusiasm for the position and the school in this interview process.

Establishing a Classroom and Teaching Tips

You should expect a variety of emotions and varied experiences as you become acquainted with teaching in K-12 schools. At some level, all new teachers experience a sense of elation at getting to put their dance education to good use, and some may also experience setbacks trying to manage their classrooms and establish strong relationships with colleagues. As a first-year teacher, growing pains are normal as you work to develop your best classroom and professional practices. Prioritize class content and positive relationships with colleagues and students.

Depending on the school in which you start teaching and how dance fits into the overall curriculum and culture, you may discover that you still have much to learn when you start teaching. Because it is atypical to teach in the same school in which you completed your student teaching, expect to recalibrate to a new school system, new colleagues and students, and common attitudes and beliefs. Show students the importance of dance through preparation, developed lesson plans, and clear and consistent communication. Many younger teachers report feeling disadvantaged by their youth upon taking their first job in K-12 schools. Don't let these feelings distract from the job you are there to do. Be confident that your education and skills have prepared you well for the career on which you are embarking.

Progression and Transitions

Dance educators in public schools receive tenure, which equates to a certain amount of job security. Tenure is achieved differently in different states and school systems, and often consists of submitting an application after a certain number of years teaching successfully in that school. Each school system also has its own system for pay raises, so make sure you understand standard procedures for your school.

Some K-12 dance educators begin and end their careers in these positions, while others transition out of public education entirely. These decisions are personal and may be determined by your dynamic interests and evolving skill set. In any case, a multitude of resources online can help guide a dance educator's career transition into, among other areas, graduate school, postsecondary education, nonprofit dance, or private studio work.

STEPS TO A CAREER IN POSTSECONDARY DANCE EDUCATION

Before applying for a job in postsecondary education, you should take into account the degrees you hold, your professional experience, and areas of expertise to determine what kind of academic job will suit you best. This requires a comprehensive search of online job listings on sites like indeed.com and higheredjobs.com and the employment opportunities page of chronicle.com as well as universities' human resources websites. In this search, get a sense of how positions are described, paying close attention to the required qualifications and expected duties of each position. Most position ads also include narratives about the kind of department and college in which the dance program resides and information about the university and its geographical location. Some ads discuss salary and benefits and others do not. All of this information will help you decide whether or not a position is a good fit for you.

Tenure-Track Versus Non-Tenure-Track Versus Visiting Versus Adjunct Positions

In your academic job search, you may notice terms such as tenure-track position, visiting professor, adjunct instructor, and non-tenure-track position. It is important to understand the differences between the terms before you begin applying for postsecondary faculty jobs.

Tenure-track positions are some of the most sought after (and most competitive) positions because they hold the potential for tenure, which equates to a lifetime appointment, job security, and academic and artistic independence. Tenure-track educators spend six years as an assistant professor and following this initial probationary period, apply for tenure and promotion to associate professor. Most other academic positions are not on the tenure track, and some are part time. A visiting assistant professor position is often a one- or two-year appointment, with the possibility of extending or being granted a tenure-track position later. Visiting faculty are encouraged (but often not required) to produce significant research, and usually contribute to departmental committees and other service duties. Professors of practice typically are full-time teachers and are not usually required to produce research.

Part-time positions in academic dance are commonly listed as adjunct faculty or adjunct professor. These educators are usually paid per course rather than per academic year and, while these positions offer excellent entry-level experience in academic dance, they are often not sustainable over the lifetime of a career because they do not pay enough to be equivalent to a livable salary. Some adjunct professors, therefore, accumulate several part-time positions or serve as adjuncts at multiple universities to make a living. Adjunct professors are typically not required to perform research or service to the university.

Teaching Versus Research Institutions, Public Versus Private Institutions

Postsecondary institutions are either public or private and usually identify as either a teaching or research institution. Generally speaking, public universities are dependent on a state's funding and local priorities, whereas private institutions rely on private contributions from individuals, foundations, and alumni. Public institutions can be more structured in the way assessments, policies, and tenure and promotion are handled because those processes are standardized by the state. Private institutions may offer unique chances for collaboration across campus and curricular innovation because these institutions are not authorized by state governments.

The differences between teaching and research institutions are important to understand when considering an academic position. While most tenure-track faculty members are required to engage in teaching, research, and service, each of these areas may be weighted differently depending on whether the institution is teaching or research based. In a research institution, faculty members must be actively engaged with research, in creative or scholarly forms, and, while teaching is still important, research may account for up to 50 percent of their workload. Research universities strive to support faculty research with grant-writing assistance, internal grant opportunities, travel funding, and graduate research assistants. In a teaching institution, faculty members' main areas of productivity and accomplishment are in teaching and the number of classes each faculty member teaches may be higher than at a research university. Teaching institutions value research and service as well and encourage faculty members to produce research related to their teaching.

Pay attention to what kind of work you're drawn to while you are in graduate school. If you are most interested in teaching, then perhaps a teaching institution will best support your goals. However, if you are more interested in choreography or scholarship, consider seeking a position at a research institution. Another consideration when choosing a postsecondary position that will best suit you is to think about how you want to relate to your students. If you envision yourself leading intimate lectures in a university where everyone seems to know each other, a private school might be a good fit for you, whereas others may value the larger systems of public state institutions. Overall, it is not just the position itself, but also the kind of institution that will be important to your success and fulfillment in academic dance.

Identifying Schools and Programs for a Good Fit

In addition to identifying each university's goals and structure, it is important to recognize the differences between various dance programs and how they can support your career interests, areas of specialty, and goals. Ensure that the institutions to which you apply match at least some of your artistic and academic values and ideas in their mission and vision statements, descriptions of programs, social media, and website and print materials.

Program Size and Scope

Most academic dance programs host websites and have a social media presence; these can give you ample information about the size and scope of its program. Note the number of faculty and their areas of specialty; this information will give you a sense of how you might fit into the program, unique perspectives you could bring, and with whom you could potentially collaborate. Additionally, examine curricular offerings, making note of courses that you could teach; review photos and videos of facilities and performances; and check out recent news and announcements to get a sense of the program's values and culture.

Consider how your work could be spread over the course of an academic year given the number of students and faculty in each program, how the program engages with other disciplines and in the community, and how dance fits into the larger structure of the university. Whereas some dance programs are paired with another discipline in a shared department, others stand alone as their own departments. Some dance programs are housed within a college of arts, while others may share a college with areas such as kinesiology, sports management, architecture, humanities, and even education. This information reveals much about each dance program's strategic planning and goals as well as funding sources and potential areas of collaboration.

Finally, decipher what each dance program is trying to do for its students by studying how it promotes and brands itself as a department. Does it place high value on training professional performers? Do you notice a lot of accomplishments in written research or grants? Do you sense an investment in international work? Do you notice interdisciplinary connections? The emphases of your institution should evoke excitement in you, and you should feel as if you have something unique to contribute to its vision.

Programmatic Mission

Most dance programs and departments are motivated by the vision and goals identified in their mission statements. A mission statement outlines the major areas of interest and focus of a particular program and can give you a sense of how this program will work in the future. Pay attention to how programs define themselves and note whether or not your own values and ideas align with these statements.

The Juilliard School, for example, has a mission to "provide the highest caliber of artistic education for gifted musicians, dancers, and actors from around the world, so that they may achieve their fullest potential as artists, leaders, and global citizens" (Juilliard School 2018, para 1). By contrast, Brigham Young University Department of Dance "prepares articulate artists in an intensive learning environment through teaching, scholarship, choreography, and performance that integrate the body, mind, and spirit" (Brigham Young University 2019, para 1). Appalachian State University's Department of Theatre and Dance aims "to facilitate transformative experiences for students and the public, which cultivate compassionate, creative and collaborative communities through theatre and dance" (Appalachian State University 2020, para 1). In these three examples, unique values and focus of each program are evidenced through the language used to convey their goals and mission. Surveying this language will help you sense your fit within particular academic environments.

Searching for Additional Information

Networking within academia can provide additional information about dance positions and departments not available in job ads or on university websites. Ask trusted colleagues or mentors what they know about certain programs or positions. If you know someone who has worked or studied at an institution of interest to you, ask pointed questions about their perceptions of faculty members working there and the school's institutional culture and reputation. Also, seek information about how faculty members are supported by the university through internal awards, grants, sabbaticals, professional development, family and medical leave, travel and research funding, and other recognition. Often, this information can be found on institutional websites and in documented policies or faculty handbooks. Seek an institution that is supportive of its faculty's needs and makes efforts to reward and acknowledge accomplishments.

Applying and Interviewing

The application and interview process in academia is extensive and strenuous because the competition for full-time tenure-track positions is intense and the hiring timeline, lengthy. Generally speaking, academic job ads are released during September, October, and November. Some schools do a round of phone or video-conference-style interviews sometime from November to February. Campus interviews are typically scheduled during the first half of the spring semester, between January and March. Job offers are usually made sometime from February to May, with some positions even being offered during the summer months.

At least a year before applying for jobs in academia, you should identify and make requests of at least three dance professionals who would be willing to write you strong letters of recommendation for these positions. For each application, you should send your recommenders an updated curriculum vitae, the position ad, recipient contact information, deadline for submission, and a brief synopsis of why you are a good fit for this position. This will help your letter writers compose a strong letter of recommendation that addresses each position specifically.

The following items may be required elements of postsecondary position applications: letter of interest; curriculum vitae; teaching philosophy statement; diversity statement; letters of recommendation; and links to videos of choreography, performance, or teaching. If your graduate program does not include course content that covers how to create these documents, find a mentor to guide you in building an application packet. This packet is important because it represents your interests and strengths and helps search committees get a sense of how you would fit into their position and department. Your application materials must be organized and clear and demonstrate your strengths.

Phone and videoconferencing interviews are used by search committees to narrow a pool of qualified candidates to a list of finalists who will be invited to visit campus for another interview. Practice reciting answers to questions you think they may ask you. Conduct extensive searches of the department's website and social media pages so that you know the position and the department inside and out and can speak about how you would enhance its existing structure. Prepare to discuss your experiences in teaching, research, and service, and expect questions about your long-term goals and plans.

If you are fortunate enough to be granted campus interviews, be prepared for them! Typically, a campus interview consists of a whirlwind two-day visit to campus, in which the following events may comprise your itinerary: interviews with the search committee, department chair, and dean; meetings with students and faculty; teaching demonstrations; a job talk or lecture about your research; tours of campus and the surrounding area; and meals with faculty and staff. Successful candidates clearly describe their strengths and how those fit within the open position's requirements. Successful candidates maintain positivity and energy throughout the campus interview and show genuine enthusiasm for their potential future colleagues and students as well as for the department and position.

Establishing Teaching, Research, and Service Agendas

Once you have secured a position in academia, your next task is to establish your teaching, research, and service activities so that they match however they are weighted in your particular position. For example, some professors' workloads constitute 40 percent teaching, 30 percent research, and 30 percent service. Your job is to strike that balance with the activities and projects to which you commit yourself. This is not an easy task. If your department doesn't assign you a mentor, find one (or several) on your own; invite this person to observe your teaching and give you feedback, read your writing, attend your shows, and nominate you for committees and awards.

All new dance faculty members face the time-consuming task of preparing new course material when they take a new position. Find out what you will be teaching as soon as possible upon accepting a job offer so that you can begin working on course preparation well in advance of your first semester. Ask how much flexibility you can have with developing course content; this varies. Invite senior colleagues and supervisors to observe your teaching. Because each institution maintains its own standard practices and pedagogical values, it will be helpful to know how your teaching style is perceived and supported by the institutional culture at large.

Another first step upon accepting a postsecondary position is to read through university policies regarding expectations and processes for tenure and promotion. This will help you sense how research and service are valued in that school. Further, pay attention to the way research is discussed on campus. These informal conversations can help you understand how the university understands and supports both scholarly and creative activity. Scholarly research may involve qualitative projects that investigate dance through empirical data such as interviews, observations, and field work or quantitative projects that analyze dance through

Neal Hinkle/TTUHSC

Ali Duffy teaching an undergraduate improvisation class at Texas Tech University.

numerical data and statistical analysis. Scholarly research products may include peer-reviewed book manuscripts and journal articles, book reviews, and editing work. Creative research yields choreography, performance, or interdisciplinary work and may include community engagement and collaborative endeavors. To understand the research expectations, keep discussions about your progress going with supervisors and mentors on campus.

Service assignments could include sitting on committees, university governance, administration, or service to a professional organization or company. Serving as a director, choreographer, or performer in on-campus performances and events may sometimes also fall under the umbrella of service. Also, any work on a project or facilitation of an event with students is considered service. For example, if you facilitate a trip to an American College Dance Association conference with your students, that should count toward your service load. Curate a range of activities for yourself so that you're meeting colleagues across campus and contributing to your home department and the dance field in your service load.

Progression and Transitions

Postsecondary educators progress through their careers differently depending on the kind of positions they hold. A tenure-track assistant professor, for example, is granted tenure and promoted to associate professor after a six-year probationary period. The progression from associate professor to professor is less defined and often contingent on the faculty member's securing a national or international profile. Faculty members in non-tenure-track positions may find career progression into full-time instructor or professor of practice positions. These positions are usually eligible for benefits, so may be more attractive to faculty wanting long-term employment.

Sometimes, dance faculty move into administrative positions, such as department chair or dean, or other administrative positions in internal institutions or centers. Usually, these positions are offered to senior faculty members with tenure. Prepare yourself for administrative positions by volunteering to serve on committees that work with upper administrators and offering to chair committees in your department. Expanding your network and gaining additional skills through service work will give you important experience leading to a future in administration.

PROS AND CONS OF DIFFERENT EDUCATIONAL ENVIRONMENTS

As in many disciplines, teaching in dance can be incredibly rewarding and also relentlessly taxing. Dance education takes sustained stamina, focus, and care for students and for the discipline. Changes in curricular standards, classroom management, student support, and work–life negotiation are often challenges that dance educators must manage. At the same time, many are grateful for the chance to teach in an area they are passionate about, continue their own creative explorations of dance in their jobs, and support their students' growth.

Teaching dance in K-12 schools offers many benefits, including job security, attractive work hours, summer and winter breaks, and full benefits. K-12 educators convey that their love for their students keeps them motivated to maintain high standards, strong work ethic, and creativity in their teaching. At the same time, K-12 dance educators are often overworked, being assigned additional (and often unpaid) tasks, such as coaching extracurricular dance teams or choreographing shows. Additionally, dance can be relegated to the physical education realm or be offered as elective classes, so it may not be considered a serious academic subject in some schools. This can be frustrating for dance educators who are highly skilled and educated.

In postsecondary dance positions, job security (for tenured professors), benefits, summer and winter breaks, and academic and artistic freedom are appealing. Additionally, many professors value the flexibility in their schedules, travel support, interdisciplinary opportunities, and an ability to conduct research while also teaching. Like K-12 educators, postsecondary faculty members often face a culture of overwork and must strive to maintain balance in their lives in order to avoid burnout or health problems. Further, as postsecondary faculty members rise through the ranks, they are often called on for added service that may seem unrelated to their work in dance and that may infringe on the work they enjoy within the discipline.

Dr. Doug Risner

Distinguished professor of dance and director of graduate studies, Wayne State University

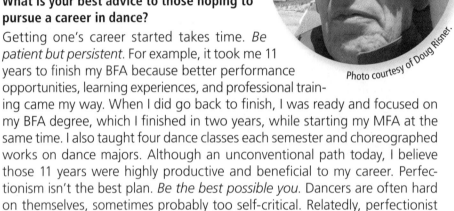

Photo courtesy of Doug Risner.

What is your best advice to those hoping to pursue a career in dance?

Getting one's career started takes time. *Be patient but persistent*. For example, it took me 11 years to finish my BFA because better performance opportunities, learning experiences, and professional training came my way. When I did go back to finish, I was ready and focused on my BFA degree, which I finished in two years, while starting my MFA at the same time. I also taught four dance classes each semester and choreographed works on dance majors. Although an unconventional path today, I believe those 11 years were highly productive and beneficial to my career. Perfectionism isn't the best plan. *Be the best possible you*. Dancers are often hard on themselves, sometimes probably too self-critical. Relatedly, perfectionist attitudes and habits can support dancers in their lives and professions, but if left unchecked can present numerous negative effects.

Some additional advice: Develop skills beyond dance performance and choreography. Research shows that undergraduate dance majors will earn nearly 70 percent of their income outside of performing. Teaching is the largest portion of that income. Be ready for unanticipated opportunities as best you can—they will come to you. Take control of your career before you even have one by always being on time, doing more than is required, stepping up when the situation arises, supporting your peers, coming to rehearsal early, assisting your teacher when needed, speaking up effectively, listening clearly, and believing in yourself.

Describe some of the greatest lessons you've learned in your dance career.

The adage, "The world is run by the people who show up," is also true in the world of postsecondary dance and speaks to the power of being engaged, prepared, and ready to do the work. I often learn most profoundly from experiences in which I've failed or fallen short. While it can be difficult to face or acknowledge, my experiences of success provide far less that contributes to my real learning. The value of collaboration is underrated and frequently misunderstood. Its value in learning can lead to humanizing experiences and meaning making. As a white male professor in academia, I know my gender and race account for a good deal of opportunities and advantages from which I have benefited. That I am a nonheterosexual dance professor diminishes my level of privilege as a white male professor.

In total transparency, dance education is not a career to pursue if you want to become wealthy. While this career can afford a comfortable living, you should understand and expect that these positions do not often come with large paychecks. Data collected through organizations such as *The Chronicle of Higher Education* and Glassdoor provide current salary figures.

SUMMARY

A career in dance education, whether at the K-12 or postsecondary level, promises to be challenging, fulfilling, and dynamic. Many teachers marvel at their students' growth and find reward in championing their successes and preparing them for bright futures in dance. At the same time, the responsibility for educating the next generation of dance participants, artists, educators, and scholars is significant and serious. Approaching a dance education career with an open mind, strong work ethic, and care for student success will bolster you as you work to create spaces for learning and achievement to happen in dance.

Reflection

DEVELOPING A TEACHING PHILOSOPHY

Before diving into a teaching career, craft a teaching philosophy statement. This can help you direct your job search efforts—aligning your values with that of your employer—as well as help guide your work in the classroom with the students. There are many ways to craft a useful teaching philosophy statement; answering the questions below will get you started. Your teaching philosophy should evolve over time. As you learn more about teaching and how to best meet the needs of your students in any given situation or circumstance, your ability to be flexible in your pedagogical approaches will determine your success as an educator. Here are questions to consider:

1. Describe the best teachers you have had. What qualities and approaches made them the best?

2. What would you like your students to achieve or learn from your teaching?

3. Are there theories of learning that guide your teaching methods or practices?

4. What unique or external circumstances (students' personal lives, class time, available resources, geographical location) might affect how your students respond to you as an educator? And what can you do about those circumstances to foster an effective learning environment?

5. Why do you think your subject matter is important? How can you create a learning environment to encourage students to share your enthusiasm and seriousness of purpose?

6. Define the teaching strategies you will employ in your classes. Why do you value these approaches instead of others available to you?

7. How do you aim to evaluate students?

8. How do you propose to measure your teaching effectiveness?

Think carefully about your responses and return to this document often, especially as your circumstances change, say, at the beginning of each new year, when you start a new job, or when you have particularly challenging students or circumstances. Reframing your work as a philosophy will provide you with a foundation that undergirds your decisions when you feel challenged.

Chapter 4

Opportunities in the Private Sector: Dance Studios and Schools

"Every child has a right to know how to achieve control of his body in order that he may use it to the limit of his ability for the expression of his own reactions to life. Even if he can never carry his efforts far enough to realize dance in its highest forms, he may experience the sheer joy of the rhythmic sense of free, controlled, and expressive movement, and through this know an addition to life to which every human being is entitled."

Margaret H'Doubler

"Teaching might even be the greatest of the arts since the medium is the human mind and spirit."

John Steinbeck

Private dance studio work is best for dance professionals interested in teaching children and teenagers outside academic environments. Studios vary widely in curricula, goals, and outcomes and focus mostly on training in technique and performance. Studio classes are held outside regular school hours in the evenings and on the weekends. Productions and competitions may be part of the expected activities in which teachers are involved. For example, many dance studios produce annual recitals to demonstrate skills learned by students throughout the year. Other schools produce full-length ballets or commissioned work by guest artists. Still others invest in competitions and conventions in which students compete by performing throughout the year in various locations.

Anisha Rajesh

Founder and director of the Upasana Kalakendra School of Indian Classical Dance

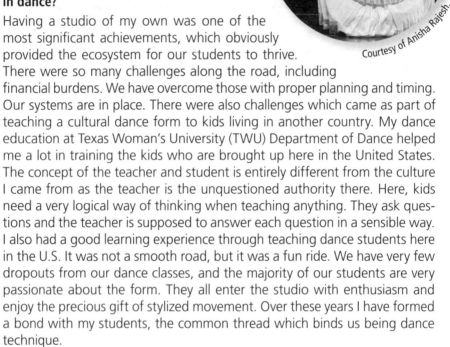

Courtesy of Anisha Rajesh.

What have been your most significant experiences as a working professional in dance?

Having a studio of my own was one of the most significant achievements, which obviously provided the ecosystem for our students to thrive. There were so many challenges along the road, including financial burdens. We have overcome those with proper planning and timing. Our systems are in place. There were also challenges which came as part of teaching a cultural dance form to kids living in another country. My dance education at Texas Woman's University (TWU) Department of Dance helped me a lot in training the kids who are brought up here in the United States. The concept of the teacher and student is entirely different from the culture I came from as the teacher is the unquestioned authority there. Here, kids need a very logical way of thinking when teaching anything. They ask questions and the teacher is supposed to answer each question in a sensible way. I also had a good learning experience through teaching dance students here in the U.S. It was not a smooth road, but it was a fun ride. We have very few dropouts from our dance classes, and the majority of our students are very passionate about the form. They all enter the studio with enthusiasm and enjoy the precious gift of stylized movement. Over these years I have formed a bond with my students, the common thread which binds us being dance technique.

What is your best advice to those hoping to pursue a career in dance?

Approach dance as a discipline; connect it with other disciplines both in teaching and performing; make it accessible and understandable.

Looking back, what have been the best decisions you have made during your career?

Upasana Kalakendra itself was one of the best decisions. Having my own institution gave me the flexibility and freedom to balance both work and family. And, of course, the PhD courses at TWU gave me access to new knowledge systems, which helped me with both teaching and performance.

Professional work in dance studios provides unique benefits for job security and flexibility not afforded by other options in the field. Similar in many ways to elementary through high schools (K-12) and postsecondary schools, dance studios often operate on the academic calendar, so summer and holiday breaks are common in this setting. Some dance studio teachers hold full-time positions while others work part time. This means that studio work could be undertaken at different points within a career to support other work in or out of the dance field. Many college students, for instance, support themselves by working part time in studios during their time in school.

Two major distinctions between education in a private studio and a public school are the diverse foci of the curricula and the wide range of quality in studio programs. Because dance studios do not follow any one curricular design model nor accreditation standards, a consistent way to measure expected outcomes or teaching methods does not exist. Therefore, research a private studio before committing to a job in it. Make sure your own pedagogical and professional standards are upheld and supported by that school. A wonderful aspect of working in studios is that they offer opportunities to explore diverse teaching and choreographic practices and to learn about business strategies.

Annual and hourly pay for dance teachers are largely dependent on geographical location, years of experience, and how established the school is in its community. Indeed reports the average hourly wage for dance teachers in the United States is $29.85 (Indeed 2020). Payscale reports a salary range of $23,000 to $60,000 for dance teachers working in the United States (Payscale n.d.). Glassdoor reports an average salary of $43,740, with the extreme ends of the pay scale at $26,000 and $75,000 (Glassdoor 2020). While opportunities for advancement in these positions are slim, most communities house multiple dance studios and consistently search for employees.

In this chapter, a description of private studios and schools is followed by a discussion of education and training requirements for dance teachers in these settings, classroom management and teaching tips, information about applying and interviewing, and maintaining a teaching career over a lifetime. Next, a section about opening a dance studio addresses the business elements of studio work. This chapter concludes with a set of reflection prompts to help you identify your goals within the area of dance education in private studios and schools.

TYPES OF STUDIOS AND SCHOOLS

Private dance studios and schools are founded for different reasons and with different purposes and goals. Whereas some are intended to provide training in a specific genre, others may include multiple genres in order to emphasize diverse experiences. Some schools feature affordable community programming for families, while others aim to compete at advanced technical levels. Some studios aim to create interdisciplinary experiences, while others endeavor to train students specifically for entrance into professional companies or university programs. More recently, studios are cropping up around the country with the sole purpose of supporting active lifestyles through dance and related activities. This diversity in purpose creates unique opportunities for you to engage as an educator in numerous ways.

Dance Studios in the Traditional Model

Many studios operate in a prescribed model that includes a range of classes at various levels that work toward a concluding recital at the end of the year. Classes are geared to children ages 3 through 18 and may include genres such as jazz, ballet, tap, lyrical, musical theater, hip-hop, modern, clogging, pointe, tumbling, and world dance forms. Classes are held in the evenings and on weekends. Dance teachers in these settings are typically expected to create choreography for recital performances during the latter portion of the year and are often hired for teaching specific genres or age groups, depending on expertise.

Competitive Studios

Studios with a competition-based curriculum usually do not differ drastically from traditional studios in the genres and teaching methods employed. The main difference is that students in competitive studios are expected to learn and rehearse often in order to compete regionally and nationally throughout the year. Some studios hold auditions to recruit dancers for elite competition companies within the studio environment. Educators interested in teaching in competitive studios should expect extended working hours and travel and should expect to produce choreography. Most competitive studios produce an end-of-year recital that includes both the choreography created in the classes and works made for the competition stage.

Genre-Specific Schools

Some schools focus solely on one genre in order to train dancers to be specialists in that form. For example, many ballet schools work to train dancers who may be suitable to feed directly into professional ballet companies. Some focus on a non-Western or world genres to pass on historical knowledge and tradition along with technical skills to their students. Some schools enhance technical training with theory-based classes such as dance history. Educators in these environments are highly skilled in the specific areas of focus the studio endorses and may need to be well-versed in theoretical elements of these techniques as well.

Conservatory Programs

Conservatories intensely train dancers for performing on the concert stage. Conservatory programs may be held year-round and during the academic school day. Some of these programs offer academic course work for students in addition to dance training. Others prioritize training during the summer months when students are out of school. Faculty members in these institutions are highly skilled and hold advanced degrees or significant professional experience.

Schools Connected to Other Organizations

Dance schools affiliated with companies or community organizations create opportunities for students to engage with different environments and populations within their training. These schools may also offer intensive experiences in which students are invited to concentrate their training in specific genres or with specific purposes. For example, Urban Bush Women's community engagement branch offers multiple workshop series geared toward leadership, community, and artistic training—deeply held company values that are forwarded through their educational initiatives (Urban Bush Women 2018). Faculty in these institutions may be company dancers or organizational staff and are trained to support the ideals of the company or organization through their teaching. Additionally, faculty may be recruited from outside the organizations in order to provide a counterperspective to students.

Community Dance Classes

Whereas many private dance schools value technical precision and performance, community dance classes may focus on different goals and outcomes. For example, some community programs are designed for toddlers and parents to dance together, some introduce dance to adults, and some focus on underserved populations of students, such as those who could otherwise not afford dance training or students with disabilities. One of the benefits of these positions is that they offer opportunities to be involved in dance as an inclusive, diverse art form that can support connections between the arts and the greater community. Some of the challenges of these positions are that the classes are often held in spaces not equipped for dance (sometimes with poorly designed floors and no sound system) and that dancers come to these classes with wide-ranging abilities and experience.

TRAINING AND EDUCATION FOR DANCE STUDIO PROFESSIONS

Preparation for teaching and choreographing in a privately owned school varies widely. If this is your goal, consider narrowing your focus to include training for teaching in the certain kinds of schools that interest you most. While most private schools and studios require an undergraduate degree in dance or a related area for full-time positions, some hire college students or dancers with significant experience on a part-time or temporary basis. In any case, an undergraduate education in dance will equip you with a foundation of pedagogical, technical, and choreographic tools you can use in studio classes.

You can also prepare for teaching in a studio by taking classes in a variety of studio environments and learning from those teachers the elements of a successful class you would like to emulate in your own. Pay attention to the methods teachers use to manage classroom behavior, bring out students' best qualities, and push students without causing injury or overuse. Ask questions of the teachers you admire most so you can better understand how and why they work the way they do.

Just as important as learning how to teach is learning how *not* to teach. No teacher will be able to please every student at all times, but teaching approaches that are harmful to students emotionally, mentally, or physically should not be replicated.

It is critical that you understand various teaching methods and ongoing issues in dance pedagogy so that you can make informed choices about how you teach. Much of this information is provided in undergraduate dance course work, but also make an effort to read books and scholarly articles about pedagogical practices in dance throughout your career.

Many dance studio owners maintain their own methods for teacher training. Some are more rigorous and involved than others. Studio owners may supply teachers with handbooks outlining their curriculum and best teaching practices, some hold regular teaching training sessions so there is consistency in how classes are structured, and some observe and provide practical feedback to the teachers in their studio. Make sure you understand and agree with a studio's practices and teaching models before signing a contract to teach there. Find a studio that will support and encourage strong teaching and lifelong growth.

TEACHING IN A DANCE STUDIO

Teaching in a dance studio can provide great professional fulfillment as you watch your students learn and develop, achieve technical goals, and receive awards and acclaim for their work, or go on to college programs or professional work in the field. On a daily basis, studio teachers may be in the process of creating new class material for their students, searching for music and costumes for class and performances, and creating choreography for productions or competition dances. Because most studio classes happen in the evenings, studio teachers are free to pursue additional work or schooling during the weekdays.

Preparation

Preparing to teach studio classes differs slightly from the way K-12 and postsecondary teachers prepare: Studio classes aim for technical proficiency, skill development, and performance. Whereas K-12 educators are required to submit daily lesson plans that adhere to the state standards in place, studio class preparation can be more individualized and, for the most part, more flexible. The standards and practices set in place by your studio director will largely determine the specificity of your preparation and your class content.

Searching for music and costumes are tasks constantly undertaken by dance studio teachers. You will be expected to find music to accompany classes, unless you have the benefit of working with an accompanist (this is rare). Many teachers find it helpful to write out counts to phrases they will teach in class and others challenge students by providing no counts and encouraging them to find their own sense of musicality. You may also be asked to find music or costumes for recital and competition dances. If you have control over music and costumes, it is important to remember that these elements should highlight the intent of the dance as well as flatter the dancers' bodies and strengths. Keep in mind the age and maturity level of the dancers with whom you are working. Your aim is to respectfully and honorably represent your students in costume and music selections and in choreography.

Ali Duffy teaching a contemporary master class at Lindenwood University.

Courtesy of Tricia Zweier.

Applying and Interviewing

Word of mouth, social media, and websites are the best resources for finding job opportunities at private dance studios. Because of the seasonal nature of some studio jobs, turnover for part-time positions is typically high, so positions open frequently. Join groups and forums on social media to be alerted when positions open in your community and stay connected with professionals working in studios to let them know of your interest. Some studios require a formal application process, including background checks, while others prefer to simply accept letters of interest for open positions.

An interview may consist of a meeting with the studio director or a teaching audition or both. Studio owners often want to meet with you to get a sense of your teaching approach, work ethic, and your personality to ensure a good fit within the current faculty. In advance of this meeting, explore the business's website and social media presence to gather information about its value system, areas of emphasis, and pedagogical approaches. Discuss how your approach and ideas align with theirs. If asked to teach, create a clear, challenging yet achievable class that shows off your skills in the studio. Praise dancers in the class and show enthusiasm for the school and the position.

Payment for dance studio teachers varies depending on the geographic location of the school, amount of work each position requires, experience requirements, and the school's reputation and level of establishment. Do your homework to understand how much someone with your level of experience at this studio should be earning and be prepared to negotiate. Because no universal standard exists for studio teaching salary, this number may be more flexible than in other parts of the dance industry.

Schedule Expectations

Studio teachers work most often in the evenings and on weekends to accommodate students' school schedules. Most classes in private studios run from one to two hours, depending on the level of the class. If you are hired on a full-time basis, expect to clock long hours in the evenings—sometimes from 3:00 p.m. to 10:00 p.m.—and weekends. Part-time teachers may benefit from flexible schedules that include only a few nights per week or weekends; often, teachers who are in school or hold other jobs are accommodated by the studio director, who schedules classes.

Teaching Tips

Many of the same teaching strategies and techniques can be effective in the studio and public school environments. Some studio owners expect specific pedagogical structures and approaches, while others are more flexible and invite variety in how their teachers conduct classes. Of course, teaching a class of three- and four-year-old children differs greatly from teaching a class of teenagers, and teaching a beginner-level class differs greatly from that of an advanced class. Further, you will vary your classroom management techniques to keep your classes inviting yet focused.

Creating Choreography for Various Levels and Purposes

Most dance studio directors require teachers to also choreograph dances for recitals, community performances, or competitions. These dances typically have requirements for genre, length, costume, and music selection. Usually, technical precision and skill level are prioritized in these dances and artistic elements may also factor into what is valued. When you're choreographing dances for children, ensure that the dance is challenging enough to demonstrate technical achievements, but not so challenging that students cannot successfully execute and perform it. Choreographic complexity, unique style, and artistic or narrative clarity enhance the technical strengths of the dancers and can teach students about the value of a rigorous choreographic process. Studio owners appreciate their teachers' ability to "clean" dances, so study carefully the lines of the dancers' bodies, quality of movements, and formations in space and make adjustments to ensure unity and clarity of intent among groups.

If you work in a school that stages full-length ballets or musicals, your approach will be very different from that of teachers choreographing for recitals and competitions. Full-length works differ in that they are restaged versions of existing work rather than creation of original work, and thus require a different kind of preparation. If you are assigned to choreograph your studio's version of an evening-length work, prepare by listening to the entire score, reading the libretto or script, viewing available versions of the production, and reading about the history of it. Then decide how you will approach the choreography; you may want to choreograph in the style of the original choreographer or to reimagine the choreography entirely. Choreography in ballets and musicals serves to continue a plotline and should be created with that intent.

Dance studios are often invited to participate in holiday parades, charity events, and arts showcases within the community. In this case, prepare choreography for alternative spaces that might not be equipped for dancing. Audiences appreciate energetic, full-bodied movement at events like these because they often occur without the benefits of stage lighting and delineation between spectators and performers. Prepare for costuming appropriate for outdoor performances and ensure there is a sound system that meets your needs. Performing in the community offers dance studios the opportunity to emphasize their brands, make connections with other organizations, and gain valuable performance experience and exposure.

Teaching Young Children Versus Teaching Teenagers

Teaching young children requires a great deal of energy, focus, and patience. Much of this job can feel like wrangling because young children have shorter attention spans than older dancers do and their responses to class activities vary widely. For example, while one three-year-old might be completely engaged and focused throughout a class, another might exhibit challenging or distracting behavior such as crying, bathroom accidents, lack of attention, and noise making. It is critical that teachers remain calm throughout class and be as clear as possible to support students' learning given their complex and differing needs. Many teachers rely on consistency within the class structure so that young students know what to expect every time they enter the space. Positive encouragement and praise also help keep a class atmosphere fun and productive. If you are offered the support of a class assistant, say yes. This person can help with classroom management while you focus on the actual content, plus it gives assistants opportunities to learn teaching strategies from you.

Teaching teenagers is uniquely fulfilling and challenging. Because at this age many teenage children experience changes in their bodies and emotional states, insecurities and behavioral issues may crop up unexpectedly. Having an array of tools for working sensitively with these students is essential. Further, while many older teenagers are advanced dancers, they can be challenged with rigor and high expectations and they may benefit from being given additional responsibility and freedom within the class structure to perform and generate new movement. Also, all students respond differently to being pushed, so try to address individual needs in your teaching, corrections, and feedback.

Whether you teach younger or older dancers, if you find yourself dealing with ongoing behavioral issues with particular students, rather than continue to distract the rest of the class, you may want to bring your studio director and the parents into difficult conversations about these issues. Reach out to your studio director or colleagues consistently to exchange ideas about how to manage classroom behavior.

Courtesy of Ali Duffy.

Creative dance classes for children and parents can include fun props and games to stimulate learning and enthusiasm.

Teaching at Every Technical Level

Most studios use their own means for assessing students' levels and differ in the ways they ask students to illustrate their readiness for advancing. Additionally, schools place different values on elements of technical precision and performance ability to determine levels for classes. Learn how a studio assigns its students to levels in order to fit your teaching to yield student success.

In teaching young children, focus on the most basic and fundamental elements of whatever technique you are teaching. Streamline the technique to its most basic elements and, when students are ready, you can add stylistic nuances or transitional steps. Another approach, if your studio is open to it, is to make early childhood dance classes about creativity and self-expression rather than technique. This option invites students to have some control over the movement they perform and supports teaching the creative potential of dance.

As students progress through levels, pay attention to what their bodies are telling you about their alignment, tensions, and qualities and to how they *feel* performing movements. Ask students how a movement feels so that they can engage holistically through a somatic awareness, learning to tune into the inner sensory cues of their bodies in space. Rather than encouraging rote replication of movement and shapes, it is helpful to guide students through conversations about how movements might look different on different bodies and that finding their interpretation of movement is valid, even expected. Further, consider incorporating imagery and metaphor into your class content as students advance to achieve nuanced physical expression. Finally, advanced students need to be taught correct terminology—the names of the steps they perform and correct anatomical language to describe what is happening as they move their bodies.

Classroom Management

Behavioral issues will arise, so the better prepared you are for diffusing tension and maintaining control of your class, the more smoothly these issues will be resolved. Every school has its own system of managing behavioral issues; become acquainted with the commonly used practices in your studio as soon as possible upon being hired. If you are not provided with training about this, ask questions of your studio director about it.

Positive reinforcement is advised because dance class should be a place where learning and enjoyment happen for children at every level. If you are dealing with disruptive students, address behavior immediately, but also find ways to keep the disruptive students engaged and busy with tasks. Reward them for meeting your expectations. Let your students know how much they have improved and voice your praise for students who are actively and enthusiastically engaged in class. Be clear in your expectations and consistent in your disciplinary measures as well so that students respect your class boundaries.

Sometimes, a child's dance teacher is the most trusted and caring adult in their life, so make sure you approach discipline from a position of genuine care. If you see a student struggling in class, and you suspect the behavior is caused by a conflict or an unresolved issue in their lives, such as mental illness, being bullied, or substance abuse, make parents aware of the situation and invite their help in resolving it. Another reason to bring parents into a discussion about classroom management is that all other strategies have been tried and have failed.

Unique Circumstances

You may encounter students with diverse challenges and abilities in your classes, so prepare for supporting these students' needs. If necessary, bring your studio director and parents in to assist you with pedagogical strategies or accommodations for students. Few training models for dance educators address teaching students with disabilities; it is the responsibility of your studio director to accommodate student needs to the best of their ability. More recently, training programs and performing organizations geared toward students and teachers with disabilities have emerged around the world. Widening the scope of who can participate in dance and who is served by dance to include people of different and unique abilities leads to dance becoming more inclusive and diverse.

MANAGING A TEACHING CAREER OVER A LIFETIME

A career in teaching can be fulfilling and provide long-term job security. One thing to anticipate and plan for, however, is how you will sustain teaching practices over the span of a decades-long career. With age and continuous stress on the body come the potential for overuse, injury, and loss of flexibility and strength. By creating strategies for self-care and thoughtful teaching to prevent some of the issues, you may extend the life of your teaching career.

Maintaining Teaching Stamina

As your teaching career takes shape, you might prioritize your teaching and neglect your body's needs. It is important that you keep up a physical training regimen so your body will remain strong, flexible, and able to perform teaching activities. It is easy to let training practices slide if other responsibilities take precedence, so make an effort throughout your career to focus on your body's progress in dance and overall wellness.

To achieve and maintain stamina in teaching, develop a routine that addresses cardiovascular endurance, strength, and flexibility. Many dance teachers cross-train in order to avoid overusing the parts of the body used most in dance classes. Cross-training methods include running, walking, weightlifting, Pilates, yoga, kickboxing, aerobics classes, and many others. Swimming is especially effective for dancers dealing with injury because it is easy on the joints. Personal trainers can help you develop an individualized plan for reaching whatever goals you have for gaining strength, stamina, and flexibility. Some teachers find at-home programs such as P90X and online programs such as those available through Fitness Blender to be especially helpful because they can be done at home when most convenient. Whatever you enjoy, stick with a routine to support your daily work as well as your overall health and well-being.

Managing Injuries and Changes With Age

Most dance educators will face changes in their bodies as they age or if they become injured during their careers. This is normal and expected in any rigorous athletic activity, so it should be expected in dance. Dance injuries can happen to anyone in a physically active position. Overuse injuries are particularly troublesome for many educators because of the constant repetition of common movements and shapes in dance. Some dance teachers demonstrate only on one side of the body, thus unevenly training themselves and may not properly warm up to demonstrate. Additionally, dance shoes are not known for being especially supportive, so they may exacerbate injuries. Be aware of your body's limitations, be able to recognize harmful pain, and be willing to slow down or stop dancing when your body is cueing you into painful sensations that could lead to injury. Seek medical attention as soon as possible when you become injured and take the advice of doctors treating you. Ignoring their advice could lead to delayed recovery and even additional injury down the road.

Dance professionals sometimes integrate care from various practitioners to treat pain, alignment issues, and injury. Physical therapists help injured patients recover strength and mobility after an injury through use of guided exercises, manual manipulations, and electronic therapies. Massage therapists support muscle relaxation and rest. Chiropractors' main emphasis is on realignment of the spine and body to rid patients of excess tension and pain. Finally, somatic practitioners, such as those working in the Alexander Technique, Feldenkrais Method, Body–Mind Centering, Kinetic Awareness, and many others, have proven to be helpful to dancers experiencing alignment problems, overuse injuries, excess tension, and stress. Each somatic technique offers a unique approach to healing or retraining the body.

Keeping Up With Trends

To stay informed of trends in the field, you must continuously seek opportunities to take new classes, view dance, and attend conferences or workshops. Whereas in K-12 and postsecondary education, dance faculty must obtain a certain amount of continuing education credit regularly, this standard doesn't often cross over into the private arena, so create these standards for yourself. For a long career in which your perspective remains relevant, it is your responsibility to stay active within the field at large, which is always changing and evolving.

OPENING A DANCE STUDIO BUSINESS

Making the significant decision to open a dance studio requires a lot of forethought and planning. You should be well-qualified in dance and well-equipped to deal with the business side of a studio. It is highly recommended that you familiarize yourself with a community for a few years, engaging deeply in its dance scene, before deciding to open a dance studio. You'll need to complete the market research necessary to understand a community's needs and gaps in its existing dance education offerings before taking a risk as big as establishing a business. Ensure that your community has a need and that you can fill that need with your dance studio. Spend time searching for the perfect location, writing a business plan, securing loans for a studio space, and gathering a team of people to help you reach your goal.

There are many financial costs and benefits to weigh when considering opening a dance studio. One of the major costs includes leasing or purchasing a building and outfitting it for studio use. Equipping a studio building involves installing sprung floors with Marley flooring, ballet barres, mirrors, curtains, sound systems, and lighting systems. Establish a reserve fund for emergency building repairs. Another major cost is insurance coverage. Select liability coverage that extends to all students, instructors, guests, and events happening in the building.

While it may seem like an uphill battle, dance studios can be lucrative investments if established in a responsible way and for the purpose of operating at a profit. Dance studios make the bulk of their money through tuition fees paid by the students in the school. Research competing businesses in your region and make sure you have calculated an ideal profit margin before deciding on pricing. Another way for dance studios to make money is to host guest residencies, recitals, and other events in the community in which participants and audience members pay for admission. Some dance studios also make money through fees related to costume purchasing, professional photos and videos, and summer camps and workshops.

Establishing a Business

Taking the time to write a business plan will help you determine realistic goals for your business and will help you lay the groundwork for the dance studio's branding and marketing efforts. A simple Internet search can give you a great deal of information about how to craft a business plan. In general, a business plan should include a mission and vision statement; description of your business; market analysis discussing how your business fits into the existing market of competitors; descriptions and qualifications of key personnel; a marketing plan; an analysis of your business's anticipated strengths, weaknesses, opportunities, and threats (SWOT analysis); a cash flow statement; and revenue projections (Hull 2013).

Invest in the assistance of a lawyer to help with other necessary legal items to attend to while you're starting a dance studio. These tasks include establishing a legal business entity, registering for taxes, setting up business accounting in preparation for annual tax filing, obtaining necessary permits, and opening a business bank account. Again, this initial investment will pay off in the long run because you will have done your due diligence to create a new business with legal and financial requirements in mind (How to Start an LLC 2018).

Building a Brand

An important task in the early days of launching a dance studio business is to establish an online presence. While the way you design and decorate your building defines your brand for your community, the way you present and promote your studio on a website and in social media identifies your business online. Website design is relatively simple and inexpensive, and creating a social media presence costs nothing. Before publicly announcing your website and social media accounts, develop your studio's brand by creating a "cohesive graphic identity that should flow from your print marketing to your website design" (Hamilton 2016, para 2). Work with a graphic designer to create a logo for your business and to decide on colors and fonts that represent the brand you wish to promote.

Your website should be the go-to location for anyone to gather information and make decisions about how to engage with your business. Always keep your website updated, choose a clean, sleek design for easy navigation, and use proper grammar and spelling. The most important elements of a studio website include location and contact information; links to social media, biographical information about studio owners, teachers, and staff; easy-to-read class schedules with class descriptions; online registration; studio policies, mission and history; and photos and video taken within your studio setting (Hamilton 2016).

Seemingly endless options for social media engagement with the public offer unique features that can help promote your dance studio. Before jumping into *all* of these platforms, research the demographic of each one and ensure the ones you activate align with your target audience. For example, Instagram and TikTok are popular among teenagers, while Facebook is more popular with parents (Marketing Charts 2019). YouTube, Snapchat, and Twitter also offer unique benefits that could attract new customers and engage your studio with the community and the industry. Be consistent in the visual images and tone of the language you use throughout all platforms so that your color palette and logo are always featured. Post regularly, interact with users, and encourage people to follow or like your page.

Gathering Resources

If you think studio ownership may be in your future, consider double majoring in business and dance or dance education in college. By the time you graduate, you will have already done much of the groundwork necessary to start and run a business. If college is already behind you, consider attending community workshops and studying online tutorials about the nuts and bolts of founding a business. Ensure you are well prepared and fully qualified to take on a professional project of this magnitude.

Once you have opened your school, stay on top of trends and new methods by remaining active in professional networks and taking advantage of continuing education opportunities. Attend competitions and conventions with your students in order to get a sense of new ideas in teaching and choreography. Invite guest teachers to your studio whenever possible to encourage community among dance professionals and expose your students to diverse styles and genres. Consider attending conferences held by professional organizations like the National Dance Education Organization and Dance/USA for a condensed experience in which you can learn about teaching strategies, advocacy and funding, and cultural and educational trends in the dance field. Staying informed as a dance educator is vital to your business's relevance and your ability to equip your students with accurate, up-to-date information about dance.

One of the best resources for researching a variety of topics related to dance studio ownership is *Dance Teacher* magazine and its affiliated website. The website contains a plethora of information about topics as wide ranging as starting a competition team, working with an accountant, facilitating efficient recital dress rehearsals, and staff management issues. As these issues arise (and they will), ensure you have a solid team of people who will provide you with information, guidance, and assistance, and make sure you know which resources you can turn to when you have questions or problems.

Marketing and Recruitment

Marketing your dance studio business is important to recruiting and retaining enthusiastic students and strong faculty. Invest in marketing, especially when your studio is new, because you need to introduce your business to the community.

Present your studio as an exciting and inviting new opportunity for dancers and families to be a part of, one that cannot be overlooked. Different communities and cities require different marketing strategies that depend on competition in your market, your geographical location, and the specific goals of your business.

One of the best ways to present an inviting space in which families will want to invest is by hosting an open house in your dance studio. An open house should be held during a weekend and a weekday and should include a registration table so that students can enroll for classes immediately. Including a series of dance classes in a variety of genres that are free and open to the public during open house events gives potential customers a taste of the amazing experience your studio offers and allows potential students and their families to meet and mingle with teachers and directors. An open house could also include opportunities for class discounts, door prizes, snacks, question-and-answer sessions, and guest appearances by VIPs in your community.

Advertising through print and media outlets can help build your business and promote upcoming events. Direct mailings, such as postcards and newsletters, can make people aware of your business when you first open your studio as well as when the beginning of the new year approaches and it is time to register students for an upcoming series of classes or special events. Fliers can target specific groups, organizations, businesses, or areas of the community in which you perceive a demand for your services. Ads in local newspapers are sometimes an effective way to spread the word about your new business. Ads on social media, television, and radio reach a variety of populations that might be interested in your studio. In general, social media ads provide flexibility and wide-ranging reach in your community and may be the most attractive marketing option upon opening a studio. This is because these ads can be easily adapted to fit any price range; they can be formatted in a variety of ways to include images, video, graphics, and text; and they can be adjusted to target specific populations of people who might be interested in your studio business. Television and radio ads tend to be more expensive, yet may increase the reach of your marketing to families not active on social media platforms. Some studio owners also advertise in newspapers and local magazines, but since print media is less popular than it used to be, these options are typically too expensive and limited in scope to be worth the added advertising cost. For specific information about cost effectiveness of the various advertising options available, *Dance Teacher* magazine's "Studio Owners" section is a terrific resource that is continuously updated with relevant information (Dance Teacher 2020).

Community exchanges and partnerships can provide excellent sources of support and publicity for your studio. Develop partnerships with local small businesses in order to create opportunities to support and promote each other. For example, a local dance wear or athletic wear business could offer parents coupons in exchange for purchasing a dedication to their child in your recital program. Hire a recital videographer or photographer for a reduced rate in exchange for a long-term contract or promotion of their business. Ask for donations of goods or services from local businesses in exchange for free or reduced-price ads in your recital program. The possibilities are endless; think creatively and present a persuasive proposal.

Actively participating in the community will help you reach areas of the market you wouldn't otherwise. For example, if your community hosts seasonal or holiday events, offer to stage a performance at them. Bring your elite group of competitive dancers to volunteer throughout the community and offer free performances and classes to the public. Showing goodwill in this way helps you establish yourself as a contributing and valuable local business and may make it more likely that you'll receive free publicity and an expanded customer base. At all of these community events, costume dancers in attire with your studio name and logo on it so the community members know who you are, and consider selling studio attire publicly: It's free advertisement!

Staffing and Managing a Dance Studio

The specific duties you assume as director of a dance studio are defined by you. Many directors also teach in their studios and may take on the role of business manager. You will likely need to hire additional staff, such as dance teachers and an administrative assistant to handle phone calls, questions, and other business while you are teaching or otherwise engaged. Depending on your approach to managing your business, you may also consider hiring a personal assistant to help with tasks related to recitals, competitions, and other events. Further, at various times, you may rely on the services of tax professionals, attorneys, plumbers, doctors, electricians, repair professionals, photographers, website designers, and lawn care professionals. Lastly, some necessary tasks can be handled by volunteers or parents of students, so keep these people in mind when you need help.

Before hiring teachers, decide how your curriculum will be designed, how many classes per week need to be taught and in what genres, and how involved you would like teachers to be in creating choreography for recitals or competitions. When you're starting out, you will benefit from advertising your studio's open positions and, eventually, you may rely on word-of-mouth referrals to recruit new teachers. Take time to interview all qualified applicants for your positions, asking specific questions about their qualifications, experience, interests, and availability. Ask applicants to teach—even just a mock class or a portion of a class—to get a sense of their teaching style and demeanor in the studio. It is not critical that all of your teaching staff adopt the same teaching style and, in fact, exposing students to diversity in teachers and styles will benefit them. Do ensure, though, that the teachers you hire are reliable, organized, experienced, caring, and clear in their teaching.

After assembling a terrific team of teaching faculty, make efforts to retain them by showing support and offering perks. Collaborate with teachers on ideas for curricular changes, recital themes, choreography, and costuming and music selections. Give them freedom to create and take ownership of their work with you. Offer incentives such as free classes for them, reduced price classes for their children, and bonuses for referrals. Additionally, at the end of each year and during the holiday season, surprise your staff with small tokens of appreciation such as a gift card with a handwritten note. These small benefits show staff members they are valued and they, in turn, will remain loyal to your business.

Create a faculty handbook that is discussed with each new faculty member at an orientation session and hold an annual retreat for all teaching staff. A faculty handbook should outline detailed studio policies and expectations for teachers. Include curricula, a student registration packet, confidentiality expectations, payment procedure, and a yearly calendar with specific expectations about and compensation structure for recitals, competitions, and other events. Also, define what professionalism means to you and detail your policies in regard to professional behavior, social media posts, photography, video, communication, attire, language, and workplace values. Include items such as contact information for reporting safety or facilities issues, inclement weather policy, parking location, attendance requirements, and communication protocols. Finally, include information about performance evaluations, behavioral consequences, and disciplinary action. All of this information should be reviewed with each new teacher. Don't just send teachers home with a big packet, discuss your expectations with them. This will illustrate to your teachers how seriously you take their work. Then, host an annual teacher retreat at your home or a cheerful gathering place where you and your staff can share ideas and stories in celebration of the past year and in preparation for the next.

Administering a Focused, Ethical Studio Business

One way to stay focused on the mission of your studio is to develop and continue to refine your curricula. First, you must survey your area to determine your target market. If, for example, there are many options in your area for ballet instruction for young children, it may be in your interest to develop a distinctive curriculum, perhaps geared toward jazz and musical theater styles or centered on the inclusion of competitive teams.

Once you've decided on your approach to dance education and training, write a teaching philosophy statement that identifies your major approaches to teaching children and your goals for your studio. Additionally, define the genres you offer and identify how each contributes to young dancers' training. List the levels offered in each genre, with the specific skills students will learn and what they will be expected to know by the end of the year. Also, describe how students are assigned to levels and the process of evaluation for continued progression through levels. If your studio includes competitive groups, identify in your curriculum how these students are selected and what additional training, if any, is required.

Another way to stay focused on the student experience in your dance studio is to create a detailed registration packet that each student receives in hard copy and can access online that outlines school policies and procedures. Specific topics should include attendance, illness, and etiquette policies; calendar; class schedule and descriptions; teacher and director biographies; tuition and payment information; registration form; and medical and photo or video release forms. You may also decide to include a dress code, facilities policies, and recital and event information. Your registration packet should be a living document, meaning you return to it every year and continually update it to reflect accurate and relevant information. You may consider giving parents only the most essential information in the registration packet to avoid information overload and then share additional information at a later date.

To maintain the integrity of your ethically led business, ensure you are well trained to manage the financial and legal elements of your job as a studio owner, or delegate some of these tasks to other professionals. Establish an annual budget and stick to it. You may prefer to purchase accounting software to help with this or you can hire an accountant, but you must begin managing cash flow right away. At first, be conservative in your spending and save for extras such as decor items and other nonessentials. Approach your business with optimism, but also prepare for the worst by building reserves in an emergency savings account. Keep your focus on student recruitment and retention and plan strategically for the long term.

In addition to financial considerations, you may want to hire an attorney to help you develop or review employee contracts, liability waivers, and releases; to ensure you have obtained all necessary permits and licenses; and to assist with annual taxes. Additionally, lawyers can help you understand whether or not you are in compliance with safety and health regulations and help you obtain appropriate music licensing and insurance policies. Doing your due diligence legally and financially will get your business off on the right foot and will support your work as an ethical and responsible leader.

SUMMARY

Working in a privately owned dance studio or school offers many benefits, including flexibility for a variety of professionals, opportunities for long-term employment, and even entrepreneurship. Part-time, temporary, and full-time opportunities are available for educators, choreographers, and administrative personnel. Witnessing the growth of students as they progress through a school is inspiring, and the opportunity to support their development as dancers and as children growing into adulthood is a significant and joyful responsibility. Approach your career in dance studio teaching or ownership or both knowing you will work hard, you will be constantly recalibrating in different schools and for different student needs, and you will be rewarded endlessly with student and teaching successes.

Reflection

QUALIFICATIONS INVENTORY FOR DANCE STUDIO WORK

Create an inventory of multiple lists to gain a sense of how you are qualified to work in a dance school or studio and what your interests and goals are in this sector. Think of this as a fun, free-writing exercise that will help you identify your strengths and can be used as a reference later.

1. Make a list of everyone you know who works in a dance studio or school. This can represent the start of establishing your network!

2. List the genres of dance, ages, and levels you are qualified to teach.

3. List your ideas for recital or competition choreography, including songs you have always wanted to use, costume ideas, movement ideas, and themes or concepts you'd like to explore.

4. Make a list of online resources that will help you conduct further research, such as competition websites, costume and prop sites, teaching blogs, and local studio reviews.

5. If you are interested in opening your own school or working as an administrator, begin making lists of people and organizations you could approach for help or advice, possible studio locations, marketing ideas, studio policies, leadership strategies, and recital themes.

As your career working in dance studios evolves, return to these lists often to remind yourself of your strengths and interests and to reassess your goals.

Chapter 5

Nonprofit Dance Companies and Organizations

"To dance is to be out of yourself. Larger, more beautiful, more powerful. This is power, it is glory on earth and it is yours for the taking."

Agnes de Mille

"Because art does for me what religion does—it organizes a seemingly chaotic world. Because it is my way of making sense of the world and its changes."

Bill T. Jones

In the past several decades, funding for nonprofit dance companies has declined; however, many opportunities still exist for working in them. Depending on the mission and vision of each company, some positions are seasonal, temporary, or part time; some include a lot of travel; and some may even begin as unpaid internships. There are also possibilities for founding your own company or organization. In complete transparency, opportunities for full-time, consistent work in dance companies are rare and are highly sought after. Job growth for dancers in the United States is projected to remain steady, with little to no change from 2018 to 2028, and employment of choreographers is projected to decline by 3 percent during that period (U.S. Bureau of Labor Statistics 2020). This data illustrates growth that is slightly slower than the average for all occupations in the U.S. However, this does not mean you should shy away from these jobs, just be aware of the state of this area of the industry.

Salary data on company dancers is minimal, but some sources estimate average annual salary at around $34,000 (Payscale n.d.; Dance Magazine 2018). The U.S. Bureau of Labor Statistics reports that the median hourly wage for dancers in the

Katherine Crockett

Dancer, actress, producer: principal dancer with the Martha Graham Dance Company, Queen from *Queen of the Night* **(off Broadway), guest artist with White Oak Dance Project, and founder and artistic director of ExquisiteMuse Productions**

Courtesy of Katherine Crockett.

What is your advice to those hoping to pursue a career in dance?

We dance because we have to dance, because our souls, our bodies, and our hearts need to move and express and communicate through the language of the body. It is not for recognition, fame, approval, and certainly not for money. It is for the pure communion with the impulse of life. And while it is this very process that brings us the fulfillment of truly being alive in the moment, it is also a path that requires you to put everything you are into it. Often there are periods of frustration and exhaustion when the body isn't able to do what we want or need it to. Keep working through this mindfully. Know that consistency is key, and an obsessive desire is a must, but also know that in order to get the most out of your body, you must treat it with love. I advise any dancer dealing with a serious injury to have a good doctor and a good physical therapist. My team of therapists have helped me get through my long career both physically and emotionally. If needed, I recommend finding a good psychotherapist too. At various points in my career I've struggled with anxiety and self-confidence issues. I found a life-changing therapist who helped give me back complete control over my emotional state using biofeedback and breathing techniques. There are also various forms of therapy and meditation and so I recommend finding what works for you. The mind and the body are connected and the best dancers know that imagination and creativity make the difference between someone who is physically executing a technical skill, and someone who is an artist, who has

United States in 2018 was $16.31, and for choreographers it was $22.98. These figures are misleading because company dancer and choreographer salaries are highly variable depending on the specifics of the contract each artist signs, how many months of the year a season comprises, and where the company is located. For example, a dancer's annual salary of $10,000 sounds very low, but if that dancer performs for only a few months out of the year and lives in a location with a low cost of living, it would still be possible to piece together a reasonable living.

This chapter provides career options in nonprofit dance companies and organizations in the areas of performance, choreography, and artistic leadership. A discus-

found a language of communication in the dance steps, which become a living, moving journey connecting to the hearts of others. This artistic depth and creativity must be nourished and developed alongside dance technique. It is not something added at the end like frosting on a cake. It *is* the cake. Seek out choreographers and teachers who encourage you to bring your unique creativity to the movement. It is not just about being a good dancer, it's about your ability to be vulnerable and courageous enough to open your heart and share what's inside with the audience. Take the risk of letting go and knowing that in the moment you might not be "perfect," but you will be creating beauty that is transformative and alive. This is often more interesting to watch and to experience. Your technique is what supports you and gives you this freedom to let go on stage.

Looking back, what have been the best decisions you have made during your career?
Deciding to take risks and work with various projects even though it meant leaving something stable and known was so important as it made me grow in ways I couldn't have otherwise and made me become better as an artist. Focus on what you love, but allow room for the unknown and remain open—for we are always learning. I believe that it's up to each of us to create our lives in ways that are fulfilling to us. If no one is casting you in what you want to dance, go create it yourself. Desire to find a way, and the way will find you. Be open to things that are outside of what you had planned. Also, I am grateful for those decisions I made to say yes to new projects and cultivate other talents I have, which has added to my artistry and to my network of connections and resources. I remain curious and keep myself inspired by seeing performances and art, reading, and trying new things and by taking time to keep a sense of discovery in my dancing . . . every day there is something new to be found. And here's a big one: I decided not to let fear keep me from what I want or from living a full happy life. My own variation on a quote I read somewhere: Fear is a dragon with a gift in its mouth; tame the dragon and the gift is yours.

sion about auditioning, branding, and networking leads to a section on founding a nonprofit organization, working with a board of directors, recruiting and managing a company, and developing marketing and budget strategies.

PERFORMING IN A DANCE COMPANY

Performing positions in dance companies are highly variable. Companies can be structured differently and take various approaches to contracting with dancers. Very few companies can hire salaried dancers because of an overall lack of funding for the arts. Many of the companies equipped to hire dancers on an annual basis are located in large metropolitan cities such as New York, Los Angeles, and Chicago. Most other U.S. communities house at least one nonprofit dance company, although the dancers in them are typically hired on a seasonal, temporary, part-time, or even project-to-project basis. This means that many company dancers must have additional means of earning a living. To prepare for securing a job in a dance company, focus on training and preparing for the audition process. Additionally, it is important to learn how to build your brand, network with other professionals, and pinpoint the kind of company for which you wish to work. Identifying your goals and working diligently toward them will assist you in your performance career.

Training and Preparation

To be competitive in the field as a performer, you must pursue rigorous, concentrated dance training. Most professional company dancers begin their training as children and progress through technical advancement in private studios and schools into adulthood. It is important for dancers to have a wide range of expertise and be able to perform multiple genres and styles of dance. Technical skill and precision are often valued as is performance presence, resilience, reliability, and overall professionalism.

Training in studios that will support your growth as a dancer or choreographer throughout your career is important. The early education you receive lays a foundation for the way you approach training your body for the rest of your career. Further, you must continue to invest in training in different studios into adulthood, continuing the trajectory of your technical growth. Select studios that value technical and artistic excellence, healthy bodies, and useful teaching methods. Research the teachers working in these studios, paying attention to their professional achievements and specialty areas. Some dancers feel that a studio with a competitive culture helps them develop grit as they approach the rigors of a career, while others prefer a serious, yet focused school geared toward technical training and performances. As you advance in your training and performance abilities, expect to spend more time in the studio. At any point in your training and professional career, if you don't feel you are progressing at the level you would like to, consider attending classes at more than one studio or change schools completely.

Class etiquette is very important and serves as a precursor to professionalism in the workplace. Ensure you take seriously every class, meeting, performance, and other opportunity related to your future dance career. When you take class, always be attentive, engaged, and polite, even if you're not feeling that way. Be aware of how you share the space with others; how you contribute to an inquisitive class environment; and how you model strong work ethic, professional behavior, and respect for yourself and others.

Maintaining a healthy lifestyle is another important element of training and preparing for a career in dance, especially because dance is extremely physically demanding, it necessitates aesthetic considerations, and is full of rejection. The way your body looks and performs is important and your health and well-being should be a top priority. Therefore, approach your diet, sleep, and cross-training as essential parts of your training regimen. Additionally, give yourself plenty of time for rest and recovery and maintain self-care strategies and friendships that will add balance and joy to your life. Prioritizing your physical, mental, and emotional well-being will enhance your abilities and continued development.

The College Choice

Some dancers who aim to perform full time in dance companies secure positions immediately following secondary education and others prefer to pursue additional or different training in a collegiate environment before pursuing company work. Collegiate dance programs provide excellent training for advanced dancers on their way to professional performing careers and can offer education in additional skills that may be beneficial to careers in the long term, such as in business, leadership, pedagogy, choreography, and technical theater. Additionally, postsecondary training environments are useful places to establish a network of like-minded colleagues and professional resources with whom you can share experiences and gain opportunities during your career. Still, some dancers feel pressured by the limited amount of time their bodies can withstand the rigors of dancing professionally and choose to put postsecondary education off if or until it becomes necessary to develop additional skills for different employment.

Finding a Community

Decide on a community in which to establish yourself before you begin actively auditioning so you will have a chance to get to know the company scene in that community before committing to any one position. Take classes at multiple studios, talk to dancers you meet, and reach out to anyone you know who is already work-ing in that city to get a sense of opportunities. If possible, take class with artistic directors of companies for which you're interested in auditioning and let them know how much you would love to work for their company. This strategy works well because it gives directors multiple opportunities to watch you dance, learn new material, and interact with others—all important elements directors consider when hiring new dancers.

If you relocate to a new community or city in which you know no one, don't let the first few months get you down. Reestablishing yourself in a new place takes time and will likely be uncomfortable for a while as you get to know the lay of the land. Embrace uncertainty by introducing yourself to new people and invit-ing them to coffee. Even if this idea sounds way outside of your comfort zone, try to engage this way as much as possible for the purpose of gaining professional contacts. You may end up with new colleagues who also become friends, which is doubly beneficial for you.

Finally, make it a priority to attend as many performances as you can afford. Not only does this continue your dance education, but it also helps you understand how each dance company in a community contributes to the overall dance scene there. Then, you'll have an even better idea of which companies would be a good fit for you so you can channel your energies in that direction.

Courtesy of Naomi Hill.

Dancer Cera Taylor of Flatlands Dance Theatre.

Researching Companies

One of the best ways to discover dance companies and better understand their goals, brand, and structure is by searching online. Examine companies' websites, paying attention to their mission and vision statements, director and dancer biographies, event calendars, and images and videos of performances or rehearsals. You might also get a sense of how much support the company enjoys by noticing expressions of gratitude to foundations, granters, corporate sponsors, or individual donors in published materials. Social media activity can illuminate many elements of a company's culture and ways of interacting with the community and the field at large. Pay attention to which social media platforms each company values, how often they post, what their posts are about, and the kind of language they use in posts.

Finally, if you are interested in working in a particular company, seek others who are already working there or who have in the past. Ask questions about their experience with the company regarding the season and events, schedules, vacation time, pay scale, working relationships, technical and training expectations, health and retirement benefits, and professional perks. Try to gather as much information as you can so you can approach auditions from an informed place.

Preparing Audition Materials

Most companies require auditioning dancers to bring a résumé and head shot with them in addition to wearing appropriate clothing and shoes for the audition. Some companies require supplementary materials such as full-length or quarter photographs or links to your website or video performance reel. If you are auditioning for a musical theater or interdisciplinary company, expect to prepare additional items related to the company's focus. For example, if you audition for a company that produces musicals, you will be asked to prepare a vocal audition (usually comprising 32 bars of music) and a brief monologue. Finally, some companies will ask you to prepare a choreographed solo to perform at the audition.

Your headshot should reflect your most authentic and professional self. Request photographer recommendations from your network and expect to spend a significant amount of money, between $400-$1,200, for quality headshots. Wear flattering clothing that is clean and pressed in solid, jewel tones that enhance your best attributes. Wear everyday makeup and wear your hair nicely. If hair and makeup are not your strong suit, hire someone to do it for the photos. Men should be clean shaven and have a recent haircut (if this is your preferred professional look). Work with your photographer to decide on the best space, which may be outdoors or indoors, and the best lighting and surrounding colors that will complement you. Keep in mind that whenever there is a major change to your appearance, such as a change in hair color or cut, tattoos, piercings, or major weight gain or loss, you should have new headshots made. Additionally, update your headshots occasionally as you age to reflect your most recent appearance.

Your résumé should include as many of your accomplishments and experiences as possible to illustrate your preparedness for company work. Include your contact information and personal website, employment history, performance and choreography experience, education and training, and special skills such as juggling or acting. Additionally, some companies want to know your height, weight, hair color, and eye color. For all entries, include locations and dates so employers can sense the timeline of your work in the field. Do a simple online search for résumé templates, which can help you organize information into an easily readable document.

Work with educators and other mentors to refine your audition materials before heading out to auditions. Work with an experienced mentor to build your résumé (sometimes limited to one page), ask other dancers for their opinions about audition attire choices, and work with coaches to perfect your danced solo, monologue, or vocal audition piece, if those are required elements of the auditions you will attend. These tasks are time consuming, so give yourself plenty of time in advance of launching into the audition circuit.

Auditioning

On the day of an audition, be prepared! Most companies will let you know what to expect. Some auditions include same-day callbacks, which can make for very long days. Therefore, pack a bag with résumé and headshot, extra clothing, dance shoes, snacks, water, first aid items, supplies for makeup and hair touchups, and a book or something else to occupy downtime. Be sure to get plenty of sleep the night before.

Attire and Appearance

You should look put together and ready to dance on the day of your audition. Your attire should be form fitting and appropriate for the style of dance the company performs. For example, if auditioning for a ballet company, women should wear a leotard and tights and men should wear tights and a formfitting tee; if auditioning for a contemporary company, attire can include formfitting tops, yoga leggings or pants that cover the knees, and even kneepads. All clothing should fit well and should be in good condition with no loose strings or holes. Keep jewelry to an absolute minimum. Hair should be secured and styled, and women should wear at least a bit of makeup. Bring extra shoes and a change of clothing if you don't have a lot of details about what to expect.

Keep a positive and energized appearance throughout the audition process. This is your chance to show company directors, choreographers, and future colleagues that you want this job and that you uphold high standards for professionalism and enthusiasm in the workplace. Be polite and friendly with others auditioning, but also be alert and attentive to those facilitating the audition. Don't sit down or chat excessively unless specifically instructed to do so.

Audition Processes

Some auditions are advertised as open, meaning, anyone can audition during the date and time scheduled. Some are appointment based, some are by invitation only, and still others require the support of an agent (see more about agents in chapter 6). Finally, some companies accept video auditions and, while this can be a helpful option for dancers unable to attend an audition, it is advisable to show up in person whenever possible.

Auditions typically begin with a process of submitting audition materials to a company representative. Some companies take photos of auditionees so directors can recall dancers based on what they are wearing that day. You may be asked to provide contact information and availability. A warm-up, either self-guided or led by a company member or director, may follow. Then, you will learn various movement material, possibly including center combinations, traveling phrases, improvisation-based scores, contact and partner work, or movement with spoken word or other theatrical elements. You may also be asked to choreograph a phrase. This is not the time for hesitation. Go for it, being as authentic and open to the experience as possible.

During the audition, there may be several rounds of learning and performing with continuous cuts being made, or the company may prefer to keep everyone together learning the same material throughout the process. Pace yourself, but remember that during the entire audition—even when you are on the side of the room waiting for your turn to perform—you are being observed and assessed for your ability to fit well into the company, enhance its strengths, and bring something unique to it.

When the audition is over, thank as many of the company representatives as possible before leaving. If you are interviewed during the process, be prepared to speak highly of the company, mentioning your favorite elements and how you will fit well into it. Depending on the needs of the company, you may know that day whether or not you will be hired, or you may experience a wait of up to several months before hearing the results. Don't spend too much time ruminating over mistakes you made in the audition and don't sit and wait for the phone to ring.

These habits can lead to self-doubt and can limit your ability to move forward. Try to focus on the things you did well and begin researching your next audition. Keep moving ahead by auditioning for as many opportunities as you are qualified for and excited about.

Branding and Networking

As an independent artist, you must take steps to promote your brand. This is your identity as defined by your unique strengths, abilities, look or type, and special relevant skills. Think of your online brand as your visual résumé. By publishing a well-constructed package of your accomplishments and activities on a personal website and on social media, you give potential employers an inside look at what it would be like to work with you and may convince them that they should hire you. Further, your network of professional colleagues will be able to keep up with your career through online sources, which could lead to future collaborative opportunities. Taking advantage of branding tools will help you home in on opportunities best suited for you and will create visibility for you as a working artist in the field.

Building Your Brand as a Performer

Career experts agree that an active online presence is the most important component of developing and promoting your brand, second only to in-person interactions and auditions (Mfuko 2019; Loucadoux and Margheritis 2017; Stevenson, Miller, and Russell 2013). Your branding materials should be visually appealing, clearly laid out, and up to date and should tell a story or elicit an emotional connection from viewers.

Personal websites are most often used for branding in dance because they are easily developed, relatively inexpensive, and can be continuously updated. The first step is to select a website-building platform such as WordPress, Wix, or SquareSpace. Some of these are free and others require a fee, so research this beforehand so you can work within your budget. Then, select a domain name (e.g., www.yournamehere.com) that clearly identifies you. Next, purchase a plan from a web-hosting provider such as InMotion Hosting, GoDaddy, or HostGator. Most plans renew annually, and you can select from a multitude of options for featuring video and photos, displaying information, sending and receiving messages, and connecting to your social media accounts.

The homepage should include your name and contact information, brief biography or tagline describing your mission as a performer, and a compelling image or video. Include drop-down menus for additional items of interest that browsers can navigate through easily. Each person organizes and groups these items differently but definitely include photos and videos of your best work, complete résumé, and links to social media pages. You can also include information about upcoming events and performances, a page dedicated to choreography or other related skills, and press coverage. If you have an agent, don't forget to include their contact information as well. Use a premade template provided by the website design platform for a clean, effective layout, and simple yet thorough navigation experience.

If you don't already participate in social media, consider joining at least a few of the following platforms: Facebook, Instagram, Twitter, and YouTube. They are free to use, easy to operate, and terrific for promoting your brand through high-quality, well-designed presentation options. Whereas your website should present your comprehensive profile, your social media should represent your everyday activities, stories, and current projects and shows. When you post someone else's choreography, make sure you seek permission to post their work. Additionally, consider how you present images and colors as part of your brand and aim to align the aesthetic of your website with that of your social media presence.

When considering what and how often to post, adopt specific strategies or goals you want to reach in your online presence. For example, one of your goals could be to illustrate the most impressive technical skills, such as extreme flexibility or a knack for complicated turning sequences. Aim to post a video or photo of yourself demonstrating these best technical attributes about once a week. Whenever you take a terrific class with a new teacher or you travel somewhere exciting to perform, document these highlights on social media and consider adding a blog feature to your website in which you could cross list these items. It is also possible within certain app settings to instantly share to several social media platforms simultaneously. This can be helpful if you engage with different groups of people on each platform, but it can also become tiresome if your followers are the same across all platforms.

Networking

It is critical for your career development and longevity to invest time and resources into growing your professional network. Ideally, your network will comprise a diversity of professionals in dance, including performers, choreographers, teachers, lighting designers, personal trainers, musicians, and people you have worked with or met at auditions or classes. People in your network will support your career by advocating for you to casting and artistic directors, sending audition announcements and other opportunities to you, and asking you to collaborate on projects.

Your classmates in high school, college, and other previous training experiences provide an automatic and potentially strong network because you have spent a great deal of time with them and they know your strengths and specialties as a performer. Upon entering a new school or program, start making connections with the people training alongside you to gauge your commonalities and potential for working together in the future. You may discover you have much in common with someone unexpected, which could lead to fruitful collaborations. At some point, you may move on to a next phase in life or relocate to a new city, so you will lose the dailiness of your interactions with these classmates; however, the dance world is small and it is likely you will continue to run into these people throughout your career.

Taking class and attending auditions is a great way to expand your network, particularly when you take class in a new city or a new school. Make a point to speak to people before and after class and consider asking a new friend for coffee or to meet up to see a show together. The larger your network, the more likely you are to hear about and even be offered unique career opportunities. Always say yes to meeting new people, whether or not they can help you now. Your career will evolve over time and your relationships will too, so you may rediscover former contacts later in your career.

Not only is social media a great tool for branding yourself, it also offers opportunities to significantly expand your network. Social media is especially beneficial for people who are introverted and for reaching out to people you've recently met. Everyone wants to expand their network, so receiving a connection request from you will be flattering to many dance professionals and would be welcomed. Further, by adding new friends and contacts, you will likely be invited to more events and know more about the field and dance in your community. In addition, use social media to support others in the field: Share their posts about upcoming shows and accomplishments. Learn now to be a champion for your fellow dance professionals.

Working in a Company

Performing in a dance company is highly variable because every company maintains a unique organizational structure, way of working together, mission, and goals. One thing is certain: Dancing with a company is sustained physical and mental work. Your body, technique, and performance skills will be challenged. Expect to spend a bulk of your time taking class, rehearsing, and performing. This may not come as news; nevertheless, many new company dancers express feeling overwhelmed by the sudden impact that full days of dancing have on their bodies. Prioritize your body's well-being and take seriously a healthy diet, proper sleep, cross-training, and self-care.

Courtesy of Naomi Hill.

Dancers Michelle Gomez, Molly Roberts, Leslie Ortiz, and Sarah Mondle of Flatlands Dance Theatre.

That said, dancing in a company can be incredibly fulfilling because of the opportunities to collaborate with other artists, explore creatively, challenge yourself physically, and perform and train with amazing colleagues. Further, dancing with a company may also include perks such as traveling, media coverage, special events, and working with guest artists.

Training

As a professional dancer, your top priority should be on the training and care of your body because it is your artistic instrument. If not in peak condition, you could lose out on opportunities for roles and advancement in the company and you could put yourself at risk for injury. Most companies that employ dancers full time hold a daily company class in which dancers continue refining technique and performance abilities and prepare their bodies for the day's rehearsals or performance. Take class seriously, but pace yourself so that you don't exhaust yourself at the beginning of the day. Class is for you—the time to explore your body's daily tensions and technical areas that need attention.

In addition to daily class, dancers incorporate cross-training and body-care practices into their routines. Many professional dancers take classes in genres outside those their company performs on their days off in order to stay relevant and trained in those forms. Cross-training methods for dancers include weight training, yoga, Pilates, cardio, and swimming. Anything that helps you maintain balance, stamina, and strength is a good choice. Professional dancers also rely on many methods of caring for their bodies, including massage, physical therapy, stretching, water therapy, meditation, and somatic practices. Overall, because your dancer's body will undertake significant daily physical challenges, scheduling time to attend to its needs outside rehearsal and class is vital for injury and pain prevention.

Performance Expectations

Dancers' performance schedules and expectations depend on how performance seasons are structured in each company. For example, according to San Francisco Ballet's online 2020 season calendar, dancers working in the company perform from January through May and tour through much of the summer (San Francisco Ballet 2019). Well-established companies tend to offer more consistent seasons, so their dancers are better able to know what events to expect. In these companies, dancers may perform 3 to 10 evenings in a row and possible matinee performances. Then, a small break may occur during which the company learns or rehearses new works to show a few weeks later. Dancers may be cast in many of the works being shown, or they may be cast as swings to rotate into roles as needed when dancers are injured or ill.

Dancers working in smaller or less-established companies, on the other hand, may be just as busy as those working in larger companies, but performances are aligned with opportunity or ongoing projects rather than based on a fixed season calendar. Finally, if you are hired on a part-time or temporary basis, performance expectations vary. For example, a company whose season runs for only a few months out of the year may require dancers to perform daily during those few months. In any case, make sure you understand and agree to performance expectations before signing a contract with a company.

Approach to Rehearsals

As in any rehearsal situation, working with different choreographers and dancers and within different technical styles presents a unique challenge. Work to support the choreographer's vision, foster positive working relationships with fellow dancers, and constantly develop technical and performance abilities. Dancers may be asked to audition repeatedly even after joining a company because choreographers often want control over casting their works. This practice is why your ongoing reputation for professionalism and strong artistic and technical abilities is important. Establish yourself as a dancer willing to take risks, open to new experiences, and with diverse technical skills and creative potential. Finally, be curious and open minded to new ideas and changes within existing works. These qualities will help choreographers and other dancers sense your commitment to the work.

The Touring Life

Touring with a company is exciting because you may have opportunities to explore new places, meet and work with different people, and perform in new spaces. Touring is often limited to the most established companies because large-scale funding for arts exchanges and traveling is scarce. Many companies schedule a handful of touring performances within the same region that occur back-to-back to maximize funding. Some companies are commission based and schedule each residency separately. Many companies travel by bus, air, car, and train, and lodging may be through hotels, Airbnb, or even in private homes. During tours, company dancers continue to take class and rehearse during the day and perform at night.

Touring presents exciting career possibilities, but there are also drawbacks to consider. Because dance companies typically operate on a tight budget, expect transportation and lodging to reflect fiscal moderation. Flying first class and lodging at extravagant hotels may not be possible. Additionally, expect each performance venue to be outfitted differently with distinct flooring, lighting, and backstage resources. Also, for some people, living out of a suitcase can become tiresome and lonely. If you have a family at home or you require a lot of alone time, a touring lifestyle may not be for you. Finally, remember that responsibilities such as bills, home repairs, family obligations, and appointments will still be waiting for you when you return home, so try to find ways to continue addressing your homelife while touring. Overall, while touring with a company can expand your creative and artistic potential, consider carefully the pros and cons of such a lifestyle to ensure it will be fulfilling for you.

Choreographing in a Company

Even more elusive than dancer positions in companies are choreographer positions in them. Some choreographers are also the artistic directors of their companies, which produce mostly or entirely their own work. Others are hired on a seasonal or commissioned basis. The hiring process, payment, schedule, and working environment vary drastically. Many choreographers first develop reputations as dancers and then shift into choreography. The ones who start careers as choreographers often found their own companies or take the reins of directing a company. Some choreographers are self-taught or mentored creatively, while others develop skills through formal education routes such as conservatory or postsecondary training. If you are passionate about pursuing a career in choreography, start developing your artistic voice now and take steps to start branding and networking.

Branding and Networking

Choreographers rely on many of the same strategies as dancers for branding and networking. Create an impactful website that highlights a video reel of your most successful choreography and lists your commissions and residencies with companies, universities, and studios. Social media is another great avenue for your work to be seen widely and for seeking opportunities for presenting it. If you also teach or choreograph in multiple genres, feature these elements as part of your brand. If you receive awards or honors, publicize them.

One way to become known for choreography is to present your work at regional and national dance and fringe festivals around the world. These festivals typically publicize a call for submissions online or through organizational email lists such as Dance/USA, *Dance Magazine*, Dance/NYC, or Dance ICONS. Sometimes these submissions require entrance fees, so weigh this cost against the likelihood of acceptance and the scope and prestige of the venue and hosting organization. Many festivals offer a choreographer stipend, production support, and advertisement for the work. Another benefit of showing work at festivals is that you will share concerts with other artists, so you will have plenty of opportunity to network and build relationships.

Another way to choreograph for companies is to progress through the ranks of a company and consistently plug your interest in dance making. Because some companies strive to maintain a historical legacy, supporting a choreographer from within the company is preferred. At first, you may be asked to prove your abilities by rehearsal directing or choreographing works for outreach or on a trial basis. These are terrific opportunities nevertheless to gain wonderful experience in developing your artistic voice and deciding how you like to work on creative projects.

Commissions

Being commissioned by a company for a choreographic work is an honor that comes with significant responsibility. After all, commissioned work represents a company and its commitment to artistic excellence and integrity. Often, a commission will include a residency unless you happen to live in the same location as the company. Make sure a commission contract includes expectations for all of the following: residency length and number of hours for rehearsal, casting and rehearsal direction procedures, technical and production support such as lighting and costuming, and details about your work postresidency such as the length of time that the company has the right to reproduce your work. Contracts should also include specific dates and payment amount and process. If the contract does not include information about transportation, lodging, or meals, ensure you have someone from the company document this agreement as well.

A company residency is intense and concentrated because it requires choreographing or setting an existing work in a brief amount of time. Preparing in advance of working with the company is critical to working efficiently. Prework could include selecting music or sound to accompany the work, deciding on a choreographic intention, writing out prompts to try with dancers in rehearsal, and spending time alone in the studio inventing movement to teach dancers when you arrive. During a residency, a choreographer's ability to be prepared, clear, and efficient is important because it allows time to complete and refine the choreography. As in any creative process, things shift and don't always work perfectly, and flexibility is required. Try not to get too bogged down in the minutia of the choreography and stay open to possibilities.

After a residency, continue to check in with directors, technical staff, and dancers as they continue to refine and prepare the choreography for performance. Ask if you can obtain video of your work for your personal archive and for including in your branding materials.

Selecting Dancers

The process of selecting dancers differs based on the circumstances of a position. A resident choreographer or artistic director can expect to have a large role in selecting the dancers who comprise their work. Further, these choreographers cast dancers however they choose by holding auditions for specific works, watching dancers take class, or by getting to know their performance abilities and ways of working through consistent interactions. Commissioned choreographers, on the other hand, may have a cast assigned to them, or casting can be done from afar. In some cases, choreographers don't know the dancers well, so learning how the abilities of the dancers available to them can fulfill their choreographic vision is a process. Sometimes, this can be a pleasant surprise if the dancers are adept and eager, while, at other times, strategies for motivating and coaxing dancers out of their comfort zones and into new styles of movement are necessary.

Establishing Expectations

At the beginning of every new creative process, expectations and goals should be shared with the dancers and other artists involved. This helps everyone in the creative team to start off working toward the same goal. Dancers want to support choreographers' methods and vision, so letting them into the process and how you think about the work can only help you achieve your best work. Define expectations in regard to reliability, rehearsal documentation, and communication. Also, describe a typical creative process, including how you prefer to invent movement, how you invite dancer involvement in creative decision making, rehearsal communication preferences (e.g., through movement, writing, speaking), and expectations for running the work (e.g., when or if marking movement is acceptable). Working with dancers who are clear about choreographic and process expectations is often a smooth, positive, fruitful process.

Process Options

The best way to discover how you like to make dance is to choreograph . . . a lot. Try new ideas, ways of working, and collaborative possibilities in order to refine your artistic voice and your preferred methods of creation. After much investigation, you may prefer to select music first and let that be the impetus for choreographic exploration. Or, you may decide on a choreographic intention, aboutness, or structure for your work before beginning to invent movement or select accompaniment. Or, you might be inspired by others—painters, poets, songwriters, sculptors, actors, scientists—and use their ideas as the starting point for your dances. You may work best by creating movement through improvisation on your own in the studio and bringing that to your first rehearsal with dancers. Or, you may want them to create the bulk of the movement through various prompts or exercises. Or, you may enjoy creating an entire dance in your mind, documenting it, and then teaching it to the dancers, manipulating and editing as needed. Or, you might appreciate variety so that every process is different. As you expand your ideas about dance making, infinite possibilities emerge. Ensure that your preferences align with the mission and philosophies of the company in which you are employed.

Other Needs: Costumes, Set, Music, Lighting

Remember that there is more to a choreographer's job than simply creating choreography. Choreographers also must work with others to make decisions about costuming, props, set design, lighting design, music, and other envisioned elements of a dance. If you are not in a position to make decisions about budgets or purchasing, communicate often with managers to ensure your vision can be fulfilled. Write a description of your vision and bring photos or drawings that can help designers support your goals. Think about the colors, materials, intensities, and tones you want in your dance. Include information about your choreographic inspiration, movement qualities, narrative arc, characters, use of stage space, and music. These elements can help designers create with you. Additionally, consider taking classes in technical theater so you will be well versed in the vernacular of these art forms as well and can better communicate with designers. Overall, developing positive working relationships with technical staff is important to the successful outcome of your choreography.

ARTISTIC LEADERSHIP

Serving a company as a leader is a massive responsibility—one that also comes with a multitude of benefits, including the ability to propel your artistry, develop and pursue an artistic vision, and support fellow artists in working toward a collective mission. Whether your goal is to fill an existing artistic or executive director role or to found your own company or organization, artistic leadership is a huge undertaking that demands rigorous preparation and consideration before pursuing it as a career. This need for considerable training often translates to artistic leaders that are already seasoned career professionals in dance. If this is a professional goal of yours, consider how your decisions in college and your early professional career could help bolster your odds of achieving director status. For example, because you will need experience in choreography, fundraising, marketing, community engagement, audience development, and grant writing, find ways in your early education to gain these skills and, at the same time, grow as an artist.

Founding a Nonprofit Organization

Starting your own dance company is a monumental undertaking; prepare for the process to take over your life for a little while. First steps may include identifying a market need and the company's mission, filing for incorporation and nonprofit 501(c)(3) tax-exempt status with the federal government (ideally, with the assistance of an attorney), raising seed money to fund the company's immediate needs, and gathering a team to help you get the company off the ground. These people can be assembled informally, or you may want to start a company with others who act as a collective, making decisions together.

Surveying your community for its dance company market is vital to future success. Unless your company offers something unique to a community or that community is underserved, it is unlikely that you will be successful if the market is already saturated. Therefore, ask yourself and those in your founding team how your company will meet a need in your community, what you hope to achieve in founding it, and how your company will distinguish itself from others. For example, you may be interested in creating a company invested in your city's unique historical and cultural elements, or a company that creates interdisciplinary or site-specific works, or a company that features emerging women artists.

In these introductory conversations and brainstorming sessions, take a hard look at the financial realities of founding a company. How will your productions, artists, and staff be funded? Some funding sources include grants, corporate sponsorships, individual donations, and ticket sales. Where will your company rehearse and perform? Are those spaces available and affordable? Do you know people in the community who could be hired for administrative tasks such as budgeting and fundraising? Is there an audience for your company and will you be able to grow your audience in this community? Create a budget and consider long-term strategies for reaching financial goals.

Once these questions are answered, establish the name of your company, develop its mission and vision statements, start a website and social media accounts, and propose a plan for raising seed money for the company's first season. Create a logo and make other branding decisions such as fonts, colors, ways of using language, and ways of presenting images that align with the company's mission. Reach out to people in your networks who could support your new endeavor. If you know studio owners, propose the possibility of donated or reduced-price rehearsal space. Ask lawyers and accountants to take you on as a pro bono client. Contact local and

Jeanne Mam-Luft

Founder and director of MamLuft&Co. Dance

What have been your most significant experiences as a working professional in dance? Through working for an outside presenting organization, I was able to gain insight into a scale of presenting and touring that my own fledgling organization will not see for years. Through this position, I was able to meet seminal and developing artists from across the country and learn about their process, their paths, and their sustainability models. So much of working in dance in America means working as a nonprofit to obtain funding. While grant writing has certainly not been my favorite aspect of my work, it is significant and, when successful, it is a great boost. In recent years, I have worked with my organization to obtain several large grants, which underscores that our work is meaningful, effective, and of high value. Collaborations with other organizations and artists have brought much knowledge and experience to the people in our organization and to me, personally. It has allowed us to create work with international artists, to present work in internationally significant spaces, and to expand our perception of dance.

Courtesy of Jeanne Mam-Luft.

What is your best advice to those hoping to pursue a career in dance?

Don't overthink it like I did and do! So many passionate and talented dancers give up on dance because they feel that they need "a real job," that dance cannot be it, and they're not sure what path to take in life. I see far too many stop themselves before they should. Whether it's pressure from yourself, your

regional media outlets to make public announcements about your new company; they may want to produce newspaper or television stories about this new addition to the community arts scene. Disseminating information about your company to people in your community and in the dance field can help strengthen its initial impact.

It may seem impossible to raise seed money without having already established a reputation in a community, but there are ways to do this (Sims 2005). For instance, staging a small showing in a donated venue and charging admission is an effective strategy for initial fundraising and audience development. Hubbard Street Dance Chicago began by staging showings in nursing homes, and the Pennsylvania Ballet held its first performance at a private home (Sims 2005). Asking board members to speak at events about the mission and importance of your company with a request for donations is advised as well. Many people and corporations enjoy being a part of an exciting new company at the outset, so offering special recognition as a

family, or your significant other, if you suspect dance is your true passion, I encourage you to release yourself from the constant worries and to allow yourself to develop and truly enjoy your growing talent. While professional gigs as dancers are few and far between (as well as generally not paid well), I believe that passion and skill will meet to find a way to work in the arts. It will take time and a great deal of patience. It may take years of struggling to make ends meet. But the exchange for that lesser income is a very special, singular kind of happiness and connection to your true self.

Describe some of the greatest lessons you've learned in your dance career.

I suffer from "imposter syndrome," which is perpetually doubting oneself. No matter where I go, I go assuming that I am the least. No matter how much I have accomplished, no matter how many times I've been proven wrong, no matter what experiences have expanded my knowledge, I can be very easily intimidated. I have to remind myself that confidence can be a virtue (that it's not always undesirable), and that I perform better when I think less about how I measure up to others and simply perform the duty at hand.

Looking back, what have been the best decisions you have made during your career?

I certainly regret a great number of decisions that I have made out of petulance or naivete. But, the best decision thus far may have been to actually take a step back in some aspects of my work and allow others to take the reins and the spotlight, allowing me to focus on other aspects. I have a tendency to want to do everything and to do it all very thoroughly and very well. Allowing others to make—in this case—the artistic choices and to develop their own work and ideas has been very freeing for me and opened the door to accomplishments in other areas.

founding donor or opportunities for discounted season tickets could also boost seed contributions. Keep in mind that raising money is an ongoing and often arduous process that is part of the responsibilities of directing a company.

Once you raise enough to cover an entire year without having to add in ticket sales, the company is ready to launch. Producing your first show is exciting and can be overwhelming. Pace yourself, but also know that you only get one chance to make a good first impression, so make that first performance as strong and inviting as possible. Remember, while you are planning and fundraising, you should also be recruiting a company of dancers, technical crew, and venue partners and creating your first show. Founding a company is tireless and can feel daunting, but once you witness your creation onstage—your company thriving in a community—those feelings are subsumed by the adoration and respect you feel for the artists and the fulfillment of sharing your work with the public.

Working With a Board of Directors

If your company is a registered nonprofit organization, it is required to operate with a board of directors who assume the fiscal and legal responsibilities of the company. As a director, you and other staff members report to the board. The board, composed of volunteers recruited from within the community, is essentially the "boss" of the company because the board is legally liable for its decisions. To that end, it is advisable to recruit people from all walks of life to serve because a board with diverse expertise can better represent a community's needs to the company and can support its extended reach and ability to grow. Board members experienced in finance, law, real estate, business, and other nonprofit organizations are particularly beneficial. Many boards are made up of smaller committees in which every member has at least one assignment. Committees meet separately from the board and report to the full board at each meeting. Dance companies often establish committees for finance, fundraising, marketing, and event planning.

Founding board members can help craft the bylaws of the organization. These outline its purpose, structure, and operational procedures and policies. Bylaws should include procedural statements about how many board members are required, how often the board meets, board responsibilities, and how members rotate on and off the board. The board should also craft a series of formal documents that outline the responsibilities of various staff members (e.g., production manager, artistic and executive directors, dancers, and guest performers).

Dance company boards typically meet at least four times per year to discuss the current and future seasons of performances, events, and fundraising ideas. The artistic and executive directors and committee chairs give reports. Additionally, the board works to create and approve bylaws, mission and vision, budgets, grant submissions, and company structure, and it facilitates staff hiring processes. Board members can also act as volunteers for the company, taking on small assignments such as ushering at shows, staffing information tables at events, and reaching out to various corporations and individuals for contributions and sponsorships.

Board members are often responsible for much of a company's fundraising efforts, so they must be well trained and well versed in the mission and goals of the company so that they can speak confidently to others about it. Create an information packet for new board members that the board president uses in orientation sessions as new members rotate onto the board. Boards operate most effectively if they gather for an annual retreat in which they and the staff review and potentially revise the company's mission, structure, long-term goals, and operating policies and procedures.

Recruiting and Managing a Company of Dancers

Recruiting and leading a company of dancers is obviously a huge part of an artistic director's job. At first, a small company could be the most manageable option until a positive reputation is developed and enough funding is obtained to support a larger group. Although the number of dancers can change, establish a target number to help you create artistic and fundraising goals. Additionally, consider whether you want to include a production manager, administrative assistant, grant writer, and a technical crew and designers as part of your company or if you would prefer to hire them on a temporary or project-to-project basis.

You may decide to recruit from within your network of close colleagues or you may approach recruitment as a way to expand your network through public auditions and referrals. Depending on the location of your company, one of these methods may prove more effective than the other. Consider whether you live in an area with a burgeoning dance scene or one that is home to collegiate dance programs from which you could recruit trained dancers. If you decide to hold annual or project-based auditions, publicize them through social media and local media outlets and ask current company dancers to help spread the word.

The process for auditioning dancers is highly variable and personal because you will be searching for dancers to fill the specific needs of your company. Many companies host traditional auditions in which someone teaches movement phrases the dancers perform for the directors and choreographers. Some companies request current members to dance alongside auditioning dancers so choreographers can get a sense of how the group would move together onstage. If improvisation or theatrical elements are important in your work, include elements of these in your audition. Ensure auditions are organized and efficient and communicate with all dancers to thank and inform them of results.

Leading a dance company requires resilience, strong work ethic, organizational skills, a willingness to embrace failure, vulnerability, and an ability to achieve buy-in from the dancers in the company. You must be able to articulate and illustrate through your actions your passion for the company, the dances you make, and the dancers themselves so that they feel a part of something special and will help you advocate and celebrate it. As with board members, company dancers should be given a proper introduction to the policies and procedures of the company. Holding regular company meetings is helpful for keeping everyone working toward the same goals and focused. Provide ample opportunities for reciprocal communication, including giving dancers evaluative feedback and asking for it from them. Consistent and frequent communication is key. Finally, show appreciation for the dancers in your company whenever you have a chance. They are fulfilling your vision!

Marketing

Marketing your company increases public awareness and ticket sales while also developing relationships with other people and organizations. As arts-marketing trends evolve at a furious pace, new ideas are a frequent discussion topic among boards and company leaders. Americans for the Arts hosts a blog devoted to marketing on its website with constant updates and articles on trending subjects. Stay up to date on marketing strategies to remain relevant, relatable, and active in your community and the field.

Some of the most effective ways dance companies advertise productions and events include email, social media, news outlets, tourism and hospitality companies, arts and culture community organizations, and paid advertisements. Join an email and marketing platform such as Constant Contact (paid) or Mailchimp (free). These sites provide design and campaign layouts for emails, newsletters, ads, invitations, and event information. In every message, offer connections to social media accounts and the company website. Circulating press releases about shows and events to area news outlets can be another important way of marketing a company. Include personal messages when you send these out asking for news coverage and interviews. Experiment with advertising in different outlets and in different media (newspaper, television, radio, online). Depending on where your company is located and the content of your upcoming production or season, certain advertisement strategies work better than others in attracting new audience members.

Marketing strategies should be deeply intertwined with branding tactics so that the aesthetic of a company is consistent in everything that is publicly disseminated. Company logo and graphic design elements (colors, patterns, shapes, fonts) should reappear in various advertisements, invitations, letters, press releases, and announcements. Use consistent and persuasive language to attract new audiences. Keep the tone professional yet down-to-earth so that the company communicates a welcoming presence through its online personality. Also, be bold yet simple in marketing; develop a clear message that can be quickly understood in marketing materials.

Budget Strategies

When determining goals for producing, purchasing, and hiring, the board and staff should use the company's budget as a guide in laying out expenses and income for each season. Ideally, if your primary interest is in fulfilling the artistic vision of a dance company, consider seeking the assistance of an executive director, assistant, or a finance-savvy board member who can help with budgets. Directors should all be intimately involved with drafting budgets because they are responsible for proposing the costs associated with productions, staffing, and commissioning.

Bylaws define the fiscal year for an organization and this calendar should be replicated in annual budgets. It is often necessary for the artistic programming of a company to be decided well in advance of a season because of the need to submit grants based on proposed budgets to help fund productions. That said, be prepared to work continuously on refining your current season of productions and events as well as planning and developing future seasons. The position of an artistic director requires the ability to formulate short-term and long-term visions.

Work closely with those whose job it is to create and approve the budget (usually, the executive director and the board) to make sure the artistic and, if relevant, educational needs are addressed. Be prepared to make a case to the board and granters for new budget line items or large increases in any one area. Finally, be prepared with backup plans in case fundraising does not go as planned. Because dance companies often grapple with funding challenges, remain flexible so that you can create terrific productions despite budgetary disappointments or surprises.

Fundraising

Dance companies that survive do so because they build fundraising strategies that work for them. Successful fundraising strategies are often dependent on the nature (size, location, and cultural circumstances) of the community in which a company operates. For example, companies in large cities such as New York and Chicago are numerous, they must compete with many others for local and state grant funding, while companies located in smaller communities may find generous grant support because the competition for that funding is not as fierce. Some companies find success by maintaining a list of individual and corporate sponsors, and others host multiple fundraising events or campaigns throughout the season. In most companies, in-kind contributions are a major source of support for dance companies.

Recruiting a strong grant writer can equate to wonderful opportunities for a company to get on its feet, maintain ongoing and new projects and facilities, and expand its reach and prestige. To apply for grants, a company must be registered with the Internal Revenue Service as a 501(c)(3) nonprofit organization. Another option is to identify an arts-focused fiscal sponsor, such as Fractured Atlas, under whom your company can apply for grants. At first, a company will be able to apply for only local foundation grants. After a company has operated as a nonprofit organization for three years, it is eligible for state and federal grant funding. For a comprehensive search of possible local, state, and federal granting agencies, search in the Guide-Star, Dance/USA, National Endowment for the Arts, and Americans for the Arts websites. Finally, when writing grants, use persuasive language and illustrate your company's need for funding, your community's need for your company's work, and the company's demonstrated reputation for professional excellence and innovation.

Individual giving and corporate underwriting are the hallmarks of many dance companies' funding tactics. There are myriad ways you can ask for individual contributions, including scheduling coffee or lunch dates with potential donors, launching crowdsourcing campaigns through Kickstarter or Indiegogo, hosting donor dinners or cocktail hours, asking patrons for donations through email or newsletters, or sending out sponsorship brochures. In a donation request, include your intention for reciprocity. People and companies want to know what's in it for them in this deal, so offer an exchange. For instance, consider offering perks and benefits for certain levels of giving such as free tickets to shows, company swag, or opportunities to mingle with company members. Further, if the company is a nonprofit organization, let potential donors know that their contributions are tax deductible.

In many dance companies, in-kind—or nonmonetary—contributions are important to developing partnerships and enhancing relationships, especially for new companies without a lot of existing resources. An in-kind donation consists of goods or services that are offered for free or at a reduced rate and could include legal or tax services, food and drink, facilities, and employee work. With your board of directors, create a proposal strategy to determine local business owners and other professionals with whom you could develop reciprocal partnerships. Also create materials to use when making these requests. These connections within the community solidify the company's value and create lasting exchanges that can greatly influence sustainability.

SUMMARY

Approaching a career in nonprofit professional dance companies can feel daunting because of the stiff competition for jobs and the instability that comes with working seasonally or part time, plus the added pressures on your body given the physical intensity of this line of work. However, dancing in or leading professional companies is, for many, a dream come true. The benefits of living a life of creativity and artistry are limitless, as many lifelong performers and company directors would affirm. As with any career option, there are considerations and planning that you should take very seriously. Forging ahead armed with this chapter's information and tips will help you make the transition into professional company work.

Reflection

RÉSUMÉ BUILDER

Complete the following prompts and then plug the information into the résumé template below. This practice is a good way to start building a clear, impactful professional résumé. In addition to including your name, contact information, and appearance details, include professional performance experience, formal education, choreography and other related experience, awards, and special skills. Some companies may also ask for professional references on a résumé. If there is too much to list on one page, you must then decide to include only the most important information that illustrates your professionalism, qualifications, and employability. Formatting is a personal choice based on your personal aesthetic and design preferences as well as how much information you want to include on the page. Find ways to maximize your use of space so you can fit as much into one page as possible and present the best of what you have to offer a company.

ONE-PAGE RÉSUMÉ TEMPLATE

Use this one-page résumé template to build your own professional résumé suitable for performer auditions. Plug in your information and important accomplishments and either insert a small headshot on the résumé or attach a headshot on the backside, whatever the company prefers.

Dancer McPirouette

dancermcpirouette@gmail.com
(888) 555-5555
www.dancermcpirouette.com

Hair: Brown   Eyes: Hazel   Height: 5'4"   Weight: 125lbs.

Professional Experience

- Company Member, ABC Dance Company, Chicago, IL — 2017-2019
- Apprentice, ABC Dance Company — 2015-2017
- Guest Artist, Sunshine Dance Theatre, Sarasota, FL — 2017
- Performer, Summer Theatre Series, Austin, TX — 2015 and 2016
- Featured Dancer, Nationally Televised Event — 2012
- "Hotbox Dancer," *Guys and Dolls*, Dosido Theatre — 2011

Dance Training

- Bachelor of Fine Arts, Dance, University of Kickballchange — 2016
  - List areas of study or professors or both here.
- Summer Dance Intensive, Seattle, WA — 2015
  - List areas of study or instructors here.
- Drop Swing School of Dance, Minneapolis, MN — 2005-2012
  - List areas of study or instructors here.

Related Experience

- Grant writer, 5678 Dance Theatre, Roanoke, VA — 2017
- Featured vocalist, Summer Theatre Series, Austin, TX — 2016
- Photographer, Summer Dance Series, Charlotte, NC — 2015

Awards and Honors

- Choreography Award, Dance Foundation — 2016
- Dance scholarships, University of Kickballchange — 2012-2016
- Best Dancer Award, National Dance Competition — 2014

Special Skills

- Vocal – mezzo-soprano, fluent in Spanish, juggling, dance photography, certified yoga instructor

Professional References

Dr. Jumps Around
Professor
University of Kickballchange
(888) 555-1234
jumps.around@uk.edu

Caitlin Elise
Artistic Director
ABC Dance Company
(888) 555-5678
Caitlin.Elise@abcdance.org

Breaking Into Commercial Dance

"You are the only one of you. From the beginning of time till the end of this world to the end of eternity, there's only one of you ever created . . . . That's pretty powerful. So why on earth would you want to look like anybody else, dress like anyone else, dance like anyone else, be someone else, when you are a legend in your own right?"

Mia Michaels

The purposes of commercial dance are primarily to entertain audiences and, sometimes, to tell stories as well. Additionally, dance as an athletic or competitive endeavor can fall under the commercial dance umbrella. All of these avenues can present wonderful career opportunities for dancers. One of the benefits of working in commercial dance is that by working on a contract basis, you can expand your network and gain a positive reputation very quickly. Once you start booking jobs in these areas and you become known as a hard worker and strong performer, more professional doors will open. Working with a variety of choreographers and directors will support your growth as a versatile dancer who can easily recalibrate your technical and performance abilities to fit whatever is needed in each position. Finally, if you consider jazz, hip-hop, musical theater, or tap dance as your preferred style, the commercial dance world emphasizes these genres, so you may find commercial dance a good professional fit.

Because each job in the commercial dance area is so different in terms of workload, prestige, pay scale, permanence, and level of competition, it is difficult to estimate how a lifelong career in commercial dance will play out. Available data suggest a wide range of pay for dancers in the commercial arena. Both union and nonunion rates for dancers in television, film, music videos, theater, and commercials change annually. SAG-AFTRA data indicate in 2019 in the United States a

Sydney Sorenson

Seasoned commercial dancer and assistant professor of dance at Allan Hancock College

What have been your most significant experiences as a working professional in dance?

With the support of my teachers and mentors, I was able to film various TV shows and movies while pursuing my education. In 2008 I was cast as a featured dancer in *High School Musical 3*. While in college I filmed both SYTYCD [*So You Think You Can Dance*] and *A Chance to Dance* with the BalletBoyz. And then in 2011 I was chosen to costar alongside Tori Spelling in a made-for-TV movie called *The Mistle-Tones*. I did all of this while maintaining a 3.872 GPA and graduating on time with 122 credit hours. Due to my love and respect for both sides of the dance world, I had a hard time choosing my next step following the completion of my BFA. Ultimately, I decided to head toward California since I knew LA offered opportunities with company work and concert dance, while it continues to thrive in the entertainment industry. I was lucky to work with LA Contemporary Dance Company, and I found this to be my base as well as my family there. Disney picked me up as a performer at the park in Anaheim, and this job continues to be a blessing for me with the many friends and connections I've made through this amazing company. I've worked with countless choreographers

Courtesy of Sydney Sorenson.

maximum daily rate of $980 for performers featured in films and about $671 per day for commercial work (SAG-AFTRA 2019b). The most recent data from Dancers Alliance indicate dancers in the United States in nonunion shows can make $500 per show day and $250 per rehearsal day (Dancers Alliance 2020). A dancer in the chorus of a Broadway show earns a salary of $2,034 per week, and a backup dancer on an elite tour earns up to $2,500 per week (Culwell-Block 2018; Pincus-Roth 2018; Berlin 2018). While these jobs can be lucrative, they are usually temporary, so dancers must piece together a career and constantly be on the search for their next gig.

The United States' "gig economy," defined as a labor market of workers on freelance or short-term, contractual bases, has boomed in the past 15 years as digitization has taken hold and businesses strive to provide flexibility and convenience for workers and clients (Rouse 2019; Hyken 2018). In 2017, the U.S. Bureau of Labor and Statistics estimated that 55 million Americans were "gig workers" (Hyken 2018). In 2017, Intuit, a financial software company, predicted that by the year 2020, 40 percent of Americans would be independent contractors. Whereas

and well-known artists: Tokyo, Talia Favia, Allison and tWitch, Alex Little, Ricky Palomino, Kate Hutter to name a few. One of the best experiences for me was traveling to Europe with Helene Fischer and the Farbenspiel Live tour, where we got to travel all throughout Germany, Switzerland, and Austria. This is where I learned that I would be happy doing anything that allowed me to dance and travel. Heading back to Germany with the Trans-Siberian Orchestra was also a huge honor for me knowing they were and continue to be creative geniuses.

What is your best advice to those hoping to pursue a career in dance?

You have to love it. Keep making work, and just don't stop doing it. If your path doesn't look like everyone else's then so be it. You have to find your own route and your own niche within the art form. If it doesn't exist, then create it. That's what we do!

Describe some of the greatest lessons you've learned in your dance career.

In the very beginning I learned I wasn't going to be everyone's top choice as a performer, but I knew I had the drive to make it. As a kid I would stay in the studio after everyone had gone home just because I wanted to be better. This also applies to the creative work you do as well; not everyone will like the thing you are creating. In order to be a true innovator, you have to do something different. Allow new information to come to you. Keep doing your research. Never stop discovering things for yourself. In fact, improvisation has been one of the greatest tools for me as a dancer, teacher, and choreographer, since it easily matches what we do in everyday life.

in the past, short-term or contract-based employment was perceived by many as risky or inconsistent, recent trends toward a growing gig economy point to ways dancers can take advantage of the benefits of contracted work in dance. In addition to temporary and project-based employment, the commercial dance sector also offers many job opportunities with long-term stability and consistency. For example, talent agents (paid by commission) and casting directors or producers for film or theater companies are often long-term employees. While these career paths would veer away from performance, they typically offer the benefits of financial stability and job security.

This chapter covers the specific paths dancers can take toward an exciting career in commercial dance, including training, auditioning, and branding tips; advice about how (and whether) to sign with an agent and join a union; and how to manage rejection and the commercial dance lifestyle. With planning and organization, creating a long-term career in commercial dance can be rewarding and exciting in many unique ways. This chapter provides strategies to start a commercial dance career with the advantages of awareness and preparedness.

CAREER OPTIONS IN COMMERCIAL OR ENTERTAINMENT-BASED DANCE

Taking stock of the many job opportunities within commercial dance brings to light the abundance found in the industry and may help you discover professional paths to pursue. Many of these jobs are contract based and freelance, and keeping track of and deciding which among the multitude of auditions to attend can feel overwhelming. However, understanding your brand can help you choose the auditions most likely to get you hired. The following survey of various areas within commercial dance can help illuminate the areas you can pursue.

Broadway and Musical Theater

Being hired as a dancer in a Broadway production would be, for many, a dream come true. Musical theater work requires advanced jazz, ballet, and tap experience as well as vocal and acting abilities. Many dancers perceive New York City as the center of dance in the United States because of the sheer number of job opportunities for dancers in the city. However, if musical theater dance is your greatest strength, consider that all large U.S. cities host touring companies and house theaters of their own, so consider the many opportunities in musical theater around the country. Also, consider touring companies of Broadway productions that travel around the country and internationally. Broadway and touring performers are usually contracted for the length of the show run, unless dancers are cast on special replacement or swing contracts, which could be short term.

Cruise Ships, Resorts, and Theme Parks

The tourism industry features many opportunities for performers on cruise ships, at resorts, and in popular vacation spots like Las Vegas and Branson, Missouri. Dancers on cruise ships have the benefit of traveling around the world for free while also gaining professional performance experience. Dancers performing in vacation spots also benefit from living in a beautiful location with much to do and learn. Often, these jobs are contractual and may range from one to six months at a time. Dancers in this area of the industry rely on their training in musical theater and jazz dance genres and may also benefit from training in other areas such as aerial hoop, voice, and hip-hop. Auditions are sometimes open call and sometimes by appointment through an agent.

Music Videos and Backup Dancing

Being hired as a dancer in music videos or on tour with musical performers requires a combination of solid dance training—usually in jazz and hip-hop—acting, and modeling skills. Booking music video or backup dancing gigs usually requires the help of an agent because most auditions are by agent-invitation only. Further, some jobs are filled without an audition at all, based solely on direct booking or referrals. Therefore, building a network of professionals who can speak highly of your work is important. Later in this chapter, you can learn more about signing with an agent.

Film, Commercials, Television, and Online Work

Dancers are often hired for television commercials and shows, films, and for online content such as on YouTube and social media. Dancers featured in media can enliven advertisements, bring attention and focus to a celebrity's brand and reputation, and can also be used as dance stand-ins for actors who are not trained dancers. For example, Katherine Crockett, the professional dancer featured in chapter 5, was hired as Cate Blanchett's dance double and played opposite Brad Pitt in a few scenes in the 2008 film *The Curious Case of Benjamin Button*. Jobs in pop culture media expand your brand, your dancing strengths, your network, and opportunities for future jobs in ways you cannot predict. Most often, these positions are achieved through booking via an agent and are temporary, contract-based gigs.

TRAINING AND PREPARATION

Most jobs in the commercial dance sector do not require a college degree in dance, but do require formal, specialized training. Mark Romain, a backup dancer for multiple pop artists "learned on dance teams in college and on the job" adding that "if you start [training] late, that's okay, but train, train, train" (Spiegel 2013, para 2). His twin brother and fellow backup dancer, Donald Romain, added, "Some people train their whole lives, but some dancers move here [to Los Angeles] in their early twenties to pursue it. Once you get signed [with an agent], it's still an uphill battle to book your first job and get noticed" (Spiegel 2013, para 3). Both dancers stressed the importance of keeping up their training in the dance studio as well as cross-training in the gym to stay fit. Once dancers are hired, it is often advised by agents to retain their "look," which may require various amounts and kinds of training and a healthy lifestyle.

Deciding on a location in which to start a career in commercial dance is an important first step. Because Los Angeles is a major hub for the film and television industries, many of the commercial dance jobs in film are located there. New York City is known as the center of musical theater. Most major U.S. cities have opportunities in commercial dance, some more plentiful than others. Do your homework before making a big move. Consider your strengths, areas of interest, and existing network. After you relocate (if that is necessary), start regularly attending dance classes and getting to know your teachers and fellow dancers. This is a great way to expand your training and establish yourself in a new dance community.

Your dance training, no matter which area of the field you pursue, is never done. You should consider your career as a series of learning experiences designed to make you better. In addition, you must seek dance training throughout your career to continue learning new styles and improving on those in which you are already highly skilled. Try as many different classes as possible and, when you find one you like or you find one that is taught by someone you want to work for, become a regular in that class. Getting acquainted with teachers and other dance students is a terrific way to expand your network and improve in your dancing.

BRANDING

Producers and directors often seek to hire someone with a certain "look" rather than the best technical dancer, so this is where your ability to brand yourself and be consistent in your self-marketing becomes beneficial. First, decide what sets your look apart from the crowd: Are you especially tall or do you have a unique hair color or a distinctive pair of glasses that you always wear? The visual elements that make up your look should be visible in the way you brand yourself. Next, outline your areas of expertise: Are you strongest in a certain dance genre like hip-hop or musical theater? What technical or performance "tricks" do you have up your sleeve? Use your best technical elements to promote yourself in your branding materials.

Part of your preparation for a career in commercial dance is recognizing your strengths and being equipped and willing to capitalize on those strengths through continuous feedback, self-awareness, and self-promotion. Some dancers manage their careers by signing with talent agents who can help establish and make the most of a dancer's brand and book auditions geared to the specifics of that brand. It is possible to do these things for yourself, but you may encounter an uphill battle or fewer opportunities if you are not represented by an agent or union. In any case, consider your technical strengths, unique qualities, and the memorable aspects of your appearance that could set you apart from others. To present an impactful brand to potential employers, be clear about what your brand is and how you stand out.

Creating an online presence can be one of the best ways to promote your brand in commercial dance. Create a website that features the best of what you offer the industry in simple yet bold graphic design. Web-hosting sites like Wix and Squarespace have hundreds of design templates to choose from, so pick one and upload information, images, and videos. Be selective about the photos and videos you feature on your website; pick no more than three videos that feature unique elements of your technique and performance experience. Include contact information and a brief résumé on your website as well.

A performance reel highlighting your abilities, accomplishments, and areas of specialty can also be an effective branding tool. This reel can be posted online, and via a link in your résumé, can be quickly sent to potential agents, casting directors, and producers. Make sure that your reel is professional, high energy, and brief. It should be fun, not overwhelming, to watch. If you don't have video-editing skills, don't try to do this on your own because a poor-quality reel will detract from your strengths and skills. Work with a professional video editor whose expertise can be relied on to create a reel that will feature the best version of you as a performer.

Social media presence is important to developing and promoting your brand online. Consider participating in several social media platforms in order to gain exposure in various online communities, each of which feature different impactful ways to showcase your strengths though posts, stories, photos, and videos. Linking these platforms to your website is another helpful way to connect all the parts of your career and encourage your network of colleagues to learn more about you. Think of yourself as a curator designing an experience for someone who visits your social media pages. Always check for correct spelling and grammar, avoid controversial or overly personal posts on your professional pages, and don't post too much or too little. The general advice is to post as often as you have quality content to post. Social media experts advise that one post per day on Instagram and Facebook, 3-30 posts per day on Twitter, and one video upload per week to YouTube is ideal (Myers 2020). Overall, your goal is to present yourself as relevant, focused, and professional.

NETWORKING

Networking is extremely important to the long-term viability of your dance career. Interacting with others in the field in order to exchange ideas and develop professional relationships can have reciprocal benefits. The more people in the industry who can attest to your strong work ethic, integrity, and performance abilities, the better your chances of securing consistent work. Networking can happen anytime—in classes, auditions, and gigs and through informal social interactions. Don't be shy about reaching out to others to ask for advice, to give compliments, or to ask for help (e.g., Can you please introduce me to the casting director you know? Will you please help me review this audition combination?). Most people want to meet new people to add to their networks too, so be the first to say hello or to offer help to others. As with any relationship, it takes time to build lasting friendships, so be patient and put in the effort to expand your network of friends and colleagues.

Courtesy of Christy Cross.

Dancer Sydney Sorenson.

Once you have begun working in the industry, positive interactions and relationships with fellow dancers and management teams are important. Depending on the job, these colleagues may know you intimately, seeing and working with you every day for an extended period of time, so they can be great advocates for you in the future. However, if you don't invest in others, it is unlikely they will invest in you. Commit to fostering a strong network as a career requirement.

FINDING AN AGENT

Generally speaking, to gain access to the highest profile auditions and jobs, you must work through a talent agent who represents you to the industry. An agent's job is to send clients job announcements that fit their look and strengths; negotiate pay, working conditions, schedule, and contracts on their behalf; and serve as a liaison between production companies and their clients. Additionally, agents "advocate for the betterment of artists' conditions, compensation, credit, and creative potential" (Loucadoux and Margheritis 2017, p. 86), educate their clients about the ins and outs of the industry, and help clients expand their professional networks. In exchange, agents are paid a percentage of their clients' earnings, usually 10 percent for union contracts and up to 20 percent for nonunion projects (Loucadoux and Margheritis 2017). While talent agencies are most active in Los Angeles and New York City, you can also find agents in large cities across the country such as Dallas, Nashville, and Cincinnati (Dance Spirit 2012).

Many dancers wonder how to get signed with an agent. While this is not always an easy task because there are a multitude of dancers seeking representation, there are several ways to increase your chances of being represented. Overwhelmingly, agents seek new clients, not the other way around. It is much more likely that you will be signed by an agent who is actively recruiting new clients rather than through your initiative. Major agencies hold a few open auditions every year to search for new talent to represent; these auditions are usually listed on agency websites. Agents also attend major competitions, showcases, and classes at well-known studios to find new clients. Another way to find representation is through referrals: Choreographers or teachers can refer dancers to their own agencies. Finally, cold submissions—sending your résumé, headshot, and reel—is another way to get your foot in an agency door, although this is not the best way because it is difficult to assess a dancer on paper or video in the same way as in an audition.

It is critical to find an agent that believes in you and is willing to work hard consistently to help you land jobs and be treated well in those jobs. Therefore, be selective in your choice of agency and agent to ensure you're being represented well. Agency websites outline the kind of professionals they represent, what they look for in potential clients, and how to submit materials or audition. Check out each agency's roster of clients to see how you would fit into or enhance their clientele.

Once you receive an offer to sign with an agency, don't immediately settle for that agency. Do additional research and meet with a few other agencies. You should feel a connection with and sense of support from your agent and the agency's values. Be aware of what you're signing once you select an agency. Look carefully at the contract, paying attention to the agent's and your responsibilities, contract terms, and commission rate.

To maintain a positive and productive relationship with your agent, it is your job to remain in close communication with them, be available for auditions, be professional in the workplace, return communications promptly, and be present on the dance scene. Clients are sometimes dropped by agents if communication becomes problematic, so stay vigilant about responsiveness with your agent. Also, because your agent's job is to ensure you are hired for jobs, they will work with you to develop your look and maintain your overall well-being. Therefore, agents may suggest tweaking your look to fit the image of the niche you fill in the dance industry, and they may make recommendations for your attire, which headshot photographer to use, and even referrals to physical therapists or dermatologists. Within reason, your relationship with your agent will often go beyond the boundaries of other professional relationships because it is the agent's job to holistically represent you to the industry. Try to keep an open mind when your agent makes suggestions because it is their job to look out for your best professional interests.

Agents primarily assist clients in securing jobs within the commercial dance sector and, depending on your areas of specialty, can also expand your career options in film, television, commercials, and dance companies. If you have varied interests and talents, say, as a vocalist or actor, make sure to communicate these strengths to your agent so that they can find you potential gigs in these areas as well as in dance.

JOINING A UNION

A union is composed of a group of performers who have come together to mandate effective working conditions, fair pay, job safety, and benefits distribution. Joining a union can boost your career and create unique opportunities for success. Union membership in one of the four main dancer unions—Actors Equity Association (AEA), Screen Actors Guild-American Federation of Television and Radio Artists (SAG-AFTRA), American Guild of Variety Artists (AGVA), or American Guild of Musical Artists (AGMA)—requires that you pay initiation fees and annual dues, maintain professional credentials, and actively and consistently work in the industry. Each union has its own membership requirements and member benefits such as health care and retirement plans.

To perform in a Broadway show, you must be a member of the Actors Equity Association. National touring companies, regional theater companies, and Broadway all work under AEA, and therefore, must hold auditions solely for Equity members, which means being seen by casting directors at significant auditions even without agent representation (Loucadoux and Margheritis 2017). You can earn your Equity card in one of three ways: be offered a job that requires union membership (an unlikely, but not impossible scenario), join a sister union first (such as AGMA or SAG-AFTRA), or become an Equity Membership Candidate and earn points toward your membership by working in reputable theaters across the country. You must accrue 50 points to become a member and, generally speaking, one week of work in a union theater will earn you one point. You can also negotiate a "fast pass" to union membership as part of contract negotiations with union theaters (Loucadoux and Margheritis 2017). AEA charges an initiation fee of $1,700, which can be paid over two years (and will increase to $1,800 in 2022); $174 in annual dues; and 2.5 percent of gross earnings, taken out of your paycheck (Actors Equity Association 2020). The benefits are often worth the financial investment in the union in terms of how much money you make per contract, workload requirements, opportunity, and career longevity.

If working as a dancer in films, television, commercials, or music videos, you would likely work under SAG-AFTRA. You may join if you are already a member of a performers' union or if you have worked as a principal dancer in one gig or as a backup dancer in at least three gigs. SAG-AFTRA, like AEA, provides safe working conditions, guaranteed breaks, and shelter from the elements, and perks such as a members-only directory that could very quickly expand and enhance your network! One of the downsides to membership with SAG-AFTRA is that members are restricted from taking nonunion work, which could be prohibitive, depending on which area of the industry you anticipate focusing on in your career. Also, the one-time initiation fee of $3,000 is steep, but it can be paid over 24 months. Members also pay annual dues of $218.60 and 1.575 percent of earned income deducted from paychecks (SAG-AFTRA 2020).

The American Guild of Variety Artists serves dancers working in theme park productions, circus-style shows such as Cirque du Soleil, comedy shows, and venue-based shows such as Las Vegas productions, and it oversees the Radio City Rockettes shows and some off-Broadway and touring productions. Like other unions, AGVA ensures dancers receive proper working conditions and pay, vacation time, and sick leave. Unlike other unions, dancers may petition to join AGVA without already having a contract in hand. Dues are earnings based and range from $72-$795 per year and, although the union does charge an initiation fee, likely around $1,000 based on informal research, you have to call and ask for the updated amount because it varies (American Guild of Variety Artists 2020; Loucadoux and Margheritis 2017).

Dancers employed in modern, ballet, or opera companies work under the American Guild of Musical Artists. To join, you must have a contract with an AGMA affiliated company. The initiation fee is $1,000 to be paid by the time you earn $4,000 or after three years, whichever comes first. Also, an annual fee of $100 and 2 percent of earnings are deducted from members' paychecks. Some of the best benefits of membership in AGMA include health insurance and multiple discounts for things like Pilates classes, car rentals, and massage therapy (American Guild of Musical Artists 2020).

Whichever union you choose—or whichever union is chosen for you based on your employment—take advantage of the many perks that membership affords you. Not only do unions negotiate for your safety, health, and pay, they also ensure retirement and health care benefits and establish grievance processes. Most unions offer discount programs and other perks such as cross-training and therapy opportunities. In short, if you are working under a union contract, your working conditions are standardized to reflect well-being and professionalism and are strictly upheld.

Consider joining a union for expanded access to job opportunities, professional working conditions, and benefits that will support your career in the long-term.

AUDITION TIPS

As the saying goes, you only have one chance to make a first impression. Unquestionably, you should present the very best version of yourself at any audition but also be able to highlight your strengths as relevant to each particular call or job. Clothing, hair and makeup styling, and necessary items to bring vary depending on the audition and job. For example, an audition for a backup dancer may call for a trendy look that helps the hiring team see that your individuality and aesthetic match with the musical artist, whereas an audition for a role in a Broadway production would require you to dress and look the part of that particular role. Pay careful attention to the audition call or agent's instructions about how to best prepare for each audition.

One of the best ways to prepare for any audition is to continue honing your technical and performance skills. Attend class as often as your schedule and finances allow. Don't stick to just one teacher or style—diversify. Attend classes in multiple studios with different teachers to learn how to catch on quickly to new styles and technical skills. If a choreographer you appreciate teaches regular classes, drop in and, if presented with an opportunity after class, introduce yourself and express your enthusiasm for that person's work. If finances are a concern, consider taking a work-study opportunity offered by many studios in which you can clean studios or do administrative work in exchange for free or reduced-price classes. Overall, attending class will help you improve your dancing and expand your network and may help you get your foot in the door with people or companies who may hire you in the future.

In addition to focusing on dance training, it is crucial to cross-train and commit to a healthy lifestyle. Because your body's performance is what will get you hired, you must respect and prioritize its needs. A healthy diet of moderation and balance, including a variety of fruits and vegetables, complex carbohydrates, and protein, with minimal alcohol and a lot of water can support your body's nutritional needs, which are substantial, considering dancers' physical activity demands. Getting adequate sleep (for most, seven to nine hours per night) and taking a rest day every week to allow your body to recover is critical. Smoking is terrible for physical health—particularly that of dancers because the need for cardiovascular health and endurance is significant—so, if you smoke, make it a goal to quit for your health and your career. Whatever cross-training method you enjoy doing, whether it be walking, swimming, yoga, biking, or weightlifting, keep it up to help your muscles remain balanced and supportive of your dancing. Additionally, self-care strategies such as meditation, psychotherapy or talk therapy, gardening, knitting, or dog snuggling can enhance your quality of life. Consider how all the elements of your day contribute to how successful and fulfilled you are as a whole person.

On the day of an audition, pack a bag full of essentials: résumé and headshot, dance shoes (which could include heels or pointe shoes), extra clothes (just in case), water, healthy snacks, towel, makeup and hair supplies, and script or sheet music, if necessary. Give yourself plenty of time to arrive early. Casting directors notice when someone arrives late and will sometimes excuse dancers on the spot for that reason. Be prepared for anything once you arrive. Auditions may involve a full day of learning and performing combinations and then waiting for the next round of callbacks. Others involve merely a brief demonstration of something simple like a pirouette or leap. Sometimes, casting teams present auditioning dancers with surprising tasks to get a sense of how they work under pressure and with unexpected tasks. These surprises could include being asked to improvise, choreograph, sing, speak, or share weight with other dancers.

Casting directors and choreographers are not only looking for technical prowess, versatility, and dazzling performance skills, but they also seek to hire someone who demonstrates professional behavior and shares similar creative process values. Therefore, stay focused and alert throughout auditions and be aware of how your presence and interactions with others are telling. When you walk into an audition room, be confident, courteous, and positive with everyone you meet. If you receive feedback during the audition, take this very seriously. Often, the hiring team wants to get a sense of how you learn and how quickly and willing you are to take corrections and adapt. Because many auditions are overcrowded, find a spot in the room from where you can see demonstrations, and when you are not in the group called to perform full out for the casting team, stand to the side of the room and refrain from dancing full out until you are called. In other words, avoid being distracting until it is your turn to wow the panel.

Every auditioning company or hiring team differs in how it makes casting decisions and communicates them. Some decisions are made and communicated on the day of the audition, while you may not hear about others for weeks or even months. If a company is on a casting tour of multiple cities, you can bet that you won't hear results for a while. Sometimes, you will learn audition results face-to-face with casting directors, while other times, you may learn you booked a gig through a phone call from your agent. Don't spend too much time fretting over any one job. Rejection happens all the time in the dance industry, so your ability to demonstrate resilience and move on quickly to the next audition will help you be efficient and effective in the job market.

Contracts and Negotiations

When you receive a job contract, make sure that you (and your agent, if you're represented) look it over carefully and don't be afraid to negotiate terms if the contract is not aligned with industry standards. Ensure you understand and agree to the terms of your employment before signing. If you are not represented by an agent, make sure your contract addresses the following items: contract duration; rehearsal and performance dates and times; work hour expectations per day or week; break and overtime expectations; health and safety items such as physical therapy support and facilities information; pay rates for rehearsals, performances, and holidays; payment schedule; allowances for shoes, gym, and per diem; dispute resolution clause; termination clause; discrimination and harassment clause; and intellectual property information.

Don't be afraid to negotiate your contract. Companies expect negotiations and you should absolutely advocate for what you're worth, within reason. Before beginning negotiation requests, reach out to mentors and senior contacts in the industry to field your desires. If they believe your requests are warranted, pursue them. Keep in mind that not all of your requests may be honored, and the company may return with a counteroffer that sits between what you want and what they will give. Decide in advance your deal breakers and bottom line so that you don't make rash decisions and walk away from what otherwise could be a wonderful opportunity. Weigh the benefits of the job against the potential downsides. When communicating negotiations, always make sure they are in writing and that your tone is pleasant and professional. Once you have settled on negotiated terms, you must be given a new contract with these requests reflected in it before you sign.

While you wait for rehearsals to begin, continue to train, maintain the same appearance as when you auditioned (this requirement will likely be included in your contract), and stay on top of email and phone communications. Many companies offer new-employee training or a retreat to gather creative players together to make sure everyone understands job expectations and the schedule. Be sure to ask questions if you have them and be friendly and professional with everyone you meet. This is an opportunity to begin a new job by expanding your network and contributing to a positive community of colleagues.

Managing Rejection

Because the commercial dance sector relies on temporary and seasonal employees for gig or project-based work, there are many jobs to be had. However, this benefit also comes with the reality that every dancer will face: rejection. Learning from rejections and developing strategies to manage them will support your career and your well-being. Resilience and patience are difficult to master when you feel rejected, but they will greatly benefit you.

Learning from rejection means trying to get an objective sense of what could have gone better for the sake of improving your auditioning skills and presenting your brand (without obsessing over every tiny error you think you may have made). In some cases, you can tweak your approach to auditions in hopes that the next one will go well, or you may decide that you attended an audition that wasn't right for your specific skills, look, and abilities. So, how do you know what went wrong? Recall any feedback you received during the audition, whether through technical corrections or comments about your performance, appearance, or fit for a role. You can also gain a lot of information by watching those around you because facial expressions and other nonverbal communication can offer you important feedback as well. Finally, pay attention to who gets hired. How did they sell their brand to the casting team for this particular job? In some cases, personal ties are very strong, and a dancer is hired because she or he knows and has worked with a production team previously. This speaks to the importance of maintaining a network and developing a strong professional reputation. In other cases, dancers who are hired share a certain body shape, height, or a particular stylistic nuance and perhaps you did not fit that aesthetic or level of skill in a certain genre. Whatever the case, you can discover a lot about yourself as a dancer—what your strengths are in addition to areas of needed improvement—by being honest with yourself after a rejection.

In addition to continuously self-assessing, check in with your agent, mentors, and other dancers you trust to ask them about what they perceive to be your best qualities and abilities as a dancer. You may be surprised to discover that the way you are perceived may not be the way you intend to represent yourself in the field. This doesn't mean you will be told only negative things, but rather, that you may discover, for example, that while others see you as a hip-hop dancer, you have been focusing solely on attending contemporary auditions. By reaching out, you can gain important information from your network that can lead you to redirect your audition efforts or adjust your brand to fit your intentions and your talents.

Finally, it is critical that you build a life for yourself outside of your dance life so that you can achieve balance, rest, and recover from the difficult work of auditioning. Everyone differs in their ideas of how to create balance in their lives and how they maintain positivity and motivation. For some, establishing a group of friends helps to maintain maximum levels of fulfillment and joy. Call on friends, partners, and family when you feel down about auditioning or job searching. Prioritize self-care strategies such as meditation, bubble baths, journaling, or whatever makes your heart sing and makes time fly. These activities melt stress away and create inner calm and equilibrium. Finally, prioritize sleep, a healthy diet, water, body–mind therapies, and cross-training. It is easy to let some of these necessities fall away when you become busy. However, as a dancer, it is vital to your overall success, so keep health and well-being at the top of your to-do list.

Courtesy of Ali Duffy.

Musical theater performers dancing in a production of *Curtains*.

A DAY ON THE JOB

No day on the job in commercial dance will look the same across the industry, although you can expect working conditions to be clear and consistently adhered to if you are working under a union contract. For instance, a day in the life of a dancer in a touring production—consisting of monthslong contracts traveling to various cities—will look different than that of a dancer working a weeklong gig as a dancer in a music video. While the following descriptions of particular commercial dance jobs estimate what a typical day is like, there are always unique variances and exceptions in each company and position.

Jobs on Broadway and musical theater may include rehearsals specifically to review choreography or to work with vocal and acting coaches on songs and scenes. After a rehearsal period of a few weeks to a few months, productions begin and dancers perform six days a week, with two shows on Wednesdays and Saturdays. Dancers are called to the theater 30 minutes to an hour before showtime to warm up and prepare for the show. After performances, they go home to get sleep and do it all again the next day! Brush-up rehearsals are called when needed and when a cast member is replaced.

In union work on film, television, and commercials, the schedule revolves around the needs of the film and production crew. Rehearsals may happen on location or may happen before shooting at an offsite location. Most big-budget films take about three months to film, a season of a television show typically takes 8 to 10 months to film, and commercials usually film in two to five days. During periods of filming, featured performers are on set up to five days per week and up to 12 to 16 hours per day. Multiple takes and reshoots are often necessary, which may require long workdays, so stamina and preparedness are key to successful shoot days. Typically, in order to accommodate long days for performers and to prepare for scenes, film sets are equipped with catering services, makeup and hair stylists, a wardrobe department, and directors and coaches who facilitate scene blocking, rehearsal, and filming.

Working on cruise ships or touring productions involves extensive travel. Before taking a job on a cruise ship or with a touring production, ensure your personal life can accommodate travel and that you could thrive working and living with the same community of people, your fellow dancers, for long spans of time. Some contracts are as long as 16 months and require dancers to remain on a ship or traveling with the tour for the entirety of a contract. On cruise ships, your onboard cabin becomes your home, whereas in touring productions, dancers live out of a suitcase and make each new hotel room a temporary home. Touring dancers may find it challenging to maintain a healthy diet, self-care, and cross-training routines because there is little possibility of consistent cooking equipment and professional services such as favorite yoga instructors. However, many touring production companies hire physical therapists and other support staff who tour with cast members. The amazing benefits of touring productions include opportunities to see the world, meet new people, immerse yourself in new cultures and experiences, and perform in world-class theaters around the world.

Each branch of the commercial dance sector and, in fact, each individual company, has its own culture and ways of working together, so figuring out those individualities and adapting to them quickly will make you an invaluable employee. Make sure to ask your agent and company contacts questions in advance of taking a gig so that you are prepared to jump in on your first day ahead of the game.

SUMMARY

Commercial dancers demonstrate extremely strong work ethic and professionalism in order to entertain audiences and meet the needs of the various production companies for whom they work. While dance as entertainment sounds fun—and it is—it is also a business with deadlines, strict schedules, and rigorous demands on performers. The commercial dance industry requires dancers who are self-sufficient and are keen to work in a gig economy. Commercial dancers must also prioritize self-branding and ongoing training in dance and related skills. Working with an agency or a union can help you navigate the legal and contractual details of your employment, including pay and working conditions, but it is not required that all dancers in the sector be represented. Become acquainted with the language of contracts and be willing to negotiate your best deal for each job. It is important that you become your own best advocate, particularly if you are not represented by an agent. As in every other part of the dance industry, positivity and professionalism mean a lot. If directors and casting teams can rely on you to be punctual, dependable, and consistent in addition to being a highly skilled dancer, you will have better chances for a long, fulfilling career in commercial dance.

Reflection

PROFESSIONAL INVENTORY FOR BUILDING AN ONLINE BRAND

The following prompts guide you to create several lists to begin building a professional brand in commercial dance. These lists compile information that should be included on your website and social media because they provide casting directors and agents with your most attractive skills and assets, which can get your foot in the door of an agency or company. Consider the language you use to describe your skills in these lists as well as the colors, textures, and patterns that might represent your developing brand on a website or promotional materials.

- List all of your dance skills.
- List all of your employee skills, which may differ from those specifically in dance to include qualities such as reliability and self-motivation and special skills such as graphic design and copyediting.
- List your top 10 accomplishments in the dance field.
- List relevant experience such as acting and vocal performance.
- List five long-term career goals.

Chapter 7

Dance Journalism and Research

"Dance is not endangered—it will always find a way to express itself."

Judith Jamison

People who write about dance—researchers, critics, journalists, biographers, bloggers, and grant writers—provide critical support to the dance industry. Writers create a unique historical record of description and analysis of how dance operates and how it is perceived and experienced in different cultures and times. In today's society, the demand for quickly and easily consumable media has boomed. The field must adapt to fit the needs of that culture by training and hiring writers to promote and support dance as lively, innovative, and relevant. While typically dance is considered a visual and kinesthetic art form, best appreciated by viewing live or recorded performances, there are a multitude of opportunities to craft a career as a writer, creating both an immediate and long-term written record of dance through journalism and research. Admittedly, though, there are very few *full-time* opportunities in these areas, so if dance writing is your passion, pay close attention to the advice in this chapter about how to supplement or piece together a living wage as a dance writer.

This chapter is divided into two subsections: dance journalism and dance research. Opportunities in online and print media are coupled with guidance on how to work effectively with newspaper and magazine editors. Next, the chapter shifts into a subsection on dance research careers. Guidance for how to steer one's dance education toward a career in dance writing lays the foundation for a deeper discussion about how research is often connected to work in higher education and organizations focused on history, dance science, or advocacy. Tips on best writing practices, preparing and submitting writing for publication in peer-reviewed venues, and ethical considerations in dance research are followed by a brief discussion on the ways dance can be researched qualitatively and quantitatively.

Sarah Kaufman

Dance critic, *The Washington Post*

What have been your most significant experiences as a working professional in dance?

I'm intrigued by the creative process, and I've had the great luck to see magnificent artists at work. I've watched Justin Peck choreograph, with his glasses flying off his nose as he whips around demonstrating steps, and the New York City Ballet dancers doubling up in laughter, and Peck stopping to think, chewing on the neck of his T-shirt and casually ordering up the impossible ("Don't leave your feet on the floor too long . . ."). Paul Taylor fixed me a sandwich at his kitchen table before speaking about his work; I've sipped tea with Bill T. Jones and his husband, designer Bjorn Amelan, in their Hudson Valley home, hearing Jones' memories of his childhood in the potato fields of South Carolina. I've watched Mark Morris drill his dancers while singing out the counts along with the piano. I've seen the great Italian ballerina Alessandra Ferri rehearse a new Broadway musical with Tony-winning choreographer Andy (*Hamilton*) Blankenbuehler. This job has allowed me to watch as art takes shape from music, sweat, and thin air. I'm constantly inspired by that, and I seek to bring that perspective and dedication home, to my own work.

Courtesy of Tony Powell.

What is your best advice to those hoping to pursue a career in dance?

Look beyond performing. There are so many other avenues to pursue with a dance background. Believe in yourself and the power of what you know. Release your gifts to the waiting world.

Looking back, what have been the best decisions you have made during your career?

I made a commitment early on to being a great dance critic. I had high standards—I wanted to be better than anyone whose work I was reading. So I kept reading the very best writers and learning from them. I studied the best choreographers' works and examined their methods and learned from them. I listened to just about everyone who had something to say about art or writing. I prepare as much as I can but mostly, I'm prepared to be surprised. Being a dance critic means you're always confronting something new and alive and moving; you have to watch carefully, think fast, and think deeply. It works every part of your brain. You never stop learning.

DANCE JOURNALISM

Dance journalists serve many important purposes, including writing reviews of concerts and events, interviewing and profiling dancers and choreographers, writing opinion pieces about current issues in dance, presenting artists' work on television, and, sometimes, even filling an advocacy role by writing in support of dance. For financially strapped publications to pool resources and money, some journalists are tasked with covering multiple art forms, including dance. Artists and companies greatly value journalistic coverage of their work because it grants them free publicity and helps confirm to funders that their work is relevant and thus, worthy of support.

Job Opportunities and State of the Field

In the interest of transparency and in order to prepare future writers for the challenges of this career, know that as of 2020, only a handful of arts journalists were paid a full-time salary in the United States. Newspapers and magazines, facing sharp declines in readership over the past few decades, are cutting arts journalism positions or folding altogether. At the same time, many online publications are thriving, which suggests that careers in arts journalism are attainable. Additionally, most news outlets still hire part-time, temporary, and contract-based arts journalists, so there are possibilities for combining part-time work in dance journalism with another position or working as a freelance journalist for multiple media sources.

Freelance arts journalists are sometimes paid by the hour, by the article or story, or by the word. Publications' pay rates vary widely, so do some investigating before pursuing work at any one outlet. For example, writing a column for a dance magazine in the United States typically secures $150 to $500 depending on level of experience, expertise, and article topic and length. Magazines and newspapers typically publicize author pitch instructions and writing guidelines on their websites and include contact information for the editor to whom you should ask questions and submit pitches.

Career Preparation

The most important preparation for a career in dance journalism is to learn about and practice different styles of writing and to learn about the journalism industry to understand how you might fit into it. There are different schools of thought about whether or not a dance journalist should have experience in the art form in order to be qualified to write about it. It is possible to write beautifully about dance without ever having set foot on a stage or in a studio, but it also doesn't hurt to have insider knowledge of how it feels to be an artist.

Arts journalists must hold a bachelor's degree. By combining a degree program in journalism with training in dance during your college years, you will be well prepared for the rigors of the field. Appropriate undergraduate degrees include a bachelor of science or bachelor of arts in the following areas: print and mulitmedia journalism, broadcast journalism, public relations, and mass communication. Also, master's degrees in arts journalism provide specific opportunities for specialization in the arts.

In addition to formal education, seek opportunities to work in the arts journalism industry as an intern or a part-time employee during your schooling. These positions can expand your network and provide invaluable experience in the field. Local newspapers, magazines, and television news networks hire temporary or part-time writers for stories about the arts. Additionally, colleges and universities often publish on-campus news and reviews, which may present opportunities to further hone your writing skills and build a portfolio. Internships can create possibilities for jobs after graduation, so take advantage of these positions. All of these opportunities provide chances to impress future employers with your valuable and diverse skills. Prove to potential employers that you have the ability to edit, blog, tweet, shoot still photos and video, write concise and clear copy, and write varied and exciting stories.

Best Writing Practices

In strong journalistic writing, efficiency and clarity are paramount. Saying a lot in as few words as possible is critical, particularly in arts journalism, where the space for arts stories in the average publication is a precious commodity. Also, it is crucial to understand each publication's readers: What is their level of education? What are their political leanings? How active are they in the arts scene? "The best writing in journalism is hard to do. It is readily understandable, instantly readable and, if it is done well, makes you want to read on" (Cole 2008, para 3). You should always strive to use active voice, positive spin (telling readers what something is, not what it isn't), and concise yet impactful quotes. Finally, hone your presentation and style by practicing writing a lot.

One way to expand reach and readership while developing a portfolio is to start a blog. Write well-researched stories that you would want to read. Eleanor Turney, blogger and editor at *ArtsProfessional* magazine offers the following advice about blogging:

> Think of yourself as a self-appointed columnist, rather than a blogger. To get more visitors to your blog, comment on other blogs. Guest post for other blogs, and get other more established bloggers to post on yours . . . . Finally, post links to your blog on Twitter and Facebook. (Groves 2010, para 9)

During her career as a dance critic for *The Village Voice*, Elizabeth Zimmer developed helpful guides for dance journalists. In her guide, "Notes Toward Concise Writing: Saying What You Want to Say in Constricted Space," Zimmer highlights four key tips for making writing stronger: (1) Avoid the passive voice, (2) Monitor use of vague, general words (i.e., this, that, is, was) in favor of exciting active language, (3) Watch use of negative constructions, and (4) Read writing aloud to catch errors or awkward language (Zimmer 2007). Zimmer, along with fellow critics Deborah Jowitt and Marcia Siegel identified a list of questions writers should ask themselves before writing about a performance. These include practical questions about formatting, space, deadline, and style requirements as well as philosophical questions about writerly voice and perspective. Decide whether your dance writing style will be infused with rich descriptions that invite readers into a multisensory experience of a dance or whether you prefer a data-based approach that calls on social and cultural context to describe dance, for instance.

Pitching Your Ideas

Before pitching a story idea to an editor, ensure your story is timely and relevant to the publication. If, for example, you want to write an interview piece that highlights a famous tap dancer, it is unlikely that pitching to a magazine whose focus is ballet would lead to a contract. Read the publications for which you want to write to gain a sense of the stories they feature and the style and tone of writing. Pay close attention to author guidelines and follow them closely in your submissions. Your goal is to make editors' jobs as easy as possible by offering strong ideas and writing and demonstrating an understanding of the publications' goals and style.

Sherry Ricchiardi of the International Journalists' Network maintains that "pitches should not be time consuming" (Ricchiardi 2018, para 4) and advises writers to create a pitch template to simplify the process and make pitching stories efficient. She recommends including the following sections in a template: headline, format, summary (the who, what, when, where, and why of the story), interviews or sources, delivery date, and a writing portfolio. For radio or video stories, editors also want to know about equipment and software needs and may want to see a storyboard or proposed shot list. Also, include a short bio and link to your personal website or blog so editors can get a sense of your credentials, interests, and experience.

A professional tone and confidence in pitches are important. Be polite and enthusiastic in your message and be clear and concise without being overly pushy in tone. Your pitch should ensure editors know why this story is important to tell right now and why you are the one to tell it. Finally, make sure the editor knows that you have prepared for writing this story—that it is not just an idea, but a story that you have already researched and planned to write. Your pitch should grab an editor's attention with its fresh angle on a topic, its succinct and clear writing, and its relevance to current trends and issues in society.

After submitting a pitch to an editor, allow about a week of reply time before following up. Editors are busy, so a follow-up email may remind an editor that they intended to reply to your inquiry or that they have forgotten about your pitch sitting in their inbox. In your email, be polite and include a brief message along these lines: I am following up to ask if you are interested in the story I pitched to you last week about (insert topic here). I know you are very busy, so if I don't hear from you in the next few days, I will assume it is not of interest at this time. Typically, a follow-up email will elicit a response one way or another, which could be an offer, or it may be a rejection. Dealing with rejection is a major part of working as a journalist. Not all pitches will be of interest to every editor, so be prepared to field your pitch to other editors or to reconsider elements of your pitch to better fit the publication. Finally, if you have submitted a pitch to several editors to be met with only rejections, you might consider writing your story anyway and posting it on your blog and including it in your portfolio for future use.

Interviewing

Investigative journalism, opinion editorials (op-eds), and profile pieces rely on interviews to strengthen ideas, arguments, and topics. Interviews can provide context, nuance, clarity, and additional information to any story. Whereas an investigative interview seeks to gather information about an event or idea in the news, a profile interview focuses on an individual. It is critical for journalists to conduct interviews ethically and responsibly so as to represent transparent and honest information, uncover truths, and represent interviewees accurately.

The four principles of interviewing are (1) to prepare thoroughly, researching background information prior to an interview, (2) to establish a trusting relationship with the source, (3) to ask relevant questions, and (4) to listen and observe the source carefully (Columbia University School of Journalism n.d.). Importantly, focus your research, interview questions, and writing on the story you pitched or that was assigned to you by an editor.

Because communication is both verbal and nonverbal, when interviewing, pay close attention to interviewees' mannerisms, gestures, facial expressions, and posturing. These bodily clues can give a strong indication of a source's attitude, mood, perspective, and level of comfort in the interview. You can use these movements and postures as a guide for how to work with each source as you navigate controversial or sensitive questions and subject matter. Use descriptions of interviewees' movements as a way to paint a rich portrait of a profile subject or to add excitement, emotion, and dimension to a story. For dance stories, in particular, including descriptions of movements and expressions invites readers into the complexity of your writing.

Ethical Considerations

The Society of Professional Journalists (SPJ) insists that "ethical journalists must act with integrity" and that being a journalist carries a weight of responsibility to deliver writing that is accurate, fair, and thorough (Society of Professional Journalists 2014, para 1). Members of SPJ honor a code of ethics that guides their work in the field and lays an ethical foundation for their daily working and writing practices. SPJ outlines in its code four main principles for ethical journalism: (1) Seek truth and report it, (2) minimize harm, (3) act independently, and (4) be accountable and transparent.

Within the principle of seeking truth and reporting it, SPJ encourages journalists to take responsibility for the accuracy of their reporting, even when under a tight deadline or with limited resources. Therefore, it is advised that journalists update stories as more information becomes available, identify sources clearly (and when anonymity is granted, explain why), diligently seek responses from those criticized, hold those in power accountable, seek to represent voices of those unheard, avoid stereotyping, and never deliberately distort facts. The public is entitled to information and the journalist's job is to report it with as much accuracy and detail as possible.

Minimizing harm is complicated because journalists must often weigh the benefits of publishing information against the potential harm or discomfort that publicizing that information may create for others. SPJ asserts that "legal access to information differs from an ethical justification to publish or broadcast" (Society of Professional Journalists 2014, para 4) and advises journalists to show compassion to people. Further, consider the long-term effects of a story on the safety and livelihood of sources and other people involved or implicated in the story.

Acting independently means that a journalist's highest obligation is to the public and not to sources or other influences. Therefore, journalists should avoid conflicts of interest; refuse gifts, favors, or money that could compromise integrity; and should never pay for information or news. Striving for impartiality is critical to journalistic writing. Being accountable and transparent involves explaining ethical dilemmas and choices to the public, acknowledging and correcting mistakes, and exposing any unethical conduct in journalism. Because it is crucial to maintain the public's trust, continuing a dialogue with them about experiences, missteps, and corrections in the journalistic process is important.

Working With Editors

A good relationship between an editor and journalist is one that centers on mutual cooperation, respect, and a shared passion for producing the best stories possible. An editor's main tasks are to research, develop, and refine stories for timely publication and to build writers' skills so that they produce stronger writing and more impactful and interesting stories. Editors also make decisions about which stories to include in a publication, how to format those stories, and whether to include graphic elements or photographs. Editors are the main points of contact for journalists and help guide a story's development.

Clear and consistent communication with an editor is key because editors and reporters work at a distance, often not seeing each other every day. Whenever possible, communicate via phone or in person rather than email because email is often easy to misinterpret. Email is ideal for sharing drafts and edits. Additionally, it is helpful for journalists to check in regularly with editors to send updates on the progress of stories and to ask nonurgent questions. Overall, consider how to make your editor's job easier by being available, communicative, and most importantly, reliable in meeting deadlines.

DANCE RESEARCH

Since, in the United States, dance research is often aligned with jobs in postsecondary education, many dance researchers (but not all) conduct research as part of postsecondary academic job requirements. So, while it is unlikely to find a full-time position specifically in dance research, postdoctoral and midcareer fellowships can temporarily support dance research full time. Additionally, some universities weigh research very heavily; therefore, that workload component may comprise the bulk of a full-time academic position.

The pay for fellowships and positions in academia vary, but in general, fellowships pay less than full-time academic positions. Postdoctoral fellowships in the United States can start as low as $23,000 per year, while the average entry-level assistant professor in dance makes around $56,950 (Glassdoor 2020). Additionally—and importantly—fellowships typically do not include full benefits, while full-time positions do.

Dance research may be structured using quantitative methods that emphasize statistical or numerical analysis of data, or by using qualitative methods, which are nonnumeric and rely on conceptual and interpretive analyses and measurements. Some dance researchers focus on one line of research that can span an entire career, while other researchers conduct research on a project-by-project basis as funding permits or as their interests and questions shift. To conduct studies, some researchers seek funding from grants, awards, or fellowships to support their work, and some also benefit from internal funding available through their universities or companies. Research outcomes include books, academic journal articles, white papers, curricula, websites, multimedia products such as video, and even the development of new companies or partnerships.

Career Preparation

Dance researchers are highly skilled and comprehensively trained, which requires years of preparation. The best groundwork you can do in preparation for a career in dance research is to obtain a doctoral degree in dance, dance education, dance studies, dance science, or performance studies. Before you can apply for doctoral programs, however, you must have earned a bachelor's degree. Most doctoral programs also require receipt of an earned master's degree in dance or a related area for acceptance.

Earning a doctor of philosophy (PhD) can take five to eight years on average, usually comprising three years of course work and additional years to complete qualifying exams and write a dissertation. PhD course work engages deeply in theory, history, literature, research methods, and writing of dance scholarship. Qualifying exams are structured differently in each institution, but typically include significant scholarly writing. This exam is then evaluated by doctoral faculty who determine preparedness for the dissertation stage. Writing a dissertation is much like writing a book in that it includes a self-directed research inquiry with a significant written component. A dissertation committee made up of graduate faculty members guide and shape this process and determine the acceptability of the final product. The dissertation, therefore, marks the transition from student to scholar.

The EdD, or doctor of education, is another doctoral degree awarded to graduate students studying dance education. The process is quite similar to that of students on a PhD trajectory, with course work, qualifying exams, and a dissertation project to complete. Whereas the EdD focuses on issues and topics related to dance education, the PhD focuses on specific issues as well depending on the subject of a degree. For example, a PhD in dance studies may center on cultural, political, and historical topics and issues related to dance, a PhD in performance studies may widen in scope to include other modes of performance.

Finding the right program in which to study is important as you consider how to make the most of your education and ensure employability after graduation. Ask mentors and people you know who hold doctoral degrees about their recommendations and experiences. Then, research websites of the programs that interest you to get a sense of what kind of course work you will undertake and how the qualifying exam and dissertation processes are facilitated. Consider traveling to visit your favorite programs to get a feel for the campus and the faculty and to assess the level of support for graduate students. Ask a lot of questions, including questions about how graduate students are supported academically and financially, whether there are opportunities to research and teach as a graduate student, and what graduates go on to do after graduation. You should select a school in which you feel supported and encouraged, but also one that will challenge you to expand your ideas and develop as a scholar.

Once you are enrolled in a doctoral program, take advantage of every opportunity to learn from faculty members who research and publish. Apply for teaching and research assistantships, which will help pay for your education and will give you invaluable practical experience and mentorship from faculty. Use this time to get to know professional organizations by joining and attending conferences; graduate student rates are always much less expensive than professional rates. Additionally, read everything you have time to read in major academic journals and take cues from these authors about writing style and tone. If possible, during doctoral studies, submit a few journal articles for publication. With a few tweaks and development, some of the writing completed in course work can be turned directly into strong articles. Finally, if a full-time job in academia is your goal, seek a mentor to show you the ropes of the job search, application, and interview processes *before* your last year in graduate school. Your last year of graduate school will be spent, in part, applying and hopefully interviewing for jobs.

Best Practices in Qualitative Research

According to practitioner Sharan B. Merriam, "qualitative researchers are interested in understanding how people interpret their experiences, how they construct their worlds, and what meaning they attribute to their experiences" (Merriam 2009, 5). Further, Merriam describes qualitative research as interpretive—it "assumes that reality is socially constructed, that there is no single, observable reality. Rather, there are multiple realities, or interpretations, of a single event. Researchers do not 'find' knowledge, they construct it" (Merriam 2009, 8-9). Qualitative research is not experimental, it does not attempt to find cause and effect, nor does it seek to predict future events or to prove or disprove a hypothesis (Creswell 2017; Merriam 2009).

Research practitioners define the approaches to qualitative research in different ways. Creswell identifies five approaches: narrative research, phenomenology, grounded theory, ethnography, and case study. Under each of these umbrella approaches, he identifies several focused approaches. Other approaches identified by theorists include action research, portraiture, and arts-based approaches. The domain of qualitative research is open to new and evolving approaches that best support the needs of the research.

Qualitative research processes include three phases, defined by Denzin and Lincoln as "theory, method, and analysis; or ontology, epistemology, and methodology" (Denzin and Lincoln 2011, 11). Creswell affirms that, in general, a qualitative research study begins with philosophical assumptions and development of a theoretical framework that shapes the research problem or questions. Then, from an emerging qualitative approach to inquiry, data is collected in natural settings and then analyzed to establish patterns or themes. Finally, the research report includes "the voices of the participants, the reflexivity of the researcher, a complex description or interpretation of the problem, and its contribution to literature or call for change" (Creswell 2017, 44).

Ethical Considerations

Because qualitative research involves working with human participants, there are many ethical considerations. Internal and external validity, reliability, and consistency are all important objectives. Also, ensuring that study participants are properly protected and accurately represented is crucial. Therefore, researchers implement various tools such as consent forms to inform potential participants about the nature of a study. If interviews or observations are included in the study, researchers aim to make interviews responsive and listen closely to participants. Further, researchers may record interviews for accuracy. Participant checks are conducted to ensure participants' reputations are unharmed, that they feel safe and respected in the research process, and that accuracy and validity are consistently prioritized; these checks will include sending the participants drafts and giving them opportunities to edit or omit any of their own words. Finally, researchers working in universities are required to obtain research approval from their school's Institutional Review Board, a governing body that ensures research is conducted safely and ethically.

Best Practices in Quantitative Research

Whereas dance scholarship is frequently written based on data collected and analyzed using qualitative research approaches, some studies require a quantitative or mixed-method approach. "Quantitative methods emphasize objective measurements and the statistical, mathematical, or numerical analysis of data collected through polls, questionnaires, and surveys, or by manipulating pre-existing statistical data using computational techniques" (Muijs 2010, 3). Quantitative research is often used in dance science studies and studies that require standardized measures to prove or disprove an existing theory or hypothesis. To conduct accurate and ethical quantitative research, researchers must have training in statistical analysis and in research methodologies because they work with numbers as well as conduct human and textual analyses.

The differences between qualitative and quantitative research come down to different conceptual and methodological approaches. For example, whereas qualitative research is concerned with understanding human behavior from the participant's perspective, quantitative research seeks to discover facts about social phenomena. Qualitative research "assumes a dynamic and negotiated reality [while quantitative research] assumes a fixed, measurable reality" (McLeod 2017, para 1). Data is collected and analyzed through the perspectives of the participants in qualitative research, while in quantitative research, data is collected through measurements and analyzed using numerical and statistical analyses. To further elucidate this difference, consider an example: The topic of cross-training methods to increase strength and stamina in dance students could be investigated both quantitatively and qualitatively. In a quantitative study of this topic, researchers might use motion capture technology and statistical analysis to numerically measure angles, force, and impact and make conclusions about the effectiveness of a training program. To study the same topic in a qualitative study might involve assigning dancers a specific training regimen to perform on their own and then interviewing them about their experiences in cross-training.

If you believe quantitative design is important to your research interests, select a graduate program equipped to teach quantitative methods and statistics. Because many doctoral programs in dance focus mainly on qualitative research design, seek additional training to ensure your educational needs are met either in a particular graduate program or by reaching across campus to take course work in other disciplines to fill gaps in quantitative research and mathematics.

Submitting Writing to Academic Journals and Publishers

Academic publishers and journals differ in some ways from commercial publishers because academic publications are peer reviewed, meaning that all submissions are vetted for publication by a group of experts in the field. This makes for a rigorous and often lengthy process for academic writers because it takes significant time to conduct the research and write it up, and even more time for reviewers to assess a submission and respond with either an acceptance (very rare), a request to revise and resubmit (common), or a rejection. It can take on average six months to a year from the time of submission to publication in a peer-reviewed journal.

Dance and dance education journals address different aims and scopes for their readers. For example, the journal *Research in Dance Education* "aims to inform, stimulate lively and critical debate and promote the development of high quality research and practice in dance education. The journal is relevant to dance academics, teachers and learners" (Research in Dance Education 2020, para 1). By contrast, each issue of the *Journal of Dance Medicine & Science* "focuses on bringing [readers] the current results of clinical and experimental research . . . . Featured articles are drawn from the fields of anatomy and physiology, biomechanics, general medicine, physical therapy, kinesiology . . ." (International Association for Dance Medicine and Science n.d., para 1). Other top journals in dance include the *Journal of Dance Education*, *Dance Research Journal*, *Dance Education in Practice*, and *Dance Chronicle*.

Additionally, depending on your research area and topic, journals and publishers outside the dance discipline may be more appropriate venues in which to publish your writing.

If you aim to target your writing to a specific journal or publisher, read several of its featured articles to ensure a good fit within your own research topic and go to its website to find author guidelines. Using these guidelines and previously published works as templates, write your article in the style and format required by that publisher. This will save you a lot of time because it will keep you from having to reformat the writing later. Usually each journal or publisher will have its own preferences in regard to formatting and style. In particular, pay close attention to how articles incorporate quotes, citations, headings, bibliographies, and tone or voice of its published authors. It is important to align the structure and style of your work with that of the publication to which you aim to submit manuscripts.

Most journals require research articles to be 5,000 to 8,000 words in length; they must include specific sections about methodologies and literature review and must include an abstract and key words. An abstract is a basic summary of the article in about 150-250 words to give readers a sense of whether or not they want to read the entire article. Publishers recommend that authors briefly include answers to the following questions in an abstract: What are your research questions? What process and methods did you use to explore those questions? What are your findings? (Purdue Online Writing Lab 2020). Journal articles also include a list of four to six key words that define the general areas or content of the article to make it easier for readers to search and find your article. Finally, prepare to submit a brief biography to accompany all articles.

One of the best resources for developing and refining a journal article for submission, review, and publication in a peer-reviewed source is called *Writing Your Journal Article in Twelve Weeks: A Guide to Academic Publishing Success* by Wendy Laura Belcher (2019). This text offers invaluable, clear, practical guidelines for how to develop a research topic and an argument, gives an overview of important writing tips, and takes readers step-by-step through the journal search, submission, review, and publication processes. The Belcher Diagnostic Test included in the book is a set of tools for improving the clarity, efficiency, and effectiveness of analytical scholarly writing.

Working With Reviewers and Editors

Each journal or publisher employs a distinct process for handling submissions and working with authors, but most are fairly similar. Once you are ready to submit a manuscript, follow author instructions explicitly to ensure appropriate submission. Many journals accept manuscripts online through independent submission sites and you will need to register for an account to submit writing. You will include a cover letter, so prepare that in advance. Your cover letter should be brief, professional, and positive in tone, and should include your name and title, the title of your manuscript, its general topic, and a reason that you think this article would be of interest to that publication's readers.

Academic writing etiquette expects authors to submit to only one journal at a time. After a manuscript submission, expect to wait a few weeks to a few months to hear back from an editor. In general, this waiting time can be stressful, so it is helpful to have a few different articles in process simultaneously to take the pressure off any one piece of writing or project. If four months pass and you have heard nothing about a submission, send a very brief follow-up email to the editor of the publication asking for an update on the review process.

When you do receive a response to your submission, it will include an acceptance notification, a request to revise and resubmit the manuscript based on reviewer comments and suggestions, or a rejection. First, if the article is rejected, don't panic. Often, rejections will include information about why the article does not fit that publication or the weaknesses found in the article. This is extremely important information to consider because it will help guide your next submission to a more appropriate venue or will assist you in developing the article into a stronger piece. If you are asked to revise and resubmit the article, the message will likely include information about how to revise and resubmit along with reviewer comments, questions, and suggested edits, omissions, or additions. Take these suggestions seriously and adhere to as many of the reviewers' comments as you can. Reviewers' feedback is valuable and can often make your writing stronger and clearer. This is your research, though, so if you do not agree with some of the reviewers' ideas, you can present a case to the editor about why you chose not to address certain changes. However, in general, editors tend to agree with the reviewers' suggestions, so by not making reviewers' changes, you risk facing a rejection.

After revision and resubmission, expect to wait (although not as long this time) for the editor's response. There may still be one or even a few more rounds of edits to make before you (hopefully) receive an acceptance notice. Then, congratulations, after a round of final proofs to check, you are officially a published author! Typically, journals provide authors with a certain number of free copies of their articles to share with colleagues and friends and to archive. Some publishers offer open-access publishing, which can be very expensive, so do research before committing to open-access publishing.

Overall, academic journals and publishers are more likely to publish writing that has been rigorously and ethically researched and that follows the venue's style and formatting practices. Reviewers and editors work to ensure precision and innovation in new scholarship and are there to help writers make their work clearer and stronger. After a few successful publications, you may be asked to serve as a reviewer for a journal or publisher. Consider offering this important service to the profession to reciprocate support to your scholar colleagues who have supported your writing.

SUMMARY

Careers in dance journalism or research present exciting possibilities to ask important questions, create new knowledge, and expand others' ideas of what dance is and how it operates. Job opportunities in dance journalism for print and online publications, television, and radio, while often part time, can financially supplement other

Dr. Ann Dils

Scholar and chair of the Department of Dance, University of North Carolina at Charlotte

Looking back, what have been the best decisions you have made during your career?

I followed my own sensibilities about how to live my life and when to take opportunities, rather than relying on well-meaning advice. While I am sure some of my decisions harmed aspects of my career, I followed my understanding of what was right for me. I jumped in and took opportunities as they arose, not necessarily when it was reasonable to do so. I was president of the Congress on Research in Dance as an assistant professor and served as editor of *Dance Research Journal* as an associate professor. I worked on *Moving History/Dancing Cultures*, despite a dean's caution that collaborative work is not well regarded during promotion and tenure decisions and have continued to work on collaborative projects. Ideally, I might have developed my work as a dance studies scholar fully by producing single-author monographs before taking on these responsibilities. I had no way of knowing if these opportunities would recur and remain happy with that work and its timing and impact on my career. Finally, I greatly value leading the Department of Dance at UNC Charlotte. Department heads are notoriously overworked and underappreciated, stuck, as they are, between the needs of the university and the desires, and egos, of faculty and students. Still, it's a privilege to work with colleagues to shape a dance department: to enact long-held beliefs about dance as inquiry, to see the humanistic benefits of a broad dance curriculum attuned to cultural competency, to see young scholars and artists advance in their careers, and to think about the relation-

dance work or can be enhanced by a holistic journalistic approach that includes all of the arts and entertainment. An entrepreneurial, self-motivated approach is key to creating a full-time career in dance journalism. Approaching a career in academic publishing with an understanding of its unique processes, including how to conduct qualitative or quantitative research and how to work with editors, will help you navigate its challenges and work toward goals effectively. Knowing that most research work is connected to careers in postsecondary education is important so you can prepare for an academic position that may also require skills in teaching, performance, and choreography. Dance researchers and journalists maintain the field's historical record, influence trends and global dialogue about dance, and inspire readers to engage with dance.

ship between a department and the people and institutions in the region it serves. It's a wonderful place to be as I contemplate retirement, more time with grandchildren, and, again, pursuing those writing projects.

What is your best advice to those hoping to pursue a career in dance?

My bits of advice are contradictory and suggest working in a deliberate, strategic way that isn't always clear when you're in the midst of a career. Collaborate. Collaboration is wonderfully energizing, allowing you to push your own thinking and marshal the energy and resources needed to complete a project. Working with other scholars opens up reflective space, especially about habitual ways of working and repeated use of theories and scholarly sources that I wouldn't get to alone. My best work has been coauthored, coedited, or otherwise done in collaboration. Take control of your own interests. For a variety of personal and institutional reasons, I moved away from daily dance practice and from studio-based creative engagement over the years. While I hadn't thought it possible, I have lost the ready kinesthetic empathy of my younger self. This impacts my work with colleagues and students interested primarily in studio practice and the ways in which I witness and respond to dance. This is a small example of the many gulfs that occur among faculties and in organizations that contain artists, scholars, and pedagogues with different backgrounds and priorities. And it leads me to another bit of advice: Realize that your ways of seeing and pursuing questions, and your understandings about the field are your own and not necessarily shared. Establish a trajectory and stick with it. When you're a young scholar and get requests to contribute to volumes, serve organizations, or collaborate on projects, it's easy to put aside your own research interests. I have two book projects in various stages of completion that I wish I'd finished. It's difficult to ask for research leave—I've only had one in my career—if you don't have a publication project near completion. I may not get back to these projects until retirement. By that time, my ideas and materials may lose currency.

Reflection

WRITING PROMPT: STORY IDEAS

Create a list of 10 ideas for stories that you would be interested in pitching to editors. Under each entry, include the names of at least two publication venues to which you could pitch your story idea. Include relevant information that could help you develop your pitch such as possible sources to interview, people to feature, companies or productions that interest you, and a timeline or deadline for the completed piece. This exercise will help you begin the work of a dance journalist by encouraging you to articulate your goals in a concrete way. Then, when you feel prepared, consider taking at least one of these ideas forward by pitching it to an editor.

WRITING PROMPT: DEVELOPING A RESEARCH TOPIC

Developing an effective research topic takes skill and time. The size and scope of a project, the amount of time you have to complete it, and the number of words or amount of space you have to present your findings will help you determine how broad or narrow to make your topic. For example, if you are writing a journal article, you may want a narrow topic, while a book topic can be broader. An example of a broad topic might be jazz dance. To narrow that topic, determine what piece of the broader topic is interesting to you. An example of a narrower topic could be queer jazz dancers working in 1920s Parisian nightclubs. Searching for source material to assess what already has been written about your topic can help you focus it as well.

In this writing exercise, first spend time making a list of topics in dance that interest you. Don't think too much about this, just write freely, constructing a list of ideas that you would like to study further. Then, select one of these ideas from your list in which to delve further. From your idea, create three to five search terms or key words and use these terms to search online in Google Scholar, on library websites, and publishing archives to find articles related to your topic. Save or document every resource you feel could contribute to your future research. As you discover what already exists in the scholarly record, you may find that your original idea is already saturated in published scholarship. In that case, add another search term or key word to your idea to further narrow it. Read some of what is already published and decide where you stand on the issues surrounding your topic. From this initial review of literature, add your more fully developed research topic to your list.

WRITING PROMPT: DEVELOPING A SCHOLARLY ARGUMENT

One of the challenges of framing a qualitative research study is in developing a scholarly argument (sometimes called a thesis). An argument should be a statement to which you can respond with agreement or disagreement and should establish a position. Practitioner Steven Posusta created a handy template for developing a strong, clear scholarly argument called the Instant Thesis Maker (Posusta 1996). Use the following template to practice developing scholarly arguments incorporating the research topics developed in the writing prompt, Developing a Research Topic: Although (general statement or opposite opinion), nevertheless, (your thesis, your idea) because (examples, evidence).

Here is an example of an argument developed through the Instant Thesis Maker: Although scholars have long surmised that Dr. Dancer's work represents the most effective ballet pedagogy; nevertheless, Dr. Ballet presents innovative ideas that challenge common weaknesses found in ballet teaching because her ideas dispel the stubbornly maintained hierarchy between teacher and student.

Chapter 8

Dance Administration and Advocacy

"I define a leader as anyone who takes responsibility for finding the potential in people and processes, and who has the courage to develop that potential."

Brené Brown

"Dance is for everybody. I believe that the dance came from the people and it should always be delivered back to the people."

Alvin Ailey

Dance advocates and administrators in K-12 and postsecondary education, dance companies, and nonprofit organizations provide important work to the industry and, in many ways, keep dance operating effectively in the United States. These jobs require a particular set of skills and a passion for dance that can be integrated and articulated into vision, action, and results. Routinely, professionals working in dance administration and advocacy adopt these roles later in their careers after acquiring comprehensive critical training and knowledge of the field and profession. Above all, dance administrators and advocates should desire to support their teams of colleagues. Letting others shine, spurring innovation in the field, fostering connections, and promoting innovation in dance are the primary goals of an administrator or advocate.

This chapter delves into the ins and outs of dance administration and advocacy, with particular foci on leadership roles in education, executive roles in companies and organizations, grant writing, and opportunities in nonprofit and government agencies. Reflective writing prompts are provided to support investigation of various leadership styles.

Dr. Melonie Buchanan Murray

Associate dean for faculty and academic affairs and associate professor of dance, University of Utah

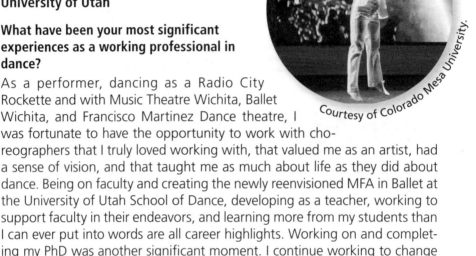

Courtesy of Colorado Mesa University.

What have been your most significant experiences as a working professional in dance?

As a performer, dancing as a Radio City Rockette and with Music Theatre Wichita, Ballet Wichita, and Francisco Martinez Dance theatre, I was fortunate to have the opportunity to work with choreographers that I truly loved working with, that valued me as an artist, had a sense of vision, and that taught me as much about life as they did about dance. Being on faculty and creating the newly reenvisioned MFA in Ballet at the University of Utah School of Dance, developing as a teacher, working to support faculty in their endeavors, and learning more from my students than I can ever put into words are all career highlights. Working on and completing my PhD was another significant moment. I continue working to change the culture of ballet and the culture of dance in higher education for the better through my writing, presenting, and serving on national organization boards. This sense of trying to be a positive agent for change is meaningful and fulfilling for me.

What is your best advice to those hoping to pursue a career in dance?

Be kind, respectful, and honorable. Always. Take enough pride in all that you do so that you never settle for mediocrity. Listen more than you speak and listen to hear rather than to respond. Respect is something that you earn. Lose the blinders. Planning ahead is fine but be careful not to have such a narrow view or plan of your future that you miss opportunities just on the periphery of your vision. Take care of your whole self (body, mind, soul). No one has as much of a vested interest in your health and wellness as you do. Describe some of the greatest lessons you've learned in your dance career. First impressions never go away. No matter what anyone says, they matter. Stand up for what you believe in, but pick your battles carefully and wisely. If you find yourself getting overly emotional, you are too close to the situation. Take a breath and a step back. I call this "zooming out" (like a camera lens). Whenever possible, take the high road.

CAREERS IN DANCE ADMINISTRATION

Dance administrators work in a variety of settings and their jobs require strong leadership abilities. Primary responsibilities include budgeting, fundraising, marketing, student or dancer recruitment and retention, audience development, community engagement, and staff management. Strong dance administrators must be visionary leaders and outstanding communicators. They must be motivational and organized and must understand broad trends in dance artistry, dance education, scholarship, public relations, and resource management (Larson 2013; Whiteman 1991). Overall, administrators must be adept at recognizing opportunity and strategically working with colleagues to improve an organization, school, or company to fully realize its mission.

The most common professional settings for dance administrators are in educational institutions. Universities and colleges offer opportunities for employment as chair or director of a department, head of an undergraduate or graduate program, and additional roles within college and university administration, such as dean or provost positions. Also, many universities host performance series and house arts centers on campus, which necessitate additional administrators. In K-12 education, dance programs are led by directors, and many schools also have a need for coaching leadership for dance or drill teams.

Full-time dance administrators in public and private four-year and two-year postsecondary institutions typically enjoy annual salaries and benefits. In the United States, dance department chairs and heads of dance programs can expect a salary in the range of $65,000 to over $150,000 per year (Dance Magazine 2018). This largely depends on the circumstances of the position—whether or not the administrative role is full time or if part-time duties are added to an existing position. Dance directors and coaches working in K-12 public school can earn from $16,500 to $85,000 per year (ZipRecruiter 2020; Firth n.d.; Dance Magazine 2018).

DANCE ADMINISTRATION CAREERS IN EDUCATIONAL INSTITUTIONS

Whether your goal is to become a dance director and drill team coach at a secondary school, the chair of a postsecondary dance department, or any of the myriad other administrative jobs available, the skills and experience required of strong dance leaders in educational institutions are similar. Dance administrators in academic institutions, first and foremost, must be willing to serve a program holistically to support a group of students, faculty and staff members, fellow administrators, and alumni. Academic leadership is about championing the collective and individual achievements of a team of colleagues. This differs from the approaches of individual faculty members, whose positions require that they work toward individual agendas and accomplishments. Additionally, academic leaders must be able to envision and enact new ideas and initiatives, manage teams of faculty and staff, support student and faculty interests, recruit new students and faculty members, budget and design seasons of performances and events, collaborate with others across disciplines, and market the program to the community and the field at large.

Both secondary and postsecondary institutions require degreed administrators. In K-12 schools, an undergraduate degree in dance, education, or a related area qualifies, while in postsecondary institutions, a terminal graduate degree in dance, dance education, or related area is mandatory for administrative positions. Additionally, search committees look for previous experience in administration, teaching dance, university service, choreography, performance, scholarship, and student advising and recruitment. If you can demonstrate experience in course and curricular development and assessment, budgeting, marketing, grant writing, community engagement, and accreditation processes, your chances of being hired are even better. Seek ways to gain these experiences while serving as a faculty member or even during graduate studies if administrative opportunities arise.

One of the most important success strategies administrators rely on is their experience learning and working their way up through an educational system, getting to know the history, culture, values, operational policies, and systemic processes of an institution. While these elements can be learned along the way, it is typically much smoother to go into an administrative position knowing some of the ins and outs of that school. This way, your main focus upon entering an administrative position can be your colleagues, students, and dance program.

Postsecondary Program Coordinator, Department Chair, and Dean Positions

Universities and colleges provide myriad opportunities for leadership and administration. Depending on the organizational structure of each university and department, there may be opportunities for dance administrators as department chairs, directors, or dance program coordinators. These leaders manage staff and student recruitment and advancement, represent the dance area across campus and in the community, and organize the day-to-day administrative elements of dance programs and departments such as scheduling classes, planning events, and fundraising. Deans, on the other hand, oversee various elements of multiple disciplines and areas, often with a focus on how departments work together and as separate entities, including working with budgets, curricula, and other college leadership.

In some ways, the structure of the dance program in which administrators work influences their day-to-day tasks and long-term goals and strategies. For example, some college dance programs are housed in shared departments with other disciplines such as theater and music while others stand alone as independent dance departments. When dance is an independent department, it doesn't compete with other disciplines for budgetary needs, so its leaders can focus on dance-specific necessities such as class accompanists and sprung studio floors (Caldwell 2016). On the other hand, some standalone dance departments don't have their own production staff, so these administrators are tasked with the extra responsibilities of creating temporary production crews and securing theater space for each dance production (Caldwell 2016). Independent dance department chairs have the advantage of crafting a dance-specific vision, yet they face additional responsibilities in budgeting and resource management.

When a dance program is part of a larger department, it can benefit from its potentially larger impact and presence on campus overall, but there are also drawbacks to leaders who must negotiate for dance-specific funding and resources (Caldwell 2016). For instance, when dance and theater programs share a department, dance students and faculty have opportunities to be involved in crossover productions like musicals and interdisciplinary work. Further, because these departments are typically well staffed with production teams, dance concerts are guaranteed to be fully produced. However, dance administrators in joint departments often face the challenges of addressing unfair allocations among the various areas, scheduling conflicts, and confusing bureaucratic channels of communication (Caldwell 2016). Although there is no perfect model for a dance program, understanding which kind of department you would like to lead and which circumstances you feel best fit your strengths is important before seeking an administrative job.

Beyond positions within the dance discipline, other career possibilities exist for administrators in postsecondary schools. University dance departments and programs are housed within larger structures called colleges alongside other disciplines. Each college maintains its own team of staff made up of a dean and sometimes associate or assistant deans. Serving as an academic dean involves creating synergy among the various departments in the college, overseeing programmatic developments and assessments, and implementing policies and procedures related to students and faculty. Usually, professionals in these positions have already developed successful faculty careers and maintain distinguished reputations in their discipline. However, many deans rarely teach and research minimally because workload expectations are mostly administrative. The benefits of dean positions are that they engage with the arts, including dance, and that the pay is considerably higher than that of faculty members.

Because administrative positions require significant experience and because these positions are likely to take professionals away from their personal artistic, scholarly, or teaching practices, many leaders choose to wait until later into their careers to pursue such positions. Dance scholar Sue Stinson emphasized that administrators "who try to climb the tenure track while simultaneously taking care of everyone but themselves" (Stinson 1998, 124) sacrifice much of their individual work toward tenure and other professional goals in order to be effective leaders. At the same time, according to scholar Doug Risner, "in the quest to keep dance at the center of focus while meeting the accelerating demands of the increasingly corporate-driven world of academia, effective leadership becomes progressively more important" (Risner 2017, 5). Therefore, it is important that administrators take on these leadership positions at the right time in their careers. There is no one right or wrong way to follow the administrative path, but be aware administrative requirements diverge from those of faculty members. Be prepared for these differences and be ready to let the research and teaching parts of your working self take a back seat to your administrative duties.

Stephanie Milling

Interim department chair and head of dance education, University of South Carolina; chair of NDEO Dance Advocacy Committee

Courtesy of University of South Carolina.

Describe some of the greatest lessons you've learned in your dance career.

First, be aware of what you want, but also be sensitive to what others see in you. Then, capitalize on the opportunities that are presented to you in reference to both perspectives. When I started pursuing a career in higher education, I had an advisor who recognized that I had certain skills to succeed in administration. I was not sure if I wanted to pursue that route at the time, but she introduced me to opportunities that have helped me develop my skills that have contributed to my work in several positions that I have occupied: program director, assistant dean, associate chair, etc. Second, love what you do, but make sure that you respect the need for downtime. I have always had an insatiable work ethic and passion for dance, ever since I was a young child. While it is wonderful to have a job that I love, it also makes it challenging to focus on other things at times. I feel that working in dance allows me to have a hobby and career all in one. However, it is important to nurture your personal life, which can also enhance your work. Human activities like reading a book, being aware of the dynamics of your relationships with others, and recognizing how you navigate other situations in your personal life can also enhance how you succeed in your work life. Third, nurture the relationships you have with teachers that you respect, and look to them as forever mentors. I have mentors who have continued to provide me with sound advice and wisdom for the last 20 to 30 years. I have not made many career-changing decisions without their advice or input. It has been amazing to reflect on how these people have led me along a productive and fulfilling path from student to professional, artist to educator, and dance citizen to advocate.

What have been the best decisions you have made during your career?

Becoming more involved with arts advocacy started out of necessity, but I did not realize that it would end up being one of my main areas of focus. Not only have I enjoyed learning about how policy and funding impacts the arts and arts education at local, state, and national levels, but I also have enjoyed advocating on behalf of the right of every child and citizen to have opportunities to appreciate and participate in the arts. Understanding the intricacies of policy have enabled me to actively participate in the political process as a citizen and teach my students how policy will impact their future practice teaching in K-12 classrooms. I also have found great fulfillment in contributing to the continued presence and opportunities within dance and arts education for future generations.

Many of the same interview processes apply to university and college administrators as to dance faculty in academia. Applicants are customarily asked to submit a curriculum vitae, leadership or teaching philosophy statement, and professional recommendations. Interviews typically include multiday on-campus visitations in which candidates are interviewed by the search committee, faculty, staff, students, and administrators. Candidates also usually offer a lecture or a research talk. This process can be time-consuming and lengthy; however, it is important to ensure a good fit when a university is hiring a new leader.

K-12 Dance Program and Department Director Jobs

Public and private K-12 schools across the United States differ in how they offer dance education. Some schools require dance classes for every student, some offer dance as an elective or extra, and some offer club or team-based dance programs such as dance or drill teams. All of these programs demand strong administrative leadership. Whereas there is much standardization in postsecondary dance education, there is less in secondary schools. Therefore, administrators must be proficient in developing curricula, proposing and advocating for new programs, managing student behavioral and retainment issues, and working with other administrators and faculty across campus. Additionally, because many secondary dance programs are small, dance leaders typically don't have a large number of colleagues, so they have to wear many hats, often serving as leader, teacher, advisor, and coach. Dance administrators in secondary schools are, in other words, very busy!

Secondary school dance administrators are required to hold an undergraduate degree in dance or other area, provided they have significant dance and education experience and state teacher certification or licensure. Some administrators are hired to create new programs, which requires a tremendous commitment to advocacy because much of the job, at least initially, centers on "selling" ideas about a new program to a school and its district and recruiting students into classes and initiatives. Others are hired to fill an existing leadership role in a dance program.

Often, administrative jobs in K-12 schools are advertised through traditional channels such as job and school websites. Typically, applicants submit a résumé, licensure credentials, and professional recommendations. An interview with the school principal or with current dance faculty members is required and sometimes a master class or teaching demonstration is requested as well.

Leadership Positions in Professional Organizations

Professional organizations provide invaluable services to dance workers across sectors. Typically, these are established as nonprofit organizations and they require leadership to communicate with members, work with a board of directors, organize annual conferences and other programming, budget and fundraise, and oversee committees that address items specific to the organization's mission such as advocacy, research, and education. Many organizations are led by an executive or operational director with support from other staff members who oversee specific areas of the organization such as its peer-reviewed publication or archiving. Administrative roles in national dance organizations can be part time or full time, and they require administrative experience, knowledge of the discipline and the organization, and an advanced degree in a related area. The Dance Studies Association (DSA), for example, hired a new executive director in 2019. In its job advertisement, the DSA estimated its executive director would be expected to work 60 hours per month at a rate of US$30 to US$40 per hour (Dance Studies Association 2019).

The disciplinary and professional foci of each organization and its breadth and reach in the field largely determine its size and scope and thus, the significance of its administrative needs. The National Dance Education Organization, for example, founded in 1998, has a membership of over 4,000 and, through national and state organizational branches, serves dance educators across the United States (National Dance Education Organization 2020). The Dance Studies Association was "formed in 2017 as the merged entity of the Congress on Research in Dance (CORD) and the Society of Dance History Scholars (SDHS) . . . . DSA advances the field of dance studies through research, publication, performance, and outreach to audiences across the arts, humanities, and social sciences" (Dance Studies Association 2019, para 1). The International Association for Dance Medicine and Science (IADMS) was founded in 1990 and now serves over 900 dance medicine practitioners around the world (International Association for Dance Medicine and Science n.d., para 1). Dance/USA, established in 1982, "champions an inclusive and equitable dance field by leading, convening, advocating, and supporting individuals and organizations" (Dance/USA n.d., para 1). Given the unique goals and mission of each of these major dance organizations, the roles and responsibilities of each administrative team varies as well.

ADMINISTRATIVE CAREERS IN DANCE COMPANIES AND NONPROFIT ORGANIZATIONS

The success of dance companies and nonprofit organizations largely depends on executive leadership in partnership with artistic staff and a board of directors. An executive director's key responsibilities include fundraising and development initiatives such as grant writing, donor cultivation, contracting, event planning, board development, adoption of policies and procedures, financial planning and bookkeeping, budgeting, and coordination of other executive staff such as booking agents, press representatives, and tax and insurance agents. Additionally, depending on the structure and mission of the company, an executive director may also be responsible for advocacy efforts, community engagement initiatives, touring productions, or human resources assignments. Finally, it is critical that an executive director work closely with and support the company's artistic director with the goal of a shared and cohesive vision.

Strong executive directors don't always have dance experience, but an appreciation and commitment to dance is a must. Executive leaders who exhibit cultural competence and a vision for how to create synergy between an organization and its local, regional, and even national community are coveted in dance. The executive director must be well attuned to the language and aesthetic of dance and be able to share ideas and goals with the artistic director. As a team, the directors report to the board of directors which, in turn, governs the company. Occasionally, a company's artistic director will also serve as its executive director, but because both roles require an enormous amount of work in distinct areas, it is advisable to separate these positions whenever possible.

Salaries for dance company executive administrators are more variable than those for educational administrators because there is less standardization among companies as compared with the educational system. This is because companies vary widely in their financial stability and strategic goals based on each company's size, operating budget, and geographical location. In its Local Arts Agency Salaries 2018 report, Americans for the Arts collected over 1,100 anonymous responses from professionals working in arts agencies. In this document, self-reported salaries for full-time nonprofit executive directors in the United States ranged from $16,980 to $260,875, with a median salary of $62,000 (Americans for the Arts n.d.). It is important to note that many nonprofit dance companies are small and operate with part-time staff, so the wages for those administrators are likely lower than these published by Americans for the Arts, since this report also includes data from larger organizations and across art forms.

PREPARING FOR A CAREER AS A DANCE COMPANY EXECUTIVE ADMINISTRATOR

Most executive director positions require, at minimum, a bachelor's degree, which can be in dance or in a discipline specific to executive leadership such as business or nonprofit management. Multiple universities offer arts administration degrees at the undergraduate and graduate level. Arts administration degrees are especially helpful in preparation for a career in dance company leadership because the course content is relevant to executive leadership in the arts. For example, Columbia University's Master of Arts in Arts Administration degree requires course work in arts-specific marketing, development, fundraising, law, and business policy (Columbia University n.d.). Because the arts represent a distinct area of administration, with structures and goals different from those of traditional business models, it is imperative to gain experience in these particular areas.

Knowledge and appreciation of dance, prominent dance companies and artists, and the community in which a company is located must be demonstrated to search committees. Therefore, many executive directors are recruited from within the community in which a company is located. Being able to discuss a vision with specific ideas for how a dance company can thrive in its community and beyond is important to articulate as well. Research successful dance companies in similar communities to get a sense of how they can make a great impact and what strategies their leaders employ. Borrow strategies that have worked previously for other leaders, and don't be afraid to think creatively as well about how dance companies can construct new organizational models and innovative programming and audience building. Consider your preferred leadership style and how you envision working with a production team and board of directors. All of this visionary planning should happen before interviews so that you are prepared to step immediately into an executive leadership role.

Additional Administrative Roles in Nonprofit Dance

Thriving dance companies maintain a large staff to accommodate expanded programming, including large-scale productions, community engagement, and touring performances and residencies. These companies require management from more than just an executive and artistic director. Depending on a company's mission and budget, there may be opportunities for part-time or full-time work in grant writing, marketing, event planning, audience relations, production management, and community engagement. These positions are important to the success of a dance company and these leaders work closely with the directors and board to fulfill the mission and vision of a company.

Grant Writing

Grant writing and fundraising can be a lucrative line of work because many dance companies and organizations rely on grants and contributions for survival. Grants are available through private foundations and state and federal institutions, and they may cover the operational expenses of a dance company or organization, including production costs, facilities expenses, staff stipends, travel expenses, and new programs and partnerships. Many grant-writing and fundraising positions are part time, but there are also full-time opportunities with larger companies and organizations whose missions are to fulfill multiple functions across the arts.

To apply for grants, a company must either be established as a nonprofit organization under IRS tax code 501(c)(3) or else partner with a fiscal sponsor under whose nonprofit umbrella the company can apply for grants. If the former, a company can write a grant to meet its specific needs within the boundaries of that grant program. On the other hand, when partnering on a grant with a fiscal sponsor, the umbrella organization may have a say in the grant expenditures and outcomes. Grants are offered in periodic cycles and include strict deadlines for applying and reporting. Most granters require recipients to follow a specified budget, and grant writers are responsible for keeping track of expenditures and reporting this to the granting organization within deadlines determined by the granter.

Grant writers must be fully attuned to the needs of a company before writing a grant and must be aware of the foci of various grant programs in order to help steer a company in the direction of a grant that will suit their needs. Therefore, consistent communication with the artistic and executive directors is very important in order to compose grants that will be useful to the company in addressing its goals and mission. Some grant writers even attend board meetings and interact with company members to better acquaint themselves with the company culture.

To be prepared for grant writing, educate yourself, practice writing, and stay up to date on trends and changes in dance funding. Hone your skills in writing persuasively and efficiently and practice writing descriptive narratives and budgets for various projects by doing field research on the kinds of work companies are creating and the pricing of the various elements involved. Some organizations host workshops on grant writing. Attend these if you think you might send grant applications to these organizations because they can often provide hints about their formatting preferences and pet peeves. Maintain positive relationships with funding organizations by writing strong, clear grant applications, meeting or beating deadlines, and attending their events and workshops.

Marketing

Marketing directors are hired by companies looking for support in the following areas: communications, media design, public relations, branding, strategic planning, and audience development. Marketing specialists are hired to increase the presence and impact of a company by generating interest and fostering connections both within the company and in the larger community and field. Marketing directors can create synergy between an artistic director's vision, a company's strengths, and a community's needs in order to build attendance and revenue. More specifically, some of the duties a marketing director might be assigned include developing press kits, coordinating media interviews and story pitches, creating social media and website content, overseeing email and newsletter marketing, and producing graphic design.

Strong applicants for marketing director jobs are experienced in marketing for the arts and culture sector, can demonstrate a keen eye for detail and aesthetic uniqueness, are organized and dependable, and may hold a degree in marketing or a related area. Additionally, marketing directors are usually required to be proficient in the latest design and email marketing software and platforms and must be proficient writers and editors. Applications typically require a résumé, professional references, and a portfolio of marketing materials.

Event Planning and Audience Development

Event planning and audience development roles are often shared by multiple people and relate to most of the members of a company's staff. However, occasionally a company will hire a professional on a contract or part-time basis to oversee large events such as fundraising dinners or galas, community festivals, community engagement or educational events, or company celebrations. Further, because these events often serve the dual purpose of developing donor relationships and recruiting new audiences, having experience in audience relations is especially beneficial.

Event planners do not necessarily need to be well versed in dance, but they must understand the mission and brand of the company they represent and must have established connections in the community in order to make the event-planning process as financially and artistically effective as possible. In collaboration with a company's staff and board of directors, an event planner books event locations, food, drink, and entertainment; orders supplies; organizes invitations and RSVPs; and coordinates with on-site staff for an easy, efficient setup and cleanup. Additionally, event planners may be responsible for communicating with guests before and after the event in order to develop relationships with them and seek sponsorships and other contributions on behalf of the company. An event planner with experience in audience relations can also help companies build their base of loyal supporters and production attendees. Hiring someone who can develop relationships both face-to-face through events and through online and print communication is important to a company's expanded presence in a community.

Production Management

Many companies have a production manager (or company manager) on staff to coordinate with the artistic director on technical and logistical aspects of productions. Production managers coordinate the behind-the-scenes elements of a production such as lighting, video, sound, scenery, costumes, stage management, and choreographers' specific needs. This person must coordinate these elements within budget and according to the artistic director's overall vision. If a company tours, the production manager liaises with touring venues to address technical needs, disseminates publicity materials to local promoters, arranges company travel and lodging, and may also travel with the company to assist with technical needs (Dance Consortium n.d.). Full-time production manager positions in the United States offer steady employment, with a salary in the range of $45,000 to $85,000 per year. An added benefit of production manager positions is that they are easily transferable across the arts. For example, someone who has worked as a production manager for a dance company could also be qualified to work for a theater company.

Highly qualified production managers have experience in all elements of technical theater and direction: lighting, sound, video, projection, scenery, costuming, and stage management in addition to experience in writing technical riders and contracting with various venues. Additionally, some positions may require a college degree in technical theater or related area, experience in touring management, and a vision for technical theater elements of dance.

Community Engagement and Education Coordinator Jobs

Some dance companies seeking to enrich and enhance the quality of life in their communities devote a branch of their company to community engagement through education, partnerships, and other programming. These goals necessitate leadership from a community engagement or education coordinator who plans events and develops partnerships. Established companies hire full-time employees in this role, while smaller companies may have opportunities for part-time or project-based work in this area. Full-time community engagement coordinators in the United States are salaried within a range of $30,000 to $67,000 per year; however, many of these positions are paid by the hour or per project, so these numbers vary depending on the structure and permanence of each position (Payscale 2020; Glassdoor 2020).

Requirements and qualifications for these positions typically include experience in community engagement or educational initiatives specifically for nonprofit arts organizations. Additionally, community engagement coordinators should be strong

Courtesy of Naomi Hill.

Dancers Kris Olson, Ali Duffy, and Allison Beaty of Flatlands Dance Theatre.

communicators, writers, and speakers and enjoy working closely with teams of people and different populations. An ability to envision and develop new initiatives with other company administrators based on the strengths of a company and the needs within a community is a necessary skill. A bachelor's degree in an area related to dance, education, or nonprofit administration is usually preferred, but not always required. Many organizations such as American Dance Festival, Jacob's Pillow, and American College Dance Association offer community engagement internships. All of these are excellent opportunities to gain experience for future careers in this area.

CAREERS IN DANCE ADVOCACY

In the wake of massive federal budget cuts and declining arts attendance in the last two decades of the 20th century, growth in the dance sector has since plateaued and then began declining (Stubbs 2014, 2). Despite nominal increases in funding at the local, state, and national levels since the mid-1990s, public funding of the arts has not kept pace with inflation. The nonprofit arts sector has taken an especially big financial hit from the latter half of the 20th century to today (Miller 2000). According to the National Arts Index, as of 2013, 42 percent of U.S. arts nonprofits were operating at a deficit (Arts Index 2016). This fact is in no small part because of the 31 percent funding cut by local, state, and national governments to nonprofit arts since 1992 in addition to the financial hit and postrecession recovery efforts that nonprofits across the country experienced from 2007 to 2011 (Arts Index

2016). Considering that dance is less funded than many other disciplines and art forms and that federal funding for dance has declined rapidly since the late 20th century (Arts Index 2016; Miller 2000), the need for educated, resourceful dance advocates is crucial.

Dance advocacy happens in multiple arenas and for various reasons, including in public and private schools and at the local, state, and federal level. Professionals working in dance advocacy may be tasked with, among other things, building relationships with elected officials and other community leaders and determining advocacy strategies to adopt pro-arts policies (Americans for the Arts n.d.a). Dance companies and artists require advocacy to gain funding and prestige, dance educators incorporate advocacy to justify the need for resources and funding for their programs, dance presenters must call on advocacy skills to provide evidence of dance's impact and importance, and even dance researchers use statistical and theory-based arguments to expand the conversation about dance in scholarship and critical dialogue. Professionals who understand and incorporate elements of dance advocacy in their work are highly coveted in many areas of the field.

From salary data compiled by Americans for the Arts in 2018, it is difficult to say exactly how much money dance advocates make because, while many jobs include advocacy responsibilities, job titles rarely include the term advocacy explicitly. What *can* be deduced from the data is salary averages within public and private policy and research and government affairs staff positions. According to Americans for the Arts, the average full-time salary in 2018 at the management level was $84,470, and at the program staff level it was $55,409 (Americans for the Arts 2019). As in any area of the dance industry, job salaries in advocacy are highly variable given geographical location and level of prestige of the company or organization. For example, based on recent job postings on the ZipRecruiter website, arts advocacy salaries in the United States are estimated on a scale ranging from $13,500 to $101,500 per year (ZipRecruiter n.d.).

When searching for jobs in dance advocacy, key terms and position titles might include vice president for advocacy and strategic partnerships, director of government affairs, and manager of advocacy and creative affairs (Americans for the Arts 2019). Elements of advocacy may be included in jobs listed within programming and development coordination, arts and culture direction, and arts advising. Further, many educational programs for teenagers and college students hire arts advocacy specialists on a temporary or part-time basis. Also, jobs within these sectors are most likely to include advocacy as the primary role; however, many of the positions in administration as discussed earlier in this chapter, such as executive director and president positions, also emphasize advocacy.

PREPARING FOR A CAREER INVOLVING DANCE ADVOCACY

Successful dance advocates are informed about current practices, policies, and legalities regarding as many areas of the dance field as possible. They are able to articulate why dance is important as a discipline, as an art form, as entertainment, as social practice, as cultural legacy, and as a significant contributor to the economy. Being able to articulate these ideas persuasively in writing and verbally, both in prepared speeches and extemporaneously, is critical to educating others about how dance operates, what its purposes are, and why it should be funded, studied, taught, practiced, created, performed, and archived. These skills prepare advocates for writing grants, developing and proposing policy, educating the public, and speaking with elected officials and business leaders who can offer positive support and change for dance.

Obtaining an undergraduate education in arts administration or graduate study in arts management is advisable. Course content in accredited programs includes arts law, policy, and history; community arts; and analytical and persuasive writing. Additionally, multiple organizations provide a wealth of information to the public about arts advocacy, which can adequately prepare dance advocates to gather and share information and to challenge existing funding structures and laws to better suit the needs of artists, students, consumers, and communities. Dance/USA, Americans for the Arts, and The Kennedy Center, for example, provide publicly available arts advocacy toolkits on their websites (Harmon 2019). Because much of arts advocacy is done at the grassroots level, it is possible and important to self-educate in this area. Dance professionals benefit from training in dance advocacy because they can capitalize on the multitude of jobs in the field that require advocacy skills.

SUMMARY

Dance administrators and advocates provide critical support for the field, leading teams of dance professionals in schools, companies, organizations, and government. Pursuing administrative jobs in dance requires an extensive amount of experience and a keen vision for an organization's strengths, challenges, and future possibilities. Additionally, leaders in dance must be aware of how their organizations fit into, contribute to, and innovate in the dance field at large. Finally, dance administrators lead people and so must aspire to support and motivate others. While careers in dance administration are extremely demanding, they also provide the benefits of stability, opportunities to foster creativity and innovation, and chances to make a difference through visionary leadership practices.

Reflection

DESIGNING A LEADERSHIP APPROACH

Depending on the circumstances of a position such as size of company, number of staff, geographical location, organization history, or job requirements, a leader's approach or style should be adaptable and may change throughout a career. Several leadership centers and institutions feature lists of characteristics proven to be effective for leaders in general. Some of these traits seem to be inherent qualities of personality (e.g., proactive versus reactive, open-minded versus closed-minded) and others appear to be learned or attained characteristics (e.g., ability to continue to evaluate and reevaluate, privilege of being well educated). Because of the uncertainty of funding and the contextual variables that determine a dance organization's ability to survive, many administrators in dance must possess considerable resourcefulness, initiative, and adaptability to sustain their organizations. An administrator's job is often a balancing act as they negotiate several obstacles at once. Dance leaders should take advantage of opportunities while ensuring their actions contribute to a strategy that leads to their organization's success.

Identifying the most beneficial leadership styles and important leadership traits in dance is highly variable among professionals and scholars. For example, Brenda Way, artistic director of ODC/Dance, often calls on human values such as "a taste for adventure and risk, a capacity for problem solving, straightforwardness, [and] a good ear" to lead a company that "provides opportunity, challenge, and security" (Friedler and Glazer 1997, 249). For Way, "governance and collective vision are one thing" and the dancers often take on as much administrative and creative responsibility as the leaders (Friedler and Glazer 1997, 250). Anna Halprin, by contrast, creates awareness in herself and others to trigger collective creativity and activism. Awareness, perception, emotion, self-reflection, vitality, and charisma are the keys to Halprin's leadership style (Schorn 2015, 70). Community studies writer Doug Borwick highlights the importance of humility in leadership as a company establishes itself in a community. Borwick's value on humility stems from an assumption that most community members have deeply held beliefs that the arts are disconnected and elitist (Borwick 2012, 33). Sociologist Steven L. Tepper calls for leaders to build trust between companies and communities (Tepper 2008, 28).

To craft your own leadership style, take stock of your preferences, strengths, and weaknesses and let them guide your approach. Because you are a unique person with distinct goals and personality traits, you should not adopt someone else's approach because that may not work for you. Respond to the following prompts to create your own leadership manifesto that may help guide you in your future career as a dance administrator.

- Describe how you prefer to interact or engage with colleagues.
- Describe how you want to motivate yourself and others.
- Describe how you aim to reward achievements and manage failures.
- Describe some of the traits you appreciate in other leaders that you want to emulate.
- Describe some of the leadership traits you will reject in your own approach.
- How do you envision colleagues working successfully together?
- How do you work best to set and meet goals?
- Describe how you want to make your employees and colleagues feel.
- What do you feel are your greatest strengths and greatest challenges or weaknesses as a leader?
- After you have responded to the previous prompts, craft a manifesto, which may be in paragraph form, a series of statements, or a bulleted list or presented creatively as a drawing or poem. Use language, imagery, or both to affirm your approach to leadership and let these values guide your administrative work.

Chapter 9

Dance Science, Medicine, Therapies, and Somatic Practices

"When you look at the growth of the human economy and its expected growth in the twenty-first century, I expect health will be the most important market of all. Especially as we move from a concept of health which focuses on healing the sick to a concept of upgrading the healthy."

Yuval Noah Harari

"When we give ourselves the chance to let go of all our tension, the body's natural capacity to heal itself can begin to work."

Thich Nhat Hanh

Exciting career possibilities in dance science and medicine, dance/movement therapy, and somatic practices are multiplying as increased interest and need for them emerge in a health-conscious, aging population. Dancers and nondancers seek alternative healing modalities and modes of health care and self-care. Somatic practices, dance sciences, and therapies can offer unique interventions, practices, and training methods. The areas featured in this chapter require extensive and often lengthy formalized education and training processes, yet also offer the benefits of stability, financial security, and rewarding relationships with patients or clients.

Because dancers have a unique relationship with their bodies and they use (and, sometimes, *overuse*) certain muscles and joints, dance medicine specialists and

Dr. Eri Millrod

Dance and movement therapist and assistant professor, Rider University

What is your best advice to those hoping to pursue a career in dance/movement therapy (DMT)?

I believe that passion has to be there when pursuing a career in DMT. Being a dance/movement therapist is hard work, so you have to love it. From the outside, it looks like we are just dancing or having fun, but the internal process that I have when leading a DMT session is quite intense. We work with unconscious and preverbal material of the body and mind, so there is a lot to sift through before it takes on a visible form in the body through dance/movement. I am constantly feeling and sensing what is going on kinesthetically on the body level, and trying to make sense of it cognitively, so that I can find the best way for clients to address thoughts, feelings, sensations, and memories that they might be holding in their bodies. DMT truly is a blend of art and science, dance and psychology, so you have to be proficient in both. Knowledge comes in all forms, so be curious and learn through all your senses. Be open, and don't limit yourself with preconceptions. Get to know yourself as a dancer and as an artist. How far you can take your clients psychologically and developmentally in DMT will depend on how much you developed yourself as a person. As a dancer, pay

Courtesy of Eri Millrod.

somatic practitioners confront similar issues among dancers. These similarities affect the way they practice for best results in their dancer clients. For example, physical therapist Gregory Rakowski describes issues of the fibula (the long, outer bone of the lower leg) and the calf muscles as recurring often in dancers (Woodard 2016). He describes dancers as knowing their bodies well, which means they can describe clearly what they're feeling, which is helpful. However, he says, "dancers are also some of the most determined people around and [sometimes] use sheer willpower to persist in doing something that's painful and possibly damaging" (Woodard 2016, p. 3). Rakowski and others in medical and somatic professions, therefore, approach the treatment of dancers in a unique way that allows for injury management, prevention, and simultaneous retention of flexibility and strength. Of course, each body is unique, but knowing that dancers face specific challenges and common injuries that differ from those in other athletes is necessary before going into dance medicine or therapies.

This chapter features career paths in dance science, medicine, therapies, and somatic practices. Guidance is offered on how to structure college and graduate

attention to the process of becoming and know that you never truly arrive. Allow dance to show you, teach you about yourself. Always engage in self-reflection, and don't hide behind technique. Be willing to expose yourself, be vulnerable, and be more truly you when you dance. Knowing yourself through dance will ultimately help you become a better person and a better dance/ movement therapist, and it will enrich your life regardless of your career choice.

Describe some of the greatest lessons you've learned in your dance career.
The most valuable lesson I learned by being a dance/movement therapist is gratitude. Over the years, I have seen how fragile the human mind and body are, but I've also witnessed how strong and resilient they are. I have worked with patients with mental illnesses and addictions who have survived terrible conditions; yet, I am impressed with how the human spirit can overcome adversity and heal. I appreciate that the body in movement plays an important role in recovery and that DMT is a part of that transformative process. I feel privileged that patients trust me in DMT, because when we move together, we form a therapeutic rapport quickly. I am grateful that patients are willing to share their innermost thoughts and feelings with me at a time when they are feeling most vulnerable. DMT allows patients to express things that are too difficult to verbalize or are not yet in their consciousness, and I am fortunate to have become a dance/movement therapist who can work at that level. I do not take for granted the opportunities I have to work with people with diverse backgrounds. Being a dance/movement therapist has expanded my worldview. The impermanence of dance has taught me to never take these meaningful moments with others for granted.

school experience toward these careers. Also included is discussion about finding a position in these areas of the field, including job searches and interviewing, how to interact with colleagues in other disciplines, and managing patient and client care.

CAREERS IN DANCE SCIENCE AND MEDICINE

The range of opportunities for a career in dance medicine and science suggests the field is expansive and that there are many avenues to pursue. Possible career areas and disciplines include physical therapy, kinesiology, orthopedics, athletic training, massage therapy, and Pilates. Each area requires very different training and certification and offers unique specializations and areas of connection to dance and dancers.

Physical Therapists

Physical therapists, or physiotherapists provide services to dancers that help restore function, improve mobility, relieve pain, and prevent or limit permanent physical disabilities of patients (Harkness Center for Dance Injuries 2020, para 1). They provide hands-on treatment and training to patients, teaching them how to gain strength and mobility in order to restore function and prevent recurrent injury. Dance companies and organizations hire physical therapists on a full-time and temporary (during a touring season, for example) basis. Independent dancers often rely on physical therapists at some point during their career for injury recovery and prevention. Physical therapists must hold undergraduate degrees, which can be in kinesiology, exercise and sports science, or a related area, and must also earn a doctor of physical therapy (DPT) degree. This is a three- to four-year program earned after a bachelor's degree. Residencies and fellowships are optional. They may also hold a clinical doctorate in physical therapy or a specialty certification such as sports physical therapy. Additionally, all physical therapists must be licensed in the state in which they practice. Physical therapists are in high demand and bring in salaries of between $72,000-$102,500. Employment for physical therapists is expected to grow 22% from 2018-2028, much faster than the average for all occupations in the U.S. (U.S. Bureau of Labor Statistics 2019c).

Performing arts physical therapist Cecilee Fleming tours with the casts of various Broadway musicals. When asked why she decided to pursue this line of work, she said, "For me, the opportunity to specialize in performing arts physical therapy and tour with Broadway shows is the ultimate dream job. It is the combination of many of my passions: dancing, singing, physical therapy and travel" (Neuro Tour 2017, para 3). Fleming's typical workweek schedule is

> 5:30-10:15 p.m. Tuesday through Friday, 12:00-10:45 p.m. on Saturdays, and 11:00 a.m.-9:15 p.m. on Sundays. I start work two hours before every show, seeing patients one-on-one every 30 minutes until the show starts. Then I have appointments during the show for individuals that are either not performing that night or have breaks between scenes. (Neuro Tour 2017, para 5)

She also describes being available to triage injuries in the wings during shows and accompany dancers to urgent care or emergency room centers if necessary (Neuro Tour 2017, para 6).

In addition to firsthand accounts of the day-to-day life of a performing arts physical therapist, it's important to find other resources for information about this area and possible career opportunities. The Academy of Orthopaedic Physical Therapy hosts an online special interest group for performing arts physical therapists, with many resources about common dance injuries and interventions, funding, annual conferences, and policy. The American Physical Therapy Association features similar, although more generalized resources, and a particularly useful career and education search tool.

In order to be admitted and submit your most competitive application to physical therapy programs, you must meet minimum GPA requirements (at least a 3.5 is recommended); earn a high score on the GRE exam; and meet the prerequisite undergraduate course requirements, which frequently include courses in anatomy, physiology, biology, physics, psychology, and statistics (American Physical Therapy

Courtesy of Naomi Hill.

Dancers Molly Roberts and Morgan Strutton of Flatlands Dance Theatre.

Association 2019). Be thoughtful about choosing your undergraduate major(s) in order to meet these prerequisite requirements. For example, consider double majoring in dance and kinesiology or choose a major in one of the sciences and minor in dance. Since physical therapy schooling is intensive, it is most efficient and effective to begin preparing for it as soon as you know you want to pursue it.

Orthopedic Physicians and Sports Medicine Specialists

Unlike other career opportunities described in this chapter, orthopedists are medical doctors and require extensive schooling including an undergraduate degree, medical school, a three-year residency, and a sports medicine fellowship. Dance medicine is often aligned with sports medicine, a larger and longer established field, so when in training, many interns and fellows work with athletes before working with dancers. Similar to physical therapy careers, orthopedic and sports medicine specialists benefit the dance industry in numerous ways. Since dancers face acute and chronic injuries during their careers, they rely on these medical doctors to perform surgeries and prescribe healing and retraining regimens and processes that extend dancers' professional careers. Former dancers-turned-doctors claim that the discipline required to pursue dance trains them for the rigor of medical school (Samuel 2018) and that their own experiences recovering from dance injuries inspired them to pursue medicine (McAnarney 2019).

Salary estimates for sports medicine specialists in the United States range from $61,000 to $292,000 (Payscale 2020; Career Explorer 2018; Salary.com n.d.), with physician salaries comprising the top 20 percent of that range. The Performing Arts Medicine Association and the Harkness Center for Dance Injuries are excellent resources from which to learn more about specializing in dance medicine and the various certifications and trainings associated with this specialty.

In a 2012 panel presentation at the International Association for Dance Medicine and Science, Dr. Selina Shah, board certified sports medicine and internal medicine physician, offered three useful pieces of advice for those pursuing this career route:

1. In terms of acceptance rate, medical school is very competitive; therefore, it is important to volunteer in a clinic, hospital, or nursing home. Doing this early while pursuing your bachelor's degree provides valuable experience that will make you more desirable.

2. To be eligible to apply to medical school in the United States, you must complete specific prerequisite courses during your undergraduate education; therefore, you need to start early to ensure that you meet them all.

3. During your clinical years, which usually comprise the third and fourth years of medical school, explore different fields and decide which specialty to pursue, such as sports medicine or orthopedics. This is also competitive; the more specialized the practice, the fewer opportunities there are. It is therefore important to gain as much experience as possible in that specialist field and ensure that you are at the top of your class (Shah 2012). Shah and others in the field stress that if orthopedic or sports medicine is a career goal, start working toward that goal as early high school because this career takes so much preparation and education.

Certified Athletic Trainers

Certified athletic trainers specialize in injury prevention, treatment, and rehabilitation for athletes and dancers. They typically work under the supervision of physicians to treat patients and may be hired in multiple settings, including secondary or collegiate athletic facilities, sports medicine clinics, physical therapy clinics, research institutions, and other occupational environments, such as dance companies (Harkness Center for Dance Injuries 2020). To be certified, athletic trainers must hold a bachelor's degree and must pass a three-part test administered by the Board of Certification. More than 70 percent of certified athletic trainers also hold a master's degree or higher (National Athletic Trainers Association n.d.). Additionally, most states have separate requirements for maintaining certification. The U.S. Department of Labor estimates that certified athletic trainers working in entertainment or arts industries made from $49,000 to $74,180 in 2018 (U.S. Department of Labor 2019a).

According to Katie Lemmon, a certified athletic trainer who works with the Joffrey Ballet, River North Dance Chicago, and Bulls Entertainment, her work includes on-site care for a few hours before performances in which dancers schedule 10-minute appointments with her. If needed, she also responds to calls during performances if a dancer is injured and requires urgent assessment or treatment (NATA News 2014). Lemmon also offers preseason screenings to dancers in the companies with whom she is contracted and provides guest lectures and workshops across the country during summer intensive dance workshops (NATA News 2014). Although Lemmon was hired as part of a team of care practitioners, athletic trainers can also find career opportunities working independently.

Massage Therapists

A career in massage therapy is a natural fit for dancers because they comprehend at least a basic foundation of anatomical structures and concepts and the visual and kinesthetic elements and sensations of musculature, and they have an automatic community of potential clients in fellow dancers (National Holistic Institute 2018). Massage therapy schedules can be flexible, allowing for part-time or temporary employment. There is also potential for financial security. In fact, employment for massage therapists is projected to grow 22 percent from 2018 to 2028, indicating an overall market need and potential for significant income and steady work. The median salary for full-time massage therapists in the United States is $41,420, and part-time therapists average $19.92 per hour (U.S. Department of Labor 2019b).

Requirements for licensed massage therapists vary by state and often include a formal training program, practical and written examinations, and a preliminary period during which therapists gain a standard amount of experience with clients under the supervision of a manager. While a college degree is not required, massage therapists benefit from formal education in kinesiology, anatomy, and business. Massage therapists apply techniques from more than 80 codified practices that benefit dancers, including sports or deep-tissue massage, acupressure, reflexology, and connective tissue massage. Once licensed, massage therapists can practice in a variety of settings such as massage therapy clinics, health clubs, spas, or nursing homes, or they may use portable equipment and travel to clients for massage services.

Certified Pilates Practitioners

Developed by Joseph H. Pilates, the Pilates method of toning muscles and balancing muscular force does wonders for many dancers because it increases flexibility and range of motion and encourages proper musculoskeletal alignment (Harkness Center for Dance Injuries n.d., para 28). Pilates also improves coordination, increases body awareness, and may prevent injuries. Pilates instructors work in a variety of professional settings, including fitness or Pilates studios, physical therapy clinics, and physician's offices. Pilates is practiced on floor mats and on specialized equipment. Instructors teach group classes and private individual lessons. Data about Pilates instructor pay is not accurate because often, Pilates instructor data is grouped in with data related to fitness instructors and personal trainers and includes part-time employee salaries. However, an average personal trainer salary

Dr. Tom Welsh

Dance sciences professor, Florida State University

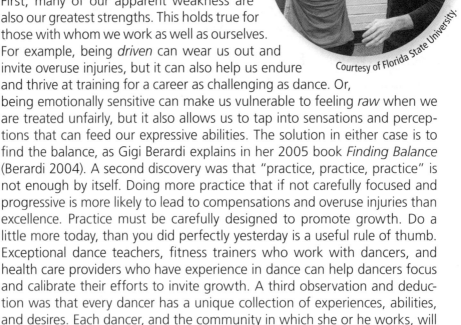

Courtesy of Florida State University.

Describe some of the greatest lessons you've learned in your dance career.

First, many of our apparent weakness are also our greatest strengths. This holds true for those with whom we work as well as ourselves. For example, being *driven* can wear us out and invite overuse injuries, but it can also help us endure and thrive at training for a career as challenging as dance. Or, being emotionally sensitive can make us vulnerable to feeling *raw* when we are treated unfairly, but it also allows us to tap into sensations and perceptions that can feed our expressive abilities. The solution in either case is to find the balance, as Gigi Berardi explains in her 2005 book *Finding Balance* (Berardi 2004). A second discovery was that "practice, practice, practice" is not enough by itself. Doing more practice that if not carefully focused and progressive is more likely to lead to compensations and overuse injuries than excellence. Practice must be carefully designed to promote growth. Do a little more today, than you did perfectly yesterday is a useful rule of thumb. Exceptional dance teachers, fitness trainers who work with dancers, and health care providers who have experience in dance can help dancers focus and calibrate their efforts to invite growth. A third observation and deduction was that every dancer has a unique collection of experiences, abilities, and desires. Each dancer, and the community in which she or he works, will be served best if they use their special abilities to make their own, unique contribution to the field.

Looking back, what have been the best decisions you have made during your career?

At each decision point, from the small ones that occur every day to the major ones at times of important life transitions, I resisted the path that would generate the greatest income, security, and convenience. Instead, I choose the path that offered the greatest potential to use my energies and my abilities to make a unique contribution to dance. "And," as Robert Frost (1916) once said, "that has made all the difference."

in the United States is about $52,000, and the salary range for fitness instructors is $18,690 to $70,180 (Metcalf 2016). Per hour, Pilates instructors can make from $20 to $42 (The Pilates Place n.d., para 8).

Pilates instructors do not necessarily need a certification, but reputable gyms and Pilates studios will not hire instructors who don't have significant training and education. Certification for mat or comprehensive teaching is available. If you think you might want to teach full time or teach private lessons, comprehensive training is the way to go. The comprehensive certification trains instructors to teach exercises on the mat and the Pilates equipment such as the Cadillac and the reformer. A reputable training program in the United States often costs about $3,000 and includes 500-plus hours of training and recognition from the Pilates Method Alliance (Long 2014). Obtaining a master's certification in advanced Pilates teaching boosts Pilates instructor salaries (Peak Pilates 2020, O'Clair 2011) and may also support a more holistic and researched approach to teaching Pilates.

Kinesiology

In general, the term kinesiology refers to the academic study of the mechanics of body movements, including the areas of "exercise science, sports management, athletic training, sport and exercise psychology, fitness and physical education, and occupational therapy" (American Kinesiology Association n.d., para 2). Obtaining a college degree in kinesiology is a terrific first step to curating an exciting career working with dancers and their physical, emotional, and psychological needs. Pairing an undergraduate education with additional training can open possibilities for being hired in roles specifically with dance companies and arts organizations. The U.S. Bureau of Labor and Statistics lists kinesiologists, also called kinesiotherapists, under the title of exercise physiologists in its occupational handbook. The job outlook is positive for kinesiologists, with expected job growth at 10% and median pay of $49,270 per year or $23.69 per hour (U.S. Bureau of Labor and Statistics 2019d).

CAREERS IN DANCE/MOVEMENT THERAPY

Dance/movement therapy is defined by the American Dance Therapy Association (ADTA) as "psychotherapeutic use of movement to promote emotional, social, cognitive and physical integration of the individual" (American Dance Therapy Association n.d., para 1). Dance therapists understand how the movement of the body can offer creative pathways to self-expression, belonging, and even healing, and they emphasize treating clients holistically through the connections between mind, body, and spirit. Dance/movement therapists practice in medical, rehabilitation, and educational settings such as private clinics, universities, nursing homes, daycare centers, and hospitals. Dance/movement therapy professionals work with children dealing with anxiety, patients with Alzheimer's disease, veterans returning from war, and people who have suffered abuse (Wingenroth 2018). Dance therapists typically work in traditional full-time positions and in the United States earn from $40,00 to $80,000 per year (American Dance Therapy Association n.d.).

Dance/movement therapists must hold an undergraduate degree with majors—or at least, experience—in dance and psychology. Additionally, the entry-level registered dance/movement therapist (R-DMT) credential is earned at the graduate level, so a master's degree from one of the ADTA-approved programs is necessary. The advanced board certified dance/movement therapist (BC-DMT) credential can be earned by gaining more experience and training beyond the graduate level and signifies preparedness for providing training and engaging in private practice (American Dance Therapy Association n.d.). Students seeking advanced degrees in dance/movement therapy should expect about 60 hours of graduate-level course work plus two internships and fieldwork (Wingenroth 2018).

CAREERS IN SOMATIC PRACTICES

Somatic practices, sometimes called somatic studies or somatics, are mind–body techniques that are intended to deepen sensory awareness of anatomical relationships in people, including dancers. Often referred to as "body therapies, body work, [or] body-mind integration," (Batson 2009, para 2) somatic practitioners help clients, including dancers, increase self-awareness and become attuned to their own bodily or sensorial cues in order to reeducate the dancing body. This training can aid dancers in developing healthy practices in technique training and performance by attuning them to their habitual muscular patterns and misalignments. Additionally, while each somatic practice emphasizes its own principles and methods, the International Somatic Movement Education and Therapy Association (ISMETA) identifies general practices that include "postural and movement evaluation, experiential anatomy and imagery, movement patterning and re-patterning, and communication and guidance through verbal cues" (International Somatic Movement Education and Therapy Association n.d., para 2). Some of the most common somatic practices that integrate well into dancer training include Ideokinesis, the Feldenkrais Method, the Alexander Technique, and Body–Mind Centering.

Many somatic practitioners work full time in a private practice teaching private and group lessons or in training institutions teaching future practitioners. Additionally, some dance professionals become certified in one or more somatic practices to supplement their dance income with part-time work. Because somatic and dance practices integrate so seamlessly, dancers often find it helpful to train in a somatic practice for their own kinesthetic development and awareness and also to become a practitioner to expand career options.

PREPARING FOR A CAREER IN SOMATIC PRACTICES

Somatic practitioners are certified through different systems and processes that are all rigorous and comprehensive. While it is not required that somatic practitioners have a college degree, it is often helpful to have prior education in kinesiology and anatomy before seeking certification in a somatic practice. Each practice requires unique training for certification. For example, to be certified in the Alexander Technique, students must complete a three-year, full-time teacher-training course that includes about 1,500 hours of instruction (Alexander Technique n.d.). By contrast, students training to become teachers of the Feldenkrais Method must complete 800 hours of training over 36 months (Feldenkrais Method 2017).

Because the training is so intensive for most somatic practice certifications, it is critical to carve out appropriate time and finances to undertake it. Additionally, before diving into training in any one somatic practice, explore a range of practices within the field in order to find your right fit. Akin to preferring one genre of dance in which you specialize as a technician, you may have a proclivity to one somatic practice or another.

SUMMARY

Careers in dance medicine, science, therapies, and somatic practices are diverse, each area requiring specific skills and credentials. Dance medicine careers require a full-time, long-term commitment to education and practice, while careers in massage therapy or somatics require intense yet more succinct certification processes leading to part-time employment opportunities that can supplement other employment in dance. Because dancing requires physical stamina and strength and because dancers inevitably experience alignment issues, injuries, and the aging process, they rely on the professionals whose jobs are described in this chapter. This contextual information provides an especially relevant career transition opportunity for current or former dancers which can be quite rewarding to support dancers' physical demands through training and healing methods.

Reflection

DEFINING YOUR INTERESTS IN ORDER TO FOCUS ON A CAREER PATH

Careers in dance science, medicine, therapies, and somatic practices require unique skills. The careers featured in this chapter require professionals who value dancers and the ability of dance and movement to contribute to wellness, good health, and healing. Because each profession highlighted is unique, requiring specific training and leading to very different day-to-day jobs, reflect on which areas interest you most. Spend time thinking and writing about the following prompts:

- Are you interested in offering medical, therapeutic, educational, or physical training services in your profession? Would you prefer to be a medical doctor, a therapist, a trainer, a researcher, or a somatic practitioner?
- How much training and education are you willing to pursue in order to reach your professional goals in this area?
- What do you want your day-to-day job to look like? Would you prefer to work full time in one space, or do you like the idea of working part-time or temporary positions on a contract basis? Note whether you enjoy working with any of the following populations: children, elderly adults, people with injuries or trauma, professional dancers, and athletes.
- How would you prefer to engage with clients and coworkers? Do you prefer to work independently or as part of a team? Would you want a job that requires a lot of hands-on work with clients or do you prefer the idea of communicating through dialogue or instruction?

By addressing some of these questions in writing, you can begin to place yourself in the various positions described in this chapter and note where you might be a good fit. By the way, it is not necessary for you to make definitive statements in this writing; it is an opportunity to lay out all of your interests and skills so that you can begin to sense where you would be most fulfilled and successful in your future career.

Chapter 10

Competitive Dance and Sports Entertainment

"Dance is certainly a sport, and they are phenomenal athletes, and they're also artists."

Neve Campbell

Exciting career possibilities in competitive dance and dance in sports entertainment abound for performers, choreographers, teachers, coaches, and administrators. Some positions are part time and can accompany other jobs in or outside of the dance field, while others are full time and require year-round commitment. Each opportunity in this chapter offers distinct benefits and, depending on your interests and strengths, may be a perfect fit for you.

Competitive dance in private studios, high schools, and colleges provide opportunities for young dancers in their early training to gain valuable performance experience and feedback. Young dancers involved in competitive dance learn how to be part of a team, develop a strong work ethic, and become versatile dancers. By emphasizing a caring yet rigorous leadership approach, competition coaches and teachers can positively influence a student's future in dance. Professionals in the competition circuit work in a condensed period of time within a competition season. Working as a competition demonstrator, judge, or teacher may also require travel to competitions around the country and for training and staff meetings at the company's headquarters. Employees on the competition circuit may need to find work with multiple companies or supplement income with another job during the off-season.

In addition to opportunities in competitive dance, this chapter describes performance jobs in the spectator sport sector. Dancing for National Football League sports teams, for example, while usually not full-time positions, can provide wonderful opportunities to explore entertainment-based performance in a unique environment.

Erin Harold Alvarado

Head pom squad coach and instructor of dance, Texas Tech University

What have been your most significant experiences as a working professional in dance?

One major highlight for me was winning Coach of the Year through the National Dance Coaches Association. A variety of students and colleagues had to nominate me for this award, which was extremely humbling. I felt like that company I was amongst was where I had aspired to be my entire career. Another highlight for me was teaching my very first college course. Again, this was a huge goal I had set for myself, and being able to impact a completely different group of aspiring dancers was extremely fulfilling to me.

Courtesy of Erin Harold Alvarado.

What is your best advice to those hoping to pursue a career in dance?

My advice would be to never put yourself in a box or decline anything (at least not the first time). You never know when your specific skill set can be used to not only better the next generation of dancers, but to better yourself as well. Growing up I always thought I wanted to own my own studio. However, saying yes to every opportunity has opened my eyes to a much bigger dance world that I never even knew existed. The people I have met, both students and colleagues, have inspired me beyond comprehension.

Describe some of the greatest lessons you've learned in your dance career.

One of the greatest lessons I have learned is that you can *always* learn more, improve, and expand as an artist and teacher. Every single day I feel like I learn something new and I thrive in that type of atmosphere. Another hard lesson I have learned is that you cannot please everyone, and you cannot find common ground with everyone—no matter how hard you try. I have learned how to utilize both my strengths and my weaknesses to help better myself as an educator in all fields.

Looking back, what have been the best decisions you have made during your career?

One of the best decisions I have made on my career path is saying yes to the dance team world when it first presented itself. I *never* could have dreamed of the doors that being in the dance team world would open to me, and I am so lucky to have it as a piece of my dance career. Another would be moving 2,000 miles away from home to take my current job at Texas Tech University. It challenged me to step out of my comfort zone and has given me so many opportunities as a coach, teacher, and mentor.

Dancers on professional teams mainly perform at sporting events and may also be required to attend publicity and touring events such as championship games for extra pay. Usually, these dancers rehearse a few times per week after regular business hours and perform whenever games are scheduled—usually in the evenings and on weekends. Often, these positions come with fun perks and can serve as a springboard to a performing career. These jobs are usually undertaken by people who also maintain full-time employment elsewhere, so they supplement other work in or outside the dance field.

This chapter outlines career paths in private competition companies, in high schools and postsecondary institutions, and as part of American spectator sports teams. At the end of the chapter is a skill inventory to help you get an idea of where you might fit into entertainment-based or competitive dance.

PRIVATE DANCE COMPETITION AND CONVENTION COMPANIES

Dance competition and convention companies are primarily geared toward young dancers training in private studios. Some competitions encompass multiple dance genres, while others focus solely on a particular genre such as hip-hop or ballet. More than 30 companies in the United States offer regional and national competitions (Dance Informa n.d.). Some of the most well-established companies include Showstopper, StarQuest, DanceMakers, Starpower, and Monsters Dance. Dancers compete for prestige, trophies, plaques, and scholarships for workshops and college study. Also, televised competitions such as *So You Think You Can Dance* may provide excellent opportunities for dancers hoping to break into the industry or to gain influence through online branding and promotion.

Competition companies hire choreographers, teachers, and adjudicators to facilitate contests and conventions around the country that each span two to seven days. Adjudicators are hired to view, evaluate, and award competing dancers. Choreographers and teachers are hired mostly for conventions and longer competitions that include workshops or master classes.

Teaching and Choreography

Dance conventions and competitions incorporate master classes and workshop experiences for participating dancers. Therefore, highly qualified teachers and choreographers are in demand, particularly those who have prominent reputations in the field. These professionals may be hired on an annual or single-event basis. Pay scale for these positions is highly variable and largely dependent on the person's status and the company's level of establishment. Many of these positions can be secured through word-of-mouth and agency connections.

The major responsibility for teacher or choreographer positions is to teach master classes to competing students. Teachers may be asked to present a diversity of dance styles, techniques, and levels and must be able to articulate modifications for various levels during class. Master classes typically last one to two hours. Because dance conventions are regularly held in ill-equipped locations without proper dance floors or mirrors, prepare for dancing on less-than-ideal surfaces such as carpeting or concrete. Further, prepare to use a microphone and at least one demonstrator for large groups of students. Finally, because the focus of competition and convention classes is to quickly learn new material and styles, prepare long combinations and plan to offer general, rather than individual, feedback to students in these settings.

Adjudication

Competition judges are tasked with considerable responsibility, so the criteria for snagging these jobs are extensive. For example, adjudicators must be experienced in performing and teaching in multiple styles of dance as well as related areas such as partnering, theatre, and acro or tumbling. so they are able to provide relevant feedback. Additionally, judges must have experience giving feedback to dancers of all ages and levels (Callahan n.d.). Being able to provide honest yet sensitive feedback that underscores the important elements of each technique and mode of performance is also essential. Finally, strong writing and speaking skills are critical to success as a competition adjudicator.

Dance competition judges are sometimes hired for a full season or annual tour of a competition circuit, or they may be hired per competition. The average judge in the United States makes $25 per hour (Dance Spirit 2013). Most adjudicators are hired based on word of mouth, so become acquainted with competition companies, network with people who already work in them, and collect information on hiring practices.

HIGH SCHOOL AND COLLEGIATE COMPETITIVE DANCE

Collegiate and secondary school dance teams represent a relatively new phenomenon in American culture. Deriving from high school drill teams beginning in the early 1900s, dance teams have emerged around the United States since then and have continued to expand to include regional and national competitions. Jobs in this area include coaching and choreography for collegiate or high school teams, adjudicating competitions, and teaching in summer camps and workshops geared toward dance and drill teams.

National Dance Alliance and Universal Dance Association

Today, most public high schools and many postsecondary institutions house competitive dance teams. To support the growth of dance as a competitive sport, two national competition circuits were established: National Dance Alliance (NDA) in 1976 and Universal Dance Association (UDA) in 1980. These organizations host regional and national competitions wherein schools can compete in various genres and in different athletic divisions. Competitions are adjudicated by a panel of judges who score each team quantitatively, as an Olympic judge would in gymnastics or pairs diving. For instance, judges scoring teams in National Dance Alliance competitions give each team a maximum of 10 points in several areas that, depending

National Dance Alliance

Dancers performing in a National Dance Alliance competition.

on the school's division and the genre being performed, may include performance impression, uniformity, quality of movement, choreography, and staging (National Dance Alliance 2019) Further, rule infractions, going over the maximum time allotment, or a dancer suffering a major fall could deduct points from a team's overall score. In addition to competitive events, NDA and UDA offer multiday intensive summer camps around the country. These camps include technical training, choreography development, team building, and informal competitions among schools and are taught by an experienced staff of dance educators (National Dance Alliance n.d.; Universal Dance Association n.d.).

Coaching

Coaching a competitive dance or drill team can be a full-time or part-time position. Many competitive collegiate teams hire full-time coaches, whereas coaches in high schools or in smaller colleges may work on a part-time or even volunteer basis. The following responsibilities are often required of competitive dance team coaches: technical training, choreography, recruitment, organization of auditions, attendance at sporting and school-related events, assistance with spirit events, collaboration with other members of the spirit team such as a band and cheerleading squad, fundraising, and sometimes budgeting and inventory of uniforms and supplies.

Working conditions, schedules, and pay scale vary depending on the school and the position. For example, some drill or dance team coaches perform their duties for free as a service to the school or as part of a service-related workload. Others are paid on a part-time or hourly basis, and still others receive salary and benefits in full-time positions. The average salary in the United States for full-time collegiate dance team coaches is from $46,000 to $49,550 per year (ZipRecruiter n.d., Dance Spirit 2013), and the average hourly wage is $21.63 (Payscale n.d.). The average pay scale for high school coaches is similar, but job requirements in this setting typically include classroom teaching as well as coaching.

Choreography and Teaching

There are several ways to capitalize on your choreography and teaching skills in the competitive dance environment. Freelance choreographers are hired to create routines for regional and national competitions. Choreographers, typically hired by word of mouth and reputation, travel for a three- to five-day residency with a team during which they teach and rehearse a routine. Choreographers and teachers are also in demand for work in summer camps and other intensive workshops for high school and college dancers. Some of these camps are sponsored by NDA and UDA, and others are facilitated through various dance schools, universities, private companies, and community programs. These jobs usually span one week to a few months, depending on the length of programming.

Adjudication

Adjudicators who work for NDA, UDA, and other competition companies are highly skilled in teaching and viewing dance and are experienced in the competitive dance scene, often having extensive prior experience as a coach, choreographer, or teacher. Judges travel to competitions, evaluate dance routines, and award dancers and teams. Strong adjudicators understand the valuable technical and artistic elements of a team performance and have a keen eye for evaluating a team's sense of space, uniformity, musicality, technical execution, visual effects, choreographic flow, creativity, and level of difficulty (Varsity n.d.).

PREPARING FOR CAREERS IN COMPETITIVE DANCE

Full-time collegiate coaches are often required to hold an undergraduate degree and must demonstrate technical and artistic ability and experience in the field. Coaches in high school programs also typically hold bachelor's degrees because they work simultaneously as teachers in the school. However, positions are available for those with a high school diploma and significant competitive dance experience. In addition to experience in dance, holding credentials in a secondary area is important for being competitive in this market. College dance team coaches collaborate with others in the spirit group and colleagues in student organizations and governance. Additionally, collegiate coaches benefit from forging strong relationships with their university's dance program.

Because dance coaches often serve in multiple advisory roles for students, a diversity of skills and qualities are necessary for success. For example, coaches work with students who are still learning how to strike a balance between challenging and caring for their bodies, how to manage interpersonal relationships, and how to prepare for their futures as students or working professionals. Therefore, many effective coaches have knowledge about basic anatomy and kinesiology, injury prevention and healing, athletic training and fitness, degree advising, study skills, career planning, and conflict management. While these qualifications do not always appear in job advertisements, they are helpful while coaching young dancers.

PROFESSIONAL SPORTS ENTERTAINMENT DANCE TEAMS

Dancing and cheering for teams such as in the National Football League (NFL) or other professional sports teams provides opportunities to perform in unique settings (sporting events), improve in technique and performance, develop a look or brand, and even tour nationally with sports teams competing in playoff games. Dancers in these settings work part time performing at games and representing teams at events. Because most NFL dancers hold additional full-time jobs, they typically rehearse for their NFL job two to five evenings per week, attend community events and tailgates to sell merchandise and make appearances on behalf of the team, and perform at games (Dungee 2015). They arrive at each game about four hours before kickoff to practice and prepare. One of the major downsides to this career option is that the pay is very low considering the amount of work completed. The average NFL dancer makes a mere $75 to $200 per game and many are unpaid or are underpaid for practices and appearances (Flanagan and Canales 2018). The benefits of this job—special perks like gym memberships and exposure on a national stage—may offer a great opportunity for dancers searching for particular possibilities in their careers. However, in all transparency, this area of the dance field has come under recent scrutiny for exploiting dancers. Lack of compensation and mistreatment related to bodily and aesthetic expectations have been cited across the NFL (Flanagan and Canales 2018). Therefore, be prepared to call on your self-advocacy skills if this career choice if of interest to you.

PREPARING FOR CAREERS ON SPORTS ENTERTAINMENT DANCE TEAMS

Significant experience in jazz, hip-hop, musical theater, and contemporary is important for pursuing a position on an NFL dance team. While a college degree is not always a requirement, it will help to have this credential in order to supplement these part-time seasonal positions. Experience as a cheerleader may help accustom NFL dancers to their role during games, such as cheering from the sidelines, understanding the game being played, and acclimating to a sports culture. NFL dance team jobs are incredibly difficult to snag; many auditions attract up to 8,000 auditioning dancers for only 5 to 10 open spots on the team (Flanagan and Canales 2018). Overall, working as an NFL dancer comes with extreme challenges and benefits that must be weighed carefully. Going into these jobs knowing how they can help launch your career is just as important as understanding when and how to negotiate and advocate.

SUMMARY

The multitude of jobs in competitive dance and in the sports entertainment arena illustrate the popularity and accessibility of entertainment-based and athletic dance. Experience in advanced jazz, hip-hop, contemporary, lyrical, and even gymnastics or cheerleading is a must, but you may also find your skills as a team player and as a leader are also great assets to demonstrate when approaching a career in this area of the field. Whether you are interested in coaching collegiate dancers for national competitions or performing on the sidelines of NFL games, opportunities in competitive dance and sports entertainment can maximize the use of your dance training and provide both long- and short-term career opportunities.

Reflection

SKILL INVENTORY: DANCER, CHOREOGRAPHER, ADJUDICATOR, TEACHER, OR COACH?

If you aim to work in the competitive dance arena but do not yet know which position may be best suited for your skills and talents, consider the prompts that follow to determine how you might fill each professional role. First, list the necessary qualities for each position. Next, list the attractive aspects of each position. Third, list the challenges or downsides of each position. Finally, take a look at which of these lists include the most positive, enthusiastic language. Gauge your level of excitement for each position with the level of skill you have in order to get a sense of how to structure your goals for future employment in this area of the dance field.

- Dancer:
- Choreographer:
- Adjudicator:
- Teacher:
- Coach:

Chapter 11

Technical Theater, Media, and Technology

"Dance till the stars come down from the rafters
Dance, dance, dance till you drop."
W.H. Auden

Job opportunities in technical theater, media, and technology can enhance dance careers and expand possibilities for working in the field. Learning how to support companies and productions by developing skills in lighting, sound, media, and scenic design increases your chances of being hired in the industry overall. By broadening your idea of what a dance career entails, you open possibilities for growing your network and gaining future employment in production and management.

This chapter brings to light the professional benefits of acquiring skills in technical theater, media, and technology. Advice for how to brand yourself online, how to seek part-time or seasonal gigs that could help support other work in dance, and how to stay abreast of the latest trends and innovations are included. Because much work can be found in these areas, it is important to foster these skills as students in K-12 education and in studio settings. Additionally, postsecondary dance degree programs are often aligned with other arts disciplines and thus, present opportunities to gain skills and experience through production assignments and course work while in college. As an aside, while costume design and construction are out of the scope of this book and will not be discussed in detail, this is yet another area of potential focus for theater and dance technicians.

Emmett Buhmann

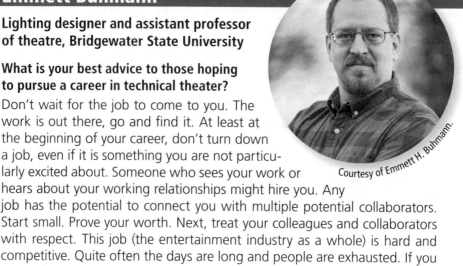

Lighting designer and assistant professor of theatre, Bridgewater State University

What is your best advice to those hoping to pursue a career in technical theater?

Don't wait for the job to come to you. The work is out there, go and find it. At least at the beginning of your career, don't turn down a job, even if it is something you are not particularly excited about. Someone who sees your work or hears about your working relationships might hire you. Any

Courtesy of Emmett H. Buhmann.

job has the potential to connect you with multiple potential collaborators. Start small. Prove your worth. Next, treat your colleagues and collaborators with respect. This job (the entertainment industry as a whole) is hard and competitive. Quite often the days are long and people are exhausted. If you can make it through those challenges with a smile on your face, and excitement for the next round, others will notice. Having quality skills is incredibly important, but being a good person and colleague is critical. If people don't have a positive experience with you, there is a good chance that you won't get asked back. Also, don't "tell stories" about people or talk about them behind their back. This is an incredibly small industry, and negative things that you say can easily find their way back to haunt you. Finally, find something that you love about every project. Teach yourself something with every project. Push your comfort zone. These things will keep you from becoming disenchanted, bored, or stagnant.

Describe some of the greatest lessons you've learned in your career.

In high-pressure situations, recognize that everyone is under the same pressure that you are under. Be in sync with your choreographer. You cannot tell a story together if you are both telling different stories. Lighting is not more important than movement. Movement is not more important than lighting. In my most successful collaborations, I have thought of light as a component that works alongside the movement to help tell a story. At moments the movement takes focus. At moments the spectacle of lighting takes focus. But ultimately, we are both on the same team, striving to achieve the same goal . . . to tell the story as clearly and effectively as possible. To affect an audience. Also, know what a stage manager does and be prepared to step into that role from time to time. I can pretty much guarantee that at some point you will be calling the show you designed, while coordinating the actions backstage and running your own lights, audio, and projection.

OPPORTUNITIES IN TECHNICAL THEATER

Well-produced shows operate with support from an experienced team of technical theater professionals. Technicians fill a variety of roles in theater production, including light and sound design, board operation, prop handling, costume design, carpentering, scenic design, and stage and production management (Princeton Review n.d.; Gillette 2012). Positions in technical theater require a high school diploma and specific expertise in lighting, sound, scenic design, costuming, or production management. Additionally, a college degree in technical theater can increase your marketability. Technicians are in high demand, have the benefit of working in exciting and enjoyable environments closely related to dance, and can often negotiate substantial salaries and stipends for their work. The United States Institute for Theatre Technology (USITT), an organization devoted to "promoting dialogue, research, and learning among practitioners of theatre design and technology," (United States Institute for Theatre Technology n.d., para 1) is a valuable resource that supports and connects theater technicians across the country. USITT is a terrific resource for theater technicians searching for networking, education, and job opportunities.

Lighting Design

A lighting designer's job spans the length of the creative process of building and launching a new show. The lighting designer collaborates with other technicians, choreographers, and directors to bring an artistic vision to life through lighting (Gillette 2012; Carter 1994). Dance productions often require specific lighting plots because it is important to prioritize lighting the contours of three-dimensional moving bodies rather than focusing on actors' faces as might be the priority in a theater production. Clear communication, collaboration, knowledge of lighting design theory and various art forms, and the ability to follow someone else's vision are particularly important qualities of a good lighting designer.

At the beginning of a lighting designer's job, they first meet with the team members responsible for developing a vision for a production, whether they be choreographers, directors, or producers. Once they have a sense of the visionary direction, goals, facilities details, and budget for the production, they begin designing by creating a light plot (Theatrecrafts.com n.d.; Gillette 2012). This is a visual document similar to an architectural blueprint that identifies the type and amount of lighting equipment needed in each area of the stage space. The light plot is read and used by the lighting designer, director, choreographer, electricians, and other technical crew as they work together to develop a show. Lighting designers attend rehearsals and continue working to refine the plot, adding written cues to document decisions about the color, position, focus, and flow of lighting. A major component of the lighting designer's job happens during technical and dress rehearsals, when the production is refined in the space in which it will premiere.

Lighting designers are trained through secondary and postsecondary institutions and community organizations. Some lighting designers gain critical experience through internship or apprenticeship experiences and even self-training or informal mentorship under an experienced designer. On average, lighting designers in the United States earn about $21 per hour for part-time work or, if salaried, $53,000 per year (Payscale n.d.b.). Once you have training and experience in theatrical lighting design, you may be qualified for work in dance and theater companies as well as additional opportunities in designing and operating lights for television, film, and online content for platforms such as YouTube.

Sound Design

A sound designer's job is to obtain and edit recorded sound, set up playback equipment, manage microphone selection and placement, mix sounds for the best audience experience during a live production, and, if not operating the sound board, train someone else to manage the task (Berklee College of Music n.d.; University of Oregon Department of Theatre Arts n.d.). The sound designer is also responsible for creating sound cues, ensuring consistent and appropriate flow of sound throughout a production, and staying up to date on sound software and systems. A sound designer's creative process is very similar to that of a lighting designer in that they use a director's or choreographer's ideas as a starting point for creation and development and work throughout the process alongside a team of technicians and artists. They attend regular rehearsals with the cast as well as all technical and dress rehearsals. Sound designers must have a "well-developed sense of hearing; a comprehensive understanding of musical history and genre; a musician's sensitivity to balance, timbre, rhythm, melody, and musical structure; and a deep understanding of psychoacoustics, system engineering, computer networking, component integration, and of the systems for sophisticated audio distribution" (Association of Sound Designers n.d., para. 3).

Sound designers are typically independent contractors, working for individual producers and companies on a show-by-show basis, although many companies have a go-to designer that they continue to hire or retain on salary. Average hourly pay for theatrical sound designers in the United States is $50 to $75, and salary average for a midcareer sound designer is $51,425 (Payscale n.d.c.). Once you have earned the credentials and skills required of a sound designer, you may be qualified for jobs in film, television, radio, music, video games, and even forensic audio (Daley 2004).

Scenic Design

Scenic designers are responsible for the visual appearance and function of the set elements used in a production (Gillette 2012). As in lighting and sound design, scenic designers take creative and budgetary cues from choreographers and directors. To translate scenic design ideas to the creative team, set designers present sketches and three-dimensional scale models to illustrate the function and appearance of their designs (Appalachian State University Department of Theatre and Dance n.d.). Additionally, depending on the makeup of staff, scenic designers may also be responsible for building, painting, and installing scenery.

Scenic designers work in various settings, including theater and dance companies, universities, community organizations, and K-12 schools. Additionally, scenic designers are hired to work on film sets and in other industries that value spatial sensitivity and artistic aesthetics, such as real estate, architecture, and interior design. In dance, scenic design work is most often found in ballet companies and organizations working with interdisciplinary design elements such as large-scale set pieces, props, or equipment. Theatrical scenic designers in the United States average $19 per hour for part-time jobs and, if salaried, from $21,000 to $87,000 per year (Payscale n.d.d).

Production Management

The role of a production manager involves planning and organizing production and touring schedules, contracting technical crew, troubleshooting technical issues, assisting with production budgets, communicating with artists and technical crew about production needs, and hiring technical staff. In general, production managers serve as liaisons between cast, crew, and the director or choreographer to ensure a smooth production process (Gillette 2012). Because production managers supervise all of the technical elements of a production, it is helpful for them to have prior experience in lighting, sound, costuming, and scenic design. Further, while experience in dance or theater is not a requirement, it is helpful to have in order to intuit the needs of choreographers, directors, dancers, and other artists.

Some production managers are independent contractors, working temporary positions connected to a specific production or season, while others are retained on salary. The median salary for a production manager in the United States is $49,112 (Study.com 2019) and average hourly pay is $49 (Salary.com n.d.a.). Production managers are equipped with unique skills in production and leadership, which make them prime candidates for other positions, including management opportunities in film, television, radio, and online media. Additionally, production manager responsibilities sometimes overlap those of a technical director, whose job is to oversee all technical elements of a production.

Stage Management

A stage manager's role involves ensuring that rehearsals and performances run smoothly and communicating a director's or choreographer's wishes to the technical crew, cast, and staff during the rehearsal and production process. Stage managers schedule and run rehearsals, call cues during rehearsals and performances, record notes about blocking and technical elements, and oversee every aspect of each performance (American Association of Community Theatre n.d.). Because of the unique nature of the job, often in a busy and high-stress environment, successful stage managers rely on particular qualities and strengths such as effective communications skills, organizational ability, patience, and a calm yet focused demeanor. Additionally, previous experience in all elements of production is usually desired of stage managers.

Some stage managers are hired per show, others are hired for a season of productions, and still others are salaried employees. The average stage manager salary in

Courtesy of Naomi Hill.

Dancer Rachel Ure of Flatlands Dance Theatre.

the United States is $43,043 (Salary.com n.d.a.) and average hourly pay for part-time workers is $16.08 (Indeed n.d.). The weekly base salary for a Broadway stage manager averages about $3,000 (Culwell-Block 2018). The skills developed as a stage manager transfer easily to other jobs such as production manager and technical director and into other fields such as film, television, and media.

PREPARING FOR CAREERS IN TECHNICAL THEATER

Much of the preparation and credentialing required for careers in technical theater can be obtained through programs in postsecondary institutions and through pre-professional work or apprenticeships in theaters and companies. Undergraduate and graduate degrees in technical theater usually include concentrations in one or more areas such as lighting, sound, scenic design, production management, costuming, or stage management. Students working toward degrees in technical theater gain additional experience by working on productions in their degree-granting programs and by taking advantage of internship and research opportunities with faculty members and community organizations.

Many of the contracted or production-specific opportunities in technical theater are more lucrative than those in performance. Therefore, gaining skills as a technician or manager can make a big difference in your ability to make enough money to sustain a performance career. There are a multitude of opportunities to gain training and experience that don't involve completing a college degree in technical theater. For example, postsecondary dance and theater degree programs offer individual courses that provide an introduction to basic technical theater theory and principles. Practical courses in technical theater offer hands-on training and experience in design and construction. Informal training through apprenticeships with theater and dance companies can create opportunities to learn on the job and, hopefully, be hired in the future.

OPPORTUNITIES IN MEDIA AND TECHNOLOGY

The need in the dance field for people trained and skilled in media and technology is greater than ever before. Dance companies, schools, organizations, and independent professionals rely on archival and promotional video, photography, and graphic and web design to expand their networks and gain additional clients or jobs. Artists also incorporate video and other technology into hybrid or digital dance works in innovative and exciting ways. The required skills and training for careers in media and technology differ from many of the other areas discussed in this book, and the day-to-day responsibilities and alternative career prospects that can emerge from skills developed while working in media and technology are unique. Because this area of the field is still emerging and evolving, new opportunities arise all the time to engage in professional dance by incorporating media and technology.

Videography and Editing

Videographers are needed to record and archive dance. For example, private dance schools and studios often hire videographers to film and edit footage from annual recitals and showcases. Independent dancers and choreographers hire professionals to film or edit existing film to create brief, artistic reels that showcase their best work. These reels are then used by choreographers and dancers for self-promotion or to secure future employment. Dance companies and organizations hire videographers to capture archival footage of their professional concerts and also require editing services for promotional and branding purposes.

Videographers and editors are most often contract-based employees, working event to event. Word of mouth is an important way to secure jobs in this area. However, an impactful website and social media presence showcasing filming and editing skills for dance should be a priority as well. It can also be helpful to reach out to dance schools, companies, and individual dancers, particularly those new to a community who may not have already committed to working with any one videographer or company. Dance videographers in the United States make from $65,000 to $94,000 per year and average $31 per hour in part-time employment (U.S. Bureau of Labor Statistics n.d.; Salary.com n.d.c.). Additionally, videographers can earn extra income by charging for recordings, typically delivered as downloads from a website or as DVDs. A significant benefit of working as a videographer in dance is that these skills transfer to multiple job opportunities outside dance, including videography for weddings, sporting events, parties, graduations, corporate advertising, music videos, and feature film.

Photography

Promoting their work through high-quality, professional photography is critical to the success of many dance companies, schools, and businesses. Photography captures the creativity and prowess of dancers' bodies in ways that intrigue people, influencing them to attend a show, take a class, join or support an organization, or hire a dancer. Additionally, photography preserves memories of dance events such as recitals, and it archives important conferences, concerts, and interviews. Therefore, dance photographers are in demand and are hired across the dance field.

Much like videographers, photographers promote themselves through websites, social media, and word of mouth. Building a strong portfolio of dance images is important, so offering free and reduced-rate sessions might be an important step in establishing clientele. Photographers' median annual salary in the United States is $41,560 per year and averages $19.98 per hour when working on a part-time basis (U.S. Bureau of Labor Statistics 2018). Photographers earn additional income through download and print purchases. Opportunities abound for additional or supplementary work in events, advertising, and corporate and individual promotions.

Graphic Design

In the information age, value is emphasized through design elements—how websites and social media pages are easily navigated and attractively laid out, and how print designs pop to grab attention. Graphic designers are incredibly important to dancers because they can create impact through two-dimensional products that epitomize the excitement and presence of live dance. Whether through print design, such as show posters or company apparel, website design, or social media design, it is more critical than ever for dance professionals to hire talented, reliable graphic designers. Experience and skills in graphic design for dance are transferable to jobs in practically any other industry. Graphic designers across areas of specialty in the United States earn an average of $47,305 per year or, if part-time, $19.39 per hour (Payscale n.d.a.).

Print Design

Print designers are hired to create advertising and marketing materials for dance studios, companies, and organizations. These materials can include season mailings, production posters and programs, apparel, invitations, and fundraising brochures. Working closely with directors and artistic visionaries, graphic designers can develop a unique aesthetic or brand for a company over time and can work to establish each client as distinct in the field. Additionally, graphic designers excel at presenting information in a clear, persuasively formatted way to attract potential business for their clients.

Web Design

A clear, engaging website is critical for every dance professional and company. Developing skills in web design uniquely qualifies you to work in nearly every arena of the dance field. Web designers must be adept at creating and coding web pages and associated apps for their clients. Some also help maintain websites for their customers after completion. Because software and technology change rapidly, web designers must stay current in these trends and updates. Additionally, being familiar with dance is helpful for designers working with artists and entertainers.

Social Media Design

In addition to in-depth knowledge of various social media platforms, social media designers must also work with companies or clients to develop strategic goals and timelines for spreading news and making announcements. Because social media presence is constantly evolving and bound by the framework of each platform, social media designers must understand how to make an impact consistently over time. Working intimately with directors and other administrators, social media designers align the social media aesthetic of a company with its trademark look in print and web design. Social media designers also build fundraising opportunities for companies using various tools and resources within each platform.

SUMMARY

Because jobs in technical theater, media, and technology are structured as part-time, temporary, or contract-based positions, their requirements vary. Many of these positions do not require an undergraduate degree, although university credentials definitely increase the chances of being hired and of higher pay. Postsecondary degrees are available in technical theater and graphic design and related fields such as media and communications, art, advertising, and marketing. Additionally, internship, apprenticeship, and informal mentorship experiences can offer valuable opportunities for specialization and networking. For potential videographers and photographers, degree programs in art and photography are recommended. Seeking experiences to work (even on a volunteer basis) with dancers, dance schools, and dance companies can help build a repertoire of products that can create a strong portfolio for future employment.

Reflection

EXPERIENCE AND INTEREST INVENTORY

In this reflection activity, spend time creating a list of your previous experiences in the areas of technical theater, media, and technology. Make note of experiences or skills in lighting, sound, scenic design, or stage or production management. Add experiences you have had in costuming, ushering shows, serving as front-of-house staff, attending a lecture, or watching a documentary or reading a book about these areas. No experience is too minor to include in this list. Each contributes to your knowledge and skills in these areas. Next, make a separate list of interests you have in the areas of technical theater, media, and technology. This list should include experiences you would like to have in the future, assignments you would like to learn how to do, theories you are interested in learning, people you would like to meet in the field, and credentials you would like to earn. Taking stock of the experiences you have had and activities you still need to experience is important as you consider how work in technical theater, media, and technology can take shape in the overall arc of your dance career.

Chapter 12

Interdisciplinary Opportunities

"I always find that the best collaborations are when you work with people that know what they're doing, and you leave them alone to do it."

Twyla Tharp

"To understand what I am saying, you have to believe that dance is something other than technique. We forget where the movements come from. They are born from life. When you create a new work, the point of departure must be contemporary life—not existing forms of dance."

Pina Bausch

Future dance professionals should learn about the benefits of reaching outward beyond the traditional boundaries of the dance field to create career opportunities. This chapter highlights some of the emerging possibilities for interdisciplinary work. Working across disciplines often yields fruitful results, which may lead to artistic growth, expanded networks, unexpected funding sources, and additional career opportunities, and it may propel your work in new, refreshing directions. Additionally, interdisciplinary projects are sometimes described by viewers as inclusive, accessible, and surprising because audience members who would not otherwise have interest or opportunities to participate in dance find connections to it through interdisciplinary projects. Dance pairs well with other arts disciplines such as music, theater, and visual arts and also can make unique connections with disciplines outside the arts such as education, science, math, kinesiology, architecture, and engineering. Surprising partnerships like these may emerge during a career in dance and it would behoove dance artists to take advantage of interdisciplinary work, which can only expand dance's possibilities.

Photo: Tom Kramer.

Dr. Merry Lynn Morris

**Assistant director
and faculty member,
Department of Dance,
University of South
Florida**

**What have been your most
significant experiences as a
working professional in dance?**

The realization of the Rolling Dance Chair Project is a significant highlight within my work as a dance professional. I conceived and initiated this project in 2005. It involved reconceptualizing mobility device design from a dance perspective, and I collaborated with engineers to bring several prototype concepts to fruition. This resulted in five U.S. patents and a developed wheelchair prototype in 2012, which multiple individuals with disabilities tested and explored. This project received national and international attention due to its innovative nature. In 2014, the Smithsonian Institution featured the Rolling Dance Chair as part of an Innovation Festival celebrating American innovations, and I have been honored to be a guest speaker in several events at the Smithsonian Institution due to this work. Also, I have found significance in the interdisciplinary curricula I have been involved in developing over my professional career. This includes a dance, architecture, and video course; a creative expression course involving art and dance faculty;

COLLABORATION WITH ARTISTS

Interdisciplinary collaborations between dance artists and those working in other arts media such as music, theater, visual art, or digital media can expand notions of individual art forms and enhance artists' ideas. Collectively, artists create impactful works that reach large audiences and receive significant support from granters and critics who appreciate innovation through collective effort. Collaborations may take longer to fund and produce due to the necessity for including multiple voices in planning, organization, and creation processes; however, many artists agree that the extra effort is always worth the associated costs because of the exciting results emerging from these collaborations.

Interdisciplinary collaborations are frequently initiated by a company or organization that may already have a project idea and sources of financial support in mind. If at least one of the collaborators is affiliated with a nonprofit organization, the project is eligible to be sponsored by a grant. Otherwise, sources of financial and

an art in health course series; and a dance medicine and science certificate program. Collaborating with professionals outside my immediate field offers the opportunity to continue to excavate new perspectives, new ideas, and new applications. I find it rewarding to work with different student populations and expose them to the value of exploring movement on a deeper level.

Looking back, what have been the best decisions you have made during your career?

Pursuing a college education was one of the best choices I made in terms of how the environment suited my interests and abilities and enabled me to continue along the path of cultivating dance expertise as well as becoming an effective dance educator. I feel that a college program in dance is ideal in that students are exposed to working with highly accomplished faculty and guest artists in the field of dance, while being pushed to critically think about their art form in expansive, relevant, and insightful ways. That being said, I also advocate for students to pursue the paths that truly fit their abilities and interests. A college program in dance may not be the right fit for every dance student. Obtaining a license as a sports massage therapist was also a beneficial decision in that it enabled me to advance my anatomical knowledge of the body, work directly in the body therapy field, gain valuable experience, and support my ability to make a living while serving as an adjunct at multiple universities. Additionally, my efforts to seek out collaborative and interdisciplinary initiatives and move beyond my own knowledge base has resulted in productive and exciting journeys of discovery and innovation. While these experiences have been challenging at times, I am glad I took the risks to explore the possibilities outside my comfort zone.

resource support could comprise individual contributions, corporate underwriting, and fiscal sponsorship under an umbrella nonprofit organization. To ensure a smooth, clear process between collaborators and to arrive at mutually agreeable expectations, include each person or organization on the team in initial discussions and planning. These conversations should include establishing roles and responsibilities for each party, defining a timeline for the project, outlining basic budgetary concerns, and agreeing on outcomes and other details about performances or products emerging from the collaboration. Remember, too, that there is give and take in every collaboration, so it is likely everyone in the project will negotiate and sacrifice a bit to make room for everyone's needs and desires.

The way dance collaborations take shape is constantly evolving, and artists continue to innovate through these interdisciplinary investigations. Dance maintains an easy partnership with music because many forms of dance are traditionally accompanied by music or sound in class and onstage. Collaborations with musicians may involve merging or cocreating original choreography and composition, improvisational forms, or chance operations of dance and music. Dance's partnership with theater is often played out in musical productions, but it can also result from devised explorations of existing theater works reimagined to involve dance. Dance's partnership possibilities with visual arts may involve incorporating sculpture into the dance as a set piece, projecting still or moving imagery, integrating site-specific structures or public art, or simply using a visual artist's work as inspiration for choreography. Finally, arts and fringe festivals, which have cropped up around the United States, offer unique opportunities for various arts media to merge, taking the form of performance and educational activities. Interdisciplinary works combining dance and other art forms may be performed live, filmed and screened, or some combination of these.

COLLABORATION WITH PROFESSIONALS OUTSIDE THE ARTS

Possibilities for creating interdisciplinary works involving dance and other areas outside of the arts are endless, inviting opportunities for expanding notions of dance and prospects for increased funding, networking, and audience building.

Photo courtesy of MFA Thesis Exhibition, CASP 5 &J Gallery 2015.

Dancers Gabriella Franco and Jackie Voller of Flatlands Dance Theatre in *The Choreography of Painting.*

Those dance artists willing to take risks and cross into new disciplinary territory are quickly emerging as inventive and prominent. Some of these projects stem from discipline-specific research that develops into creative work; some emerge based on the needs of a particular population of people or a community; and others propose to educate, empower, or tell stories.

Engaging in interdisciplinary dance work with partners outside of the arts is beneficial because these projects may interest and influence large populations of people and enhance communities. For example, dance's connections to education have been incorporated into many exciting projects that bring new meaning to instructional content for children in areas such as math, science, literature, and history while, simultaneously, creating opportunities for new art works to emerge and for building relationships between artists and community families. Many granting foundations prioritize funding projects whose purposes involve educating children and interdisciplinary partnerships, so finding ways to connect dance with public schools, universities, and other educational programs within communities may be particularly fruitful.

Another benefit of initiating interdisciplinary projects is that many disciplines outside the arts are well funded. The fact that dance is marginalized by U.S. federal and state funding sources cannot be ignored. Therefore, finding opportunities to increase financial support of dance through interdisciplinary work is a terrific strategy. For example, dance artists create collaborative projects with professionals working in kinesiology, biology, engineering, architecture, and many other areas to create events and performances, training regimens, educational curricula, lectures, and even new products for consumers. Amie Dowling, a choreographer based in San Francisco, has spent decades developing partnerships with area prisons and schools; these partnerships, through dance and theater workshops, generate publicly performed dance theater by people who are incarcerated (Dancers Group). Other choreographers collaborate with scientists on performance that supports conceptual understanding; they invite collaboration from professionals such as those working in the military, law enforcement, athletics, and medicine to infuse professional expertise in their art works; and they sometimes interact with professional writers such as journalists, historians, and poets to generate rich, well researched narrative structures in their choreography.

PREPARING FOR PROFESSIONAL INTERDISCIPLINARY OPPORTUNITIES

Many of the opportunities for developing interdisciplinary projects stem from work conducted in other arenas, such as in dance companies, schools, and arts organizations. Therefore, it is advisable to first secure a position in an established institution whose mission involves working with partners across disciplines and then, propose new ideas for collaboration or offer to support ongoing interdisciplinary projects.

Charlotte Boye-Christensen

Cofounder and artistic director, NOW-ID

Courtesy of Texas Tech University.

What is your best advice to those hoping to pursue a career in dance?

Be determined, passionate, curious, courageous, kind, and collaborative. Nurture your connections and interest in artists you have met along the way. Be generous, remain in contact, and be on time!

What have been your most significant experiences as a working professional in dance?

I have been fortunate to have had a diverse career so far, working with both ballet and contemporary dance companies as well as many types of organizations in the arts and otherwise. Interdisciplinary collaborations have been the bedrock of my creative research. I strive to engage artists from other disciplines and, in the process, address the need for transdisciplinary dialogue that reaches across fields. Dialogue deepens and clarifies intent; clarity of intent and substance, alongside refinement of conceptual research are preeminent goals for me. I have sought to work with multimedia artists, composers, graffiti artists, designers, opera singers, directors, writers, visual artists, scientists, and architects, all of whom contribute their unique talents and voices to the variegated chorus that is contemporary dance.

To be fully prepared for professional interdisciplinary work, it is helpful to have training in at least one art form. Seek opportunities to collaborate across disciplines through secondary or postsecondary educational experiences or through community or company events. Also, university programs across the country offer degrees that can lead to work as an interdisciplinary artist. The University of Rochester, for example, offers an undergraduate degree in interdisciplinary dance studies with concentrations that combine dance with one of the following areas: disability, gender, social justice, African American studies, religion and classics, or brain and cognitive sciences (University of Rochester n.d.). Duke University implemented its Master of Fine Arts in Dance: Embodied Interdisciplinary Praxis in 2018. This terminal degree encourages practice-based, interdisciplinary research by devoting nearly half of its curriculum to course work outside the dance discipline and encouraging students to develop interdisciplinary projects (Duke University n.d.).

SUMMARY

Working on interdisciplinary teams can provide fulfilling artistic processes and can lead to a multitude of other opportunities. By expanding your notions of how dance operates—within, alongside, or intertwined with other disciplines—you can also change the ways others participate in and support dance. Dance artists and educators who emphasize interdisciplinary work reach large, diverse audiences and find new ways to financially support their work.

Reflection

FREE WRITE: DREAMING UP COLLABORATION IDEAS

Whether you have contributed to multiple collaborative or interdisciplinary projects or not, it is the conjuring of ideas that stirs excitement and helps you identify potential collaborators to approach and projects to begin developing. Spend 10 minutes free writing using the following prompts as a guide:

- How could you envision your dance skills meshing with a collaborator's to answer a question or serve a need or purpose? For example, could you envision ways that your work combined with someone else's could serve a need in your community, bolster children's learning, assist people who are elderly or have disabilities, shed light on a cultural issue, bring people together, or expand your artistic goals?

- What people or organizations do you foresee being open to collaboration?

- How might you secure funding to enable these projects? Are there, for example, local foundations or companies that provide seed money or grants for which you could apply?

- How do you imagine that interdisciplinary works and collaboration could boost your work as an artist, scholar, educator, or human being?

- How might the interdisciplinary collaborations you envision lead to career opportunities in the distant future? How could these projects help you springboard your work into other areas and expand your network in positive ways?

Use this initial exercise as an impetus for deeper reflection about how and when to take on interdisciplinary projects of your own and how they might benefit you throughout your career.

Now What? First Steps Toward a Dance Career

"And onward, full tilt we go, pitched and wrecked and absurdly resolute . . . . Time to move out into the glorious debris."

Barbara Kingsolver

The conclusion of this book reviews the major takeaways in each section and offers suggestions for taking the first steps toward your career after graduating from high school or from a college program. A section on graduate school options in dance includes overviews of possible degrees and programs to research. Additionally, a discussion on how to acclimate yourself to life as a working professional will inspire you to get out there and do your best work on your way to a satisfying career in dance.

MAJOR TAKEAWAYS FROM THIS BOOK

Chapters 1 and 2 encouraged a combination of practical planning and training, open-mindedness, and a willingness to let go of rigid career expectations. Thinking of your career as an entrepreneurial journey that may include meandering paths, unexpected turns, and dead ends will prepare you for positive outcomes in your professional life. Being primed for a dance career also means educating yourself about how the dance field contributes to community, national, and global cultures and conversations. Approaching the field with curiosity, adaptability, and a willingness to work hard will bolster your ability to be successful and continue reinventing yourself in it.

Chapters 3 and 4 outlined the various career paths in K-12, postsecondary, community, and private studio dance education settings. Each area of dance education differs in its requirements, such as mandatory state certification for K-12 teachers and terminal degree requirements for postsecondary educators. Further, curricula may be structured in distinct ways depending on each institution's goals. For example, a dance studio may emphasize technical training in specific genres, whereas a community dance class may center on bringing diverse families together through dance for health and well-being. If becoming a dance educator is your goal, understanding the differences between these settings is important in order to focus on what interests you most.

Chapters 5 and 6 delved into the dance company and commercial dance sectors to reveal the multitude of job opportunities in them. Because a good portion of performance and choreography work is part-time, seasonal, or contract work, performers and choreographers face unique challenges such as maintaining financial stability and a consistent lifestyle. However, these professions also present chances for expanding artistry and a network and building a personal brand. Further, agents and unions can be instrumental in developing a long-term career in performance and choreography. Finally, serving as a leader of a dance organization can present opportunities to pursue an artistic vision and develop exciting new work with a company of dancers.

Chapters 7 and 8 outlined four major career areas: dance journalism, research, administration, and advocacy. More than ever, it is critical for dance professionals to embrace their abilities in these areas in order to inform, educate, and advocate for the future of our field. Careers in dance writing and research take many forms and require unique skills. These dance professionals ensure that the public is aware of dance's contributions and its needs and they work to archive the past and prepare for the future.

Chapters 9 and 10 discussed potential career trajectories in dance sciences, medicine, therapies, and somatic practices and in competitive and sports environments. Careers in dance sciences and medicine require specialized, sometimes extensive, education and certifications. Whether healing the body for improved mobility or training it for technical precision, an emphasis on the function and performance of the body is paramount in these careers. Careers in competitive dance and sports entertainment center on captivating, technically-precise performance and align with goals of team sports.

Chapters 11 and 12 feature careers that are either emerging in the field or that integrate well with jobs adjacent to the dance discipline. Opportunities in technical theater pair naturally with other jobs in dance because dancers have opportunities to train in technical theater during their dance educations. Further, contributing to productions in various positions gives dancers a better understanding of how each production role is valuable to the end product onstage. Plus, technical theater gigs provide another opportunity for engaging creatively and earning income. Dance professionals also create intersections between dance and other disciplines both in and outside of the arts. Interdisciplinary work can lead to major partnerships and important exploration in multiple fields and may expand opportunities for additional funding and fulfilling artistic challenges.

GRADUATE SCHOOL POSSIBILITIES

One of the paths to a successful and fulfilling career in dance is to earn a graduate degree in dance or a related area. The degrees most often pursued by dance artists and educators include the master of arts (MA), master of fine arts (MFA), doctor of education (EdD), and doctor of philosophy (PhD). Graduate degrees prepare students for dance careers in higher education, dance sciences and medicine, administration, and research. These degrees may also ensure higher salaries in K-12 dance teacher positions and other areas.

Before you decide to pursue graduate study, create a long-term plan for how you will pay for the degree, how your selected degree and program are a good fit for you, and how the degree will positively affect your future employability and help you reach your career goals. If a graduate degree will not support career advancement, it may be best to consider other options rather than incur debt and lost time that you could have been using toward your career. Overall, a graduate education provides wonderful chances to enhance your career but must be carefully weighed within your life's structure and goals.

Selecting the right degree to pursue and the right program in which to study are important undertakings that require research. Use resources such as Internet searches and personal connections to survey the field of degree possibilities and, once you narrow down a list of potential programs, visit those schools to get a sense of the student experience there. Reach out to individual faculty members and ask pointed questions about funding, teaching experience, mentorship, and course opportunities available for graduate students in that program. Also, ask for a synopsis of recent alumni accomplishments and employment information to understand the success rate of program graduates.

Once enrolled in a graduate program, be deliberate about developing relationships with faculty members and fellow students; these people will comprise your immediate network after graduation, so beginning to develop potentially long-term collaborations in school can pay off. Propose shadowing a faculty member in their research, ask to be considered for substitute teaching assignments, join graduate student organizations, and volunteer to perform or work with other students when the need arises. Being as involved as possible in graduate school will expand your network exponentially.

ADJUSTING TO LIFE AS A WORKING PROFESSIONAL IN DANCE

Jumping into the professional dance arena can, at first, feel intimidating and unknown. You may be acclimating to a new city or community and figuring out how to function as a bill-paying, living-on-your-own adult for the first time in addition to trying to secure a job and make your mark in the field. Know that this is a challenging transition for nearly everyone moving into the profession. This phase will pass and, given what you have learned from this book, from your family and friends, and from your education and training, trust that you are prepared for and can do this.

Relocating or Transitioning to Living on Your Own

One of the most important decisions you make upon entering the professional workforce is where and with whom to live. Depending on which area of the field you pursue, some geographical areas of the country may be more fruitful than others in terms of job availability. For example, if commercial dance is a major goal, Los Angeles, Chicago, and other large cities offer the greatest wealth of opportunities. If, on the other hand, you are interested in advocacy, living in Washington, D.C., or a state capital, where government officials are centralized, may be helpful. Dance educators can find jobs nearly anywhere in the country, but some areas offer more demand than others. Your network can help you locate potentially beneficial areas.

Of course, the most prolific area for your career pursuit may not be attainable for you yet because of financial or other concerns, so create backup plans for yourself before making big decisions. Some recent college graduates move back in with family members or remain in their college towns for some time after graduation to carefully consider and prepare for a major relocation. Others involve colleagues in their immediate plans, relocating and living with them. Pooling resources in this way can help you financially, emotionally, and professionally because you can share expenses, build relationships, and support each other's professional goals.

No matter where you decide to start your career, ensure you secure an emotional support system. If you are going to live in a place where you don't know anyone, be sure you have consistent access, via video or phone chats, to a supportive friend or family member, seek recommendations for a therapist in your new city, and quickly get involved to begin developing relationships in your new home.

Training and Health After Graduation

One of the more difficult tasks some dancers experience upon starting a career is prioritizing health and dance training. After all, many dance professionals juggle multiple part-time jobs and their personal lives, so devoting the money to take a dance class or the time to ensure proper sleep can seem impractical. Nevertheless, consider your long-term goals and how investing in your training and well-being will be worth the cost. It is important that these elements don't slide when you embark on a career. Share costs and create health accountability with roommates or friends. Seek opportunities to take dance classes through work-study programs or consider a part-time job in a health club for membership perks. Also, consider how your social life either contributes to or detracts from your career goals. To build a well-balanced life, nurture positive friendships and your network of trusted colleagues. Finally, invest in health insurance and establish yourself as a patient with local medical professionals.

On the Job Market

The first step in securing your first job in the dance industry is knowing how to search for available positions. Find out from others already working or looking for jobs where and how openings are announced and start searching there. Apply or audition for every job for which you think you might be even partially qualified.

Research agencies and unions, if those might help you reach your career goals. Continue making an effort to attend networking events, conferences, festivals, and classes to meet new people, learn more about the field, and possibly discover additional career opportunities. Networking and branding are extremely important ways to establish yourself in a new community or to reestablish yourself, no longer as a student, but as a working professional. Overall, at first, the job market can seem overwhelming and, after a few rejections, you may feel defeated and insecure. These are normal reactions, but remember, everyone struggles to find the right career fit, and your path to your best career will be unique and full of both challenges and successes.

Financial Considerations

Upon entering the workforce, it is important to use your money wisely and with the future in mind. Consider adopting a budget strategy to keep track of your earnings, your monthly expenses, and your savings. As a general rule, spend no more than 30 percent of your monthly gross income on housing, including utilities. Another common piece of advice is to save at least 20 percent of your monthly income; 10 to 15 percent of this savings should be invested in a retirement plan. Other savings should be used to build an emergency fund that could cover three to nine months of living expenses in case of lost employment and to sock away for future long-term expenses such as buying and maintaining a home, pursuing additional education, paying for a wedding, or starting a family. While budgeting and bill paying are not the most enjoyable parts of being a working professional, being mindful of your spending and saving will help you ensure your independence and self-sufficiency.

SUMMARY

One of the essential objectives of this book is to emphasize the vast number of career opportunities in dance. The dance field is rich in artistic, cultural, athletic, literary, leadership, and interdisciplinary possibilities. Even if you have never considered some of the career opportunities featured in this book, contemplate how your strengths and abilities may be a perfect fit for one or many of them. Expanding your identity and skills through additional training or education is always possible and highly encouraged in our age of constant change.

Hopefully, another major lesson you take from this book is that there are a multitude of ways to pursue and build a dance career. The path you take will be different than others' paths, and that is good and right. Your navigation strategies and specific goals will evolve as you grow as a dancer and as a complex person with multiple layers of needs and desires comprising your life. Many dance professionals exclaim that they never expected their careers to transform as they did, so remain open to the unexpected possibilities emerging as your own career and life unfold.

Overall, in reading this book, I hope you take seriously the commitments that accompany a dance career: leading a healthy lifestyle, approaching dance in the spirit of lifelong learning, embracing a sense of entrepreneurship on your professional dance journey, and respecting and serving as an ambassador of the dance field to introduce people and communities uneducated about dance to its appeal and its many benefits. It is a privilege to undertake a career in dance, and the field needs your unique perspective in it. I hope you take to heart the possibilities of unbridled joy that a dance career can bring to your life. I am convinced that there is no better way to spend your professional time. Your role in cultivating the exciting future of professional dance is just beginning. Enjoy the dance!

References

Chapter 1

American Dance Festival. n.d. "Dance Professional Workshops." Accessed February 26, 2019. www.americandancefestival.org/education/dance-professional-workshops.

Americans for the Arts. 2016. "Arts Facts: National Arts Index (2016)." www.americansforthearts.org/by-program/reports-and-data/legislation-policy/naappd/arts-facts-national-arts-index-2016.

Bonbright, Jane M. 2007. "National Agenda for Dance Arts Education: The Evolution of Dance as an Art Form Intersects with the Evolution of Federal Interest In, and Support of, Arts Education." National Dance Education Organization.

Dance/USA. 2017. "Snapshot of the Field." www.danceusa.org/snapshot-field.

Duval, Monique. 2000. *The Persistence of Yellow: A Book of Recipes for Life*. London: Compendium Publishing.

John F. Kennedy Presidential Library and Museum. n.d. "John F. Kennedy Quotations." Accessed February 25, 2020. www.jfklibrary.org/learn/about-jfk/life-of-john-f-kennedy/john-f-kennedy-quotations.

National Association of Schools of Dance. "Home." 2020. Accessed February 20, 2020. https://nasd.arts-accredit.org.

National Center for Education Statistics. 2012. "Arts Education in Public Elementary and Secondary Schools." https://nces.ed.gov/pubs2012/2012014rev.pdf.

National Dance Education Organization. 2013. "Evidence: A Report on the Impact of Dance in the K-12 Setting." Accessed February 25, 2020. https://s3.amazonaws.com/ClubExpressClubFiles/893257/documents/Final_Evidence_Report.pdf?AWSAccessKeyId=AKIA6MYUE6DNNNCCDT4J&Expires=1582663794&response-content-disposition=inline%3B%20filename%3DFinal_Evidence_Report.pdf&Signature=f1nM%2FFb4nnUMU4wiNopZAQVww0c%3D.

National Dance Education Organization. n.d. "Evolution of Dance in Arts Education." Accessed February 22, 2019. www.ndeo.org/content.aspx?page_id=22&club_id=893257&module_id=51380&sl=956872955.

National Endowment for the Arts. 2019. "Dance Fact Sheet." Accessed February 20, 2020. https://www.arts.gov/sites/default/files/Dance_FactSheet_7.15.19.pdf.

National Endowment for the Arts. 2019. "Latest Data Shows Increase to U.S. Economy from Arts and Culture Sector." Accessed February 21, 2020. https://www.arts.gov/news/2019/latest-data-shows-increase-us-economy-arts-and-cultural-sector.

National Endowment for the Arts. 2017. "Arts Data Profile." www.arts.gov/artistic-fields/research-analysis/arts-data-profiles/arts-data-profile-16.

National Endowment for the Arts. 2018. "The Survey of Public Participation in the Arts (2017)." www.arts.gov/artistic-fields/research-analysis/arts-data-profiles/arts-data-profile-18.

University of Maryland. 2020. "Minor in Arts Leadership." Accessed February 25, 2020. https://tdps.umd.edu/academic-programs/minor-arts-leadership.

U.S. Bureau of Economic Analysis. 2019. "Arts and Cultural Production Satellite Account, U.S. and States 2016." February 25, 2020. www.bea.gov/news/2019/arts-and-cultural-production-satellite-account-us-and-states-2016

U.S. Bureau of Labor Statistics. 2019. "Occupational Outlook Handbook: Dancers and Choreographers." www.bls.gov/ooh/entertainment-and-sports/dancers-and-choreographers.htm.

Western Michigan University. 2020. "Extended University Programs: Dance Studio Management." Accessed February 25, 2020. https://wmich.edu/extended/academics/dance-studio-management.

Williams, Trent. 2019. Interviewed by Ali Duffy, February 2019.

Chapter 2

Amin, Takiyah Nur. Interviewed by Ali Duffy, March, 2019.

Brandenburg, Stephan, Tim Roosen, and Mettina Veenstra. 2016. "Toward and Adapted Business Modeling Method to Improve Entrepreneurial Skills Among Art Students." *Artivate: A Journal of Entrepreneurship in the Arts*. 5:1, 25-33.

Cardone, Grant. 2017. "10 Things the Artist and the Entrepreneur Have in Common." *Entrepreneur*, February 9, 2017. www. entrepreneur.com/article/288568.

Clifton, Jim, and Sangeeta Badal. 2014. *Entrepreneurial StrengthsFinder*. New York, NY: Gallup Press.

Duchek, Stephanie. 2018. "Entrepreneurial Resilience: A Biographical Analysis of Successful Entrepreneurs." *International Entrepreneurship and Management Journal*. 14:2, 429-455.

Duffy, Ali. 2020. "Teaching Dance Techniques in an Aging Body: Perspectives and Recommendations from Dance Educators." [unpublished manuscript].

Machado, Antonio. 2006. *Campos de Castilla*. Madrid: Catedra.

Struxness, Betsy. Interviewed by Ali Duffy, February, 2019.

Vecco, Marilena. 2019. "The 'Artpreneur': Between Traditional and Cultural Entrepreneurship. A Historical Perspective." In *The Routledge Companion to Arts Management*. Taylor and Francis, 83-102.

Chapter 3

Appalachian State University. 2020. "Mission and Overview." Accessed February 26, 2020. https://theatreanddance.appstate.edu/about/mission-overview.

Brigham Young University. 2019. "Our Mission." Accessed February 26, 2020. https://dance.byu.edu.

Einstein, Albert, and Alice Calaprice. 2011. *The Ultimate Quotable Einstein*. Princeton, N.J: Princeton University Press, 99-101.

Graham, Martha.1953. "An Athlete of God." *This I Believe*. National Public Radio.

Juilliard School. 2018. "Juilliard's Mission." Accessed February 26, 2020. https://www.juilliard.edu/school/about/juilliards-mission.

National Association of Schools of Dance. 2019. "NASD Handbook 2019-2020." Accessed February 26, 2020. https://nasd.arts-accredit.org/wp-content/uploads/sites/5/2019/09/D-2019-20-Handbook-02-13-2020.pdf.

National Dance Education Organization. 2017. "State Certification for PreK-12 Education Executive Summary." Accessed February 26, 2020. www.ndeo.org/content.aspx?page_id=22&club_id=893257&module_id=194714.

Chapter 4

Dance Teacher. 2020. "Studio Owners." Accessed February 27, 2020. www.dance-teacher.com/your-studio/.

Glassdoor. 2020. "Dance Teacher Salaries in the United States." Accessed February 27, 2020. www.glassdoor.com/Salaries/us-dance-teacher-salary-SRCH_IL.0,2_IN1_KO3,16.htm.

H'Doubler, Margaret and Mary Alice Brennan. 1959. *Dance: A Creative Art Experience*. Madison, WI: University of Wisconsin Press, 66.

Hamilton, Chasta. 2016. "How to Create a Great Dance School Website." *Tututix*. December 27, 2016. www.tututix.com/how-to-create-great-dance-school-website.

How to Start An LLC. n.d. "How to Start a Dance Studio." Accessed March 30, 2019. https://howtostartanllc.com/business-ideas/dance-studio.

Hull, Patrick. 2013. "10 Essential Business Plan Components." *Forbes*, February 21, 2013. www.forbes.com/sites/patrickhull/2013/02/21/10-essential-business-plan-components/#7ae7eee25bfa.

Indeed. 2020. "Dance Studio Salaries in the United States." Accessed February 27, 2020. www.indeed.com/cmp/Dance-Studio/salaries.

Marketing Charts. 2019. "Social Networking Platforms' User Demographics Update 2019." Accessed February 27, 2020. www.marketingcharts.com/digital/social-media-108184.

Payscale. n.d. "Salary Reports." Accessed April 12, 2019. www.payscale.com/mypayscale. aspx?signedUp.

Steinbeck, John. 1955. "…like captured fireflies." In *America and Americans and Selected Nonfiction*, London: Penguin Classics, 142.

Urban Bush Women. 2018. "Engage with UBW." Accessed February 27, 2020. www. urbanbushwomen.org/engage-with-ubw.

Chapter 5

Americans for the Arts. n.d. "Arts Marketing Blog." Accessed May 3, 2019. https://namp. americansforthearts.org/get-smarter/arts-marketing-blog.

Dance Magazine. 2018. "How Much Can You Make in Dance? Here Are More Than 200 Actual Salaries" July 18, 2018. www.dancemagazine.com/dance-salaries-2587282090.html.

Loucadoux, Michelle, and Shelli Margheritis. 2017. "Branding" *Making It Werk: A Dancer's Guide to the Business of Professional Dance*. CreateSpace Independent Publishing.

Mfuko, Ashani. "Online Branding for Dancers: How to Increase Your Visibility." *All Things Dance*. Accessed April 1, 2019. http:// letstalkdance.net/online-branding-for-dancers-how-to-increase-your-visibility.

Payscale. n.d. "Average Dancer Salary." Accessed April 23, 2019. www.payscale.com/research/US/ Job=Dancer/Salary.

San Francisco Ballet. 2019. "2020 Season." Accessed April 26, 2019. www.sfballet.org/ season/2020-season.

Sims, Caitlin. 2005. "Starting Your Own Dance Company, Part 1." *Dance Teacher,* September 15, 2005. www.dance-teacher.com/start-your-own-dance-company-part-1-2392277186.html.

Stevenson, Tim, Courtney Miller Jr., and Harvey Russell. 2013. *The Business of Dance*. Mustang, OK: Tate Publishing.

U.S. Bureau of Labor Statistics. 2020. "Occupational Outlook Handbook: Dancers and Choreographers." Accessed February 28, 2020. www.bls.gov/ooh/entertainment-and-sports/ dancers-and-choreographers.htm.

Chapter 6

Actors Equity Association. 2020. "Dues and Fees." Accessed February 29, 2020. www. actorsequity.org/join/dues/.

American Guild of Musical Artists. 2020. "Explanation of Dues." Accessed February 29, 2020. www.musicalartists.org/membership/for-new-members/explanation-of-dues/.

American Guild of Variety Artists. 2020. "AGVA Dues Schedule." Accessed February 29, 2020. www.agvausa.com/dues.html.

Berlin, Erika. 2018. "11 Secrets of Backup Dancers." *Mental Floss*, January 26, 2018. http://mentalfloss.com/article/526920/11-secrets-backup-dancers.

Culwell-Block, Logan. 2018. "How Much Money Do Broadway Actors Make?" *Playbill,* April 16, 2018. www.playbill.com/article/how-much-money-do-broadway-actors-make.

Dance Spirit. 2012. "Getting an Agent." November. 14, 2012. www.dancespirit.com/ getting-an-agent-2326153543.html.

Dancers Alliance. 2020. "DA Rates." Accessed February 28, 2020. www.dancersalliance.org/ da-rates.

Hyken, Shep. 2018. "The Gig Economy Opens Door for Employment Opportunities." *Forbes*, July 29, 2018. www.forbes.com/ sites/shephyken/2018/07/29/the-gig-economy-opens-the-door-for-employment-opportunities/#64be8eb27662.

Loucadoux, Michelle, and Shelli Margheritis. 2017. *Making It Werk: A Dancer's Guide to the Business of Professional Dance*. CreateSpace Independent Publishing.

Myers, Louise. 2020. "How Often to Post on Social Media: A 2020 Success Guide." Accessed February 28, 2020. https://louisem. com/144557/often-post-social-media.

Pincus-Roth, Zachary. 2007. "Ask Playbill. com: Chorus Salary." *Playbill*, August 31, 2007. www.playbill.com/article/ask-playbillcom-chorus-salary-com-143361.

Rouse, Margaret. 2019. "Gig Economy." Accessed May 12, 2019. https://whatis. techtarget.com/definition/gig-economy.

SAG-AFTRA. 2020. "Membership Costs." Accessed February 29, 2020. www.sagaftra.org/membership-benefits/membership-costs.

SAG-AFTRA. 2019. "Production Center: Theatrical." Accessed May 31, 2019. www.sagaftra.org/production-center/contract/818/rate-sheet/document.

Spiegel, Amy Rose. 2013. "How Do You Even Become a Backup Dancer?" *Buzzfeed*, June 11, 2013. www.buzzfeed.com/verymuchso/how-do-you-even-become-a-backup-dancer.

Chapter 7

Barnett, Laura. 2007. "Portrait of the Artist: Judith Jamison." *The Guardian*, August 28, 2007. www.theguardian.com/stage/2007/aug/28/dance.

Belcher, Wendy Laura. 2019. *Writing Your Journal Article in Twelve Weeks: A Guide to Academic Publishing Success*. Chicago, IL: University of Chicago Press.

Cole, Peter. 2008. "News Writing." *The Guardian*. Accessed February 29, 2020. www.theguardian.com/books/2008/sep/25/writing.journalism.news.

Columbia University School of Journalism. n.d. "Interviewing Principles." Accessed June 19, 2019. www.columbia.edu/itc/journalism/isaacs/edit/MencherIntv1.html.

Creswell, John W. 2017. *Qualitative Inquiry & Research Design: Choosing Among the Five Approaches*. Thousand Oaks, CA: SAGE.

Denzin, Norman K., and Yvonna S. Lincoln. 2011. "Introduction" In *The SAGE Handbook of Qualitative Research*, 1-20. Thousand Oaks, CA: SAGE.

Glassdoor. 2020. "Assistant Professor, Dance Salaries in United States." Accessed March 2, 2020. www.glassdoor.com/Salaries/us-assistant-professor-dance-salary-SRCH_IL.0,2_IN1_KO3,28.htm.

Groves, Nancy. 2010. "What the Experts Said: Making It in Arts Journalism." *The Guardian Careers*, December 9, 2010. www.theguardian.com/careers/what-the-experts-said-making-it-in-arts-journalism.

International Association for Dance Medicine and Science. n.d. "Journal of Dance Medicine and Science." Accessed June 23, 2019. www.iadms.org/page/47.

McLeod, Saul. 2017. "What's the Difference Between Qualitative and Quantitative Research?" *Simply Psychology*. Accessed June 25, 2019. www.simplypsychology.org/qualitative-quantitative.html.

Merriam, Sharan B. 2009. *Qualitative Research: A Guide to Design and Implementation*. San Francisco, CA: Jossey-Bass.

Muijs, Daniel. 2010. *Doing Quantitative Research in Education with SPSS*. 2nd edition. London: SAGE Publications.

Posusta, Steven. 1996. *Don't Panic: The Procrastinator's Guide to Writing an Effective Term Paper*. Yuma, AZ: Bandanna Books.

Purdue Online Writing Lab. 2020. "Journal Abstracts." Accessed March 2, 2020. https://owl.purdue.edu/owl/general_writing/common_writing_assignments/academic_proposals/journal_abstracts.html.

Research in Dance Education. 2020. "Aims and Scope." Accessed March 2, 2020. www.tandfonline.com/loi/crid20.

Ricchiardi, Sherry. 2018. "How to Pitch Story Ideas: Tips from Journalists." *International Journalists' Network*, March 16, 2018. https://ijnet.org/en/resource/how-pitch-story-ideas-tips-journalists.

Society of Professional Journalists. 2014. "SPJ Code of Ethics." Accessed June 19, 2019. www.spj.org/ethicscode.asp.

Zimmer, Elizabeth. 2007. "Notes Toward Concise Writing: Saying What You Want to Say in Constricted Space." Dance Critics Association Kamikaze Writing Workshop.

Chapter 8

Americans for the Arts. 2019. "2018 Local Arts Agency Salary Report: Government Affairs/Advocacy." Accessed March 4, 2020. www.americansforthearts.org/sites/default/files/14_GovernmentAffairs_Advocacy2.pdf.

Americans for the Arts. n.d.a. "Advocacy Toolkit for Individuals and Organizations." Accessed March 4, 2020. www.americansforthearts.org/by-program/reports-and-data/legislation-policy/legislative-issue-center/advocacy-toolkit-for-individuals-and-organizations.

Americans for the Arts. n.d.b. "Local Arts Agency Salaries 2018." Accessed June 27, 2019. www.americansforthearts.org/by-program/networks-and-councils/local-arts-network/facts-and-figures/local-arts-agency-salaries-2018.

Arts Index. 2016. "2016 National Arts Index." Accessed on July 16, 2019. www.artsindexusa.org/national-arts-index.

Borwick, Doug. 2012. *Building Communities, Not Audiences: The Future of the Arts in the United States.* Winston Salem, NC: Arts Engaged.

Caldwell, Rachel. 2016. "Two Structures for University Dance Programs." *Dance Teacher.* August 31, 2016. www.dance-teacher.com/higher-ed-guide-two-structures-university-dance-programs-2392800166.html.

Columbia University. n.d. "Master of Arts, Arts Administration." Accessed July 15, 2019. www.tc.columbia.edu/arts-and-humanities/arts-administration/degrees--requirements/arts-administration-ma.

Dance Consortium. n.d. "Production Manager." Accessed July 15, 2019. www.danceconsortium.com/features/dance-resources/in-and-around-a-dance-company/production-manager.

Dance Magazine. 2018. "How Much Can You Make in Dance? Here Are More Than 200 Actual Salaries." July 18, 2018. www.dancemagazine.com/dance-salaries-2587282090.html.

Dance Studies Association. 2019. "About." Accessed July 12, 2019. https://dancestudiesassociation.org/about.

Dance/USA. n.d. "Advocacy and Visibility." Accessed July 16, 2019. www.danceusa.org/advocacy.

Firth, Michael. n.d.. "How Much Money Does a High School Dance Teacher Make?" *Chron.* Accessed June 28, 2019. work.chron.com/much-money-high-school-dance-teacher-make-13678.html.

Friedler, Sharon E., and Susan B. Glazer. 1997. *Dancing Female: Lives and Issues of Women in Contemporary Dance.* Amsterdam, The Netherlands: Harwood Academic Publishers.

Glassdoor. 2020. "Community Engagement Coordinator Salaries." Accessed March 4, 2020.

www.glassdoor.com/Salaries/community-engagement-coordinator-salary-SRCH_KO0,32.htm.

Harmon, Wynita. 2019. "10 Art Advocacy Resources Every Art Teacher Needs to Know About." *The Art of Education.* Accessed July 16, 2019. https://theartofeducation.edu/2019/03/13/10-art-advocacy-resources-every-art-teacher-needs-to-know-about.

International Association for Dance Medicine and Science. n.d. "About IADMS." Accessed July 12, 2019. www.iadms.org/page/A8.

Kurtzman, Joel, and Michael Distefano. 2014. "Alan Mulally: The Man Who Saved Ford." *Briefings Magazine.* Accessed October 14, 2019. www.kornferry.com/institute/alan-mulally-man-who-saved-ford.

Larson, Gavin. 2013. "Does a Dance Company Executive Director Need to Have a Dance Background?" *From the Green Room,* March 30, 2013. www.danceusa.org/ejournal/2013/03/30/does-a-dance-company-executive-director-need-to-have-a-dance-background.

Miller, Toby. 2000. "The National Endowment for the Arts in the 1990s: A Black Eye on the Arts?" *American Behavioral Scientist.* 43:9, 1429-1445.

National Dance Education Organization. 2020. "History of the National Dance Education Organization." Accessed March 4, 2020. www.ndeo.org/content.aspx?page_id=22&club_id=893257&module_id=194863.

Payscale. 2020. "Community Engagement Coordinator Salary." Accessed March 4, 2020. www.payscale.com/research/US/Job=Community_Engagement_Coordinator/Salary.

Risner, Doug, and Pamela S. Musil. 2017. "Leadership Narratives in Postsecondary Dance Administration: Voices, Values, and Gender Variations." *Journal of Dance Education.* 17(2): 53-64.

Schorn, Ursula. 2015. "The Life/Art Process: Building Blocks for Creative Action." In *Anna Halprin: Dance, Processes, Forms,* 57-92. Philadelphia, PA: Jessica Kingsley Publishers.

Stinson, Sue. 1998. "Places Where I've Been: Reflections on Issues of Gender in Dance

Education, Research, and Administration. *Choreography and Dance.* 5(1):117–27.

Stubbs, Ryan. 2014. "Public Funding for the Arts: 2014 Update." *Grantmakers in the Arts Reader.* 25:3, 8-11.

Tepper, Steven J., and Bill Ivey, editors. 2008. *Engaging Art: The Next Great Transformation of America's Cultural Life.* New York, NY: Routledge.

Whiteman, Erlyne F. 1991. "Management Competencies for Dance Administrators in Higher Education." In *Dance in Higher Education,* ed. Wendy Oliver. Reston, VA: American Alliance for Health, Physical Education, Recreation, and Dance.

ZipRecruiter. 2020. "Arts Advocacy Jobs." Accessed March 3, 2020. www.ziprecruiter.com/Jobs/Arts-Advocacy.

ZipRecruiter. 2020. "High School Dance Teacher Salary." Accessed March 3, 2020. www.ziprecruiter.com/Salaries/High-School-Dance-Teacher-Salary.

Chapter 9

Academy of Orthopaedic Physical Therapy. n.d. "Performing Arts Special Interest Group." Accessed July 22, 2019. www.orthopt.org/content/special-interest-groups/performing-arts/resources/dance.

Alexander Technique. n.d. "How to Find a Teacher or Group." Accessed July 12, 2019. www.alexandertechnique.com/teacher.

American Dance Therapy Association. n.d. "Become a Dance Movement Therapist." Accessed July 7, 2019. https://adta.org/how-to-become-a-dmt.

American Kinesiology Association. n.d. "About AKA." Accessed July 23, 2019. www.americankinesiology.org/SubPages/Pages/About.

American Physical Therapy Association. 2019. "Physical Therapist (PT) Admissions Process." Accessed March 4, 2020. www.apta.org/ProspectiveStudents/Admissions/PTProcess/.

American Physical Therapy Association. 2017. "Careers & Education." Accessed July 22, 2019. www.apta.org/CareersEducation.

Batson, Glenna. 2009. "Somatic Studies and Dance." International Association for Dance Medicine and Science. Accessed July 10, 2019. https://cdn.ymaws.com/www.iadms.org/resource/resmgr/resource_papers/somatic_studies.pdf.

Berardi, Gigi. 2004. *Finding Balance: Fitness, Training, and Health for a Lifetime in Dance.* Routledge.

Career Explorer. 2018. "Sports Medicine Physician Salary." Accessed February 4, 2020. www.careerexplorer.com/careers/sports-medicine-physician/salary.

Feldenkrais Method. 2017. "What Is Involved in Becoming a Certified Feldenkrais Practitioner?" March 16, 2017. https://feldenkrais.com/hrf_faq/involved-becoming-certified-feldenkrais-practitioner.

Harari, Yuval Noah. 2018. *Homo Deus: A Brief History of Tomorrow.* New York: Harper Perennial.

Harkness Center for Dance Injuries. 2020. "Dance Injury Prevention Programs." Accessed March 4, 2020. https://nyulangone.org/locations/harkness-center-for-dance-injuries/dance-injury-prevention-programs.

Harkness Center for Dance Injuries. n.d. "Dance Medicine and Science as a Career." Accessed March 5, 2020. https://med.nyu.edu/hjd/harkness/students/dance-medicine-science-career/career-overviews.

International Somatic Movement Education and Therapy Association. n.d. "Scope of Practice." Accessed July 12, 2019. https://ismeta.org/about-ismeta/scope-of-practice.

Long, Robin. 2014. "How to Become a Pilates Instructor." *The Balanced Life Online,* April 23, 2014. https://thebalancedlifeonline.com/how-to-become-a-pilates-instructor.

McAnarney, Casey. 2019. "Dance Injury Led to Career as Pain Management Doctor." *Star News Online.* Accessed arch 4, 2020.

Metcalf, Andrea. 2016. "Personal Trainer Salary Considerations." *American Council on Exercise,* September 14, 2016. www.acefitness.org/education-and-resources/professional/expert-articles/6093/personal-trainer-salary-considerations.

NATA News. 2014. "Keeping Dancers Dancing: The Inside Story on Working With Performing

Artists." April 2014. www.nata.org/sites/default/ files/professional-interests-performing-arts-dance.pdf.

National Athletic Trainers Association. n.d. "Career Center." Accessed July 23, 2019. www. nata.org/career-education/career-center.

National Holistic Institute. 2018. "Three Reasons Massage Therapy is the Perfect Career for Dancers." Accessed March 5, 2020. www. nhimassageblog.com/2018/02/28/3-reasons-massage-therapy-is-the-perfect-career-for-dancers/.

Neuro Tour Blog. 2017. "Q&A: Life as a Touring Physical Therapist." September 27, 2017. www.neurotour.com/blog/qa-life-as-a-touring-physical-therapist.

O'Clair, P.J. 2011. "A Career Path for the Pilates Instructor." IDEA Health and Fitness Association. Accessed March 5, 2020.

Payscale. 2020. "Average Physician/Doctor, Sports Medicine Salary." Accessed March 4, 2020. www.payscale.com/research/US/ Job=Physician_%2F_Doctor%2C_Sports_ Medicine/Salary.

Peak Pilates. 2020. "Become a Master Instructor." Accessed March 5, 2020. https:// peakpilates.com/become-a-master-instructor/.

Salary.com. n.d. "Physician – Sports Medicine Salary in the United States." Accessed July 18, 2019. www.salary.com/research/salary/ benchmark/sports-medicine-physician-salary.

Samuel, Leah. 2018. "From Rockette, Teacher, or Astronaut to Doctor: When Medicine is a Second Career." *STAT*. Accessed March 4, 2020.

Schnall, Marianne. 2010. "Exclusive Interview With Thich Nhat Hanh." *Huffpost*, May 21, 2010, updated December 6, 2017. www. huffpost.com/entry/beliefs-buddhism-exclusiv_b_577541.

Shah, Selina, Tom Welsh, Charlotte Woodcock, and Moira McCormick. "Pathways to Careers in Dance Medicine and Science." Panel presented at the International Association of Dance Medicine and Science. Singapore, October 26, 2012.

The Pilates Place. n.d. "How Much Do Pilates Instructors Make?" Accessed March 5, 2020.

www.thepilatesplace.info/how-much-do-pilates-instructors-make/.

U.S. Bureau of Labor Statistics. 2019a "Occupational Employment and Wages, May 2018: Athletic Trainers." Accessed July 23, 2019. www.bls.gov/oes/current/oes299091.htm.

U.S. Bureau of Labor Statistics. 2019b. "Occupational Outlook Handbook: Massage Therapists." Accessed March 5, 2020. www.bls. gov/ooh/healthcare/massage-therapists.htm.

U.S. Bureau of Labor Statistics. 2019c. "Occupational Outlook Handbook: Physical Therapists." Accessed March 4, 2020. www.bls. gov/ooh/healthcare/physical-therapists.htm.

U.S. Bureau of Labor and Statistics. 2019d. "Occupational Outlook Handbook: Exercise Physiologists." Accessed March 5, 2020. www. bls.gov/ooh/healthcare/exercise-physiologists. htm.

Woodard, Stephanie. 2016. "Five Things I Want to Tell Dancers: Physical Therapist." *Dance Informa*. Accessed July 20, 2019. www. danceinforma.com/2016/03/02/5-things-i-want-to-tell-dancers-physical-therapist.

Wingenroth, Lauren. 2018. "Everything You Need to Know About Becoming a Dance Therapist." *Dance Magazine*, December 26, 2018. www.dancemagazine.com/everything-you-need-to-know-about-becoming-a-dance-therapist-2623109794.html?rebelltitem=1#reb elltitem1.

Chapter 10

Callahan, Mary. n.d. "Impact Dance Adjudicators Make Dance Competition a Positive Experience." *Dance Informa*. Accessed July 12, 2019. www.danceinforma. com/2019/01/06/impact-dance-adjudicators-make-competition-a-positive-experience.

Dance Informa. n.d. "Dance Competition and Convention Guide." Accessed July 12, 2019. https://danceinforma.us/dance-competition-and-convention-guide.

Dance Spirit. 2013. "When I Grow Up: Dance Careers Beyond the Stage." November 1, 2013. www.dancespirit.com/when-i-grow-up-2326259355.html.

Dungee, Kristin. 2015. "Life as an NFL Cheerleader." *Chasse*. Accessed March 5, 2020.

www.chassecheer.com/blog/lifestyle/my-life-as-an-nfl-cheerleader/.

Flanagan, Graham, and Katie Canales. 2018. "NFL Cheerleaders Reveal What It's Really Like to Have Their Job." Business Insider, October 5, 2018. www.businessinsider.com/nfl-cheerleaders-reveal-what-its-like-to-have-their-job-2018-10.

National Dance Alliance. 2019. "Rules and Scoring." Accessed March 5, 2020. www.varsity.com/nda/school/competitions/rules-scoring/.

National Dance Alliance. n.d. "NDA Summer Camp." Accessed July 13, 2019. www.varsity.com/nda.

Payscale. n.d. "Average Dance Coach Hourly Pay." Accessed August 26, 2019. www.payscale.com/research/US/Job=Dance_Coach/Hourly_Rate.

Universal Dance Association. n.d. "UDA Summer Camp." Accessed July 13, 2019. www.varsity.com/uda.

Varsity. n.d. "Varsity All Star Dance Score Sheet." Accessed July 13, 2019. www.varsity.com/wp-content/uploads/2019/06/VAS_Dance_ScoreSheet_19.20.pdf.

ZipRecruiter. n.d. "College Dance Team Coach Salary." Accessed August 26, 2019. www.ziprecruiter.com/Salaries/College-Dance-Team-Coach-Salary.

Chapter 11

American Association of Community Theatre. n.d. "The Stage Manager's Job." Accessed September 5, 2019. https://aact.org/stage-manager.

Appalachian State University Department of Theatre and Dance. n.d. "Set Designer." Accessed September 2, 2019. https://theatreanddance.appstate.edu/scenery-and-props/scenic-designer.

Association of Sound Designers. n.d. "What Is a Sound Designer for Theatre?" Accessed August 30, 2019. www.associationofsounddesigners.com/whatis.

Auden, W.H. 1969. "Death's Echo." *Collected Shorter Poems 1927-1957*. London: Faber.

Berklee College of Music. n.d. "Sound Designer (Theater)." Accessed August 30, 2019. www.

berklee.edu/careers/roles/sound-designer-theater.

Carter, Paul. 1994. *The Backstage Handbook: An Illustrated Almanac of Technical Information*. Louisville, KY: Broadway Press.

Culwell-Block, Logan. 2018. "How Much Money Do Broadway Actors Make?" *Playbill*, April 16, 2018. www.playbill.com/article/how-much-money-do-broadway-actors-make.

Daley, Dan. 2004. "Alternative Careers for Sound Engineers." *Sound on Sound*. July 2004. www.soundonsound.com/music-business/alternative-careers-sound-engineers.

Gillette, Michael J. 2012. *Theatrical Design and Production: An Introduction to Scene Design and Construction, Lighting, Sound, Costume, and Makeup*. New York, NY: McGraw-Hill Education.

Indeed. n.d. "Stage Manager Salaries in the United States." Accessed September 5, 2019. www.indeed.com/salaries/Stage-Manager-Salaries.

Payscale. n.d.a. "Average Graphic Design Specialist Salary." Accessed September 9, 2019. www.payscale.com/research/US/Job=Graphic_Design_Specialist/Salary.

Payscale. n.d.b. "Lighting Designer Salary." Accessed August 30, 2019. www.payscale.com/research/US/Job=Lighting_Designer/Salary.

Payscale. n.d.c. "Sound Designer Salary." Accessed September 2, 2019. www.payscale.com/research/US/Job=Sound_Designer/Salary.

Payscale. n.d.d. "Theatrical Scenic Designer." Accessed September 2, 2019. www.payscale.com/research/US/Job=Theatrical_Scenic_Designer/Hourly_Rate.

Princeton Review. n.d. "Stage Technician." Accessed August 29, 2019. www.princetonreview.com/careers/159/stage-technician.

Salary.com. n.d.a, "Production Manager Salaries in the United States." Accessed September 3, 2019. www.salary.com/research/salary/benchmark/production-manager-hourly-wages.

Salary.com. n.d.b. "Stage Manager Salary in the United States." Accessed September 5, 2019. www.salary.com/research/salary/posting/stage-manager-salary.

Salary.com. n.d.c. 2017. "Videographer Salary in the United States." Accessed September 9, 2019. www.salary.com/research/salary/benchmark/videographer-hourly-wages.

Study.com. 2019. "Theatre Production Manager: Duties, Outlook, and Requirements." Accessed September 3, 2019. https://study.com/articles/Theatre_Production_Manager_Duties_Outlook_and_Requirements.html.

Theatrecrafts.com. n.d. "Lighting Design – The Process." Accessed August 30, 2019. www.theatrecrafts.com/pages/home/topics/lighting/lighting-design-process.

U.S. Bureau of Labor Statistics. n.d. "Occupational Outlook Handbook: Film and Video Editors and Camera Operators." Accessed September 9, 2019. www.bls.gov/ooh/media-and-communication/film-and-video-editors-and-camera-operators.htm.

U.S. Bureau of Labor Statistics. 2018. "Occupational Employment Statistics: Photographers." May 2018. www.bls.gov/oes/current/oes274021.htm.

United States Institute for Theatre Technology. n.d. "About USITT." Accessed August 30, 2019. www.usitt.org/about.

University of Oregon Department of Theatre Arts. n.d. "Sound Designer." Accessed August 30, 2019. https://theatre.uoregon.edu/production/sound-designer.

Chapter 12

Climenhaga, Royd. 2009. *Pina Bausch*. Oxfordshire: Routledge.

Dancers Group. 2017. "The Artistic Ensemble at San Quentin Prison." Accessed March 8, 2020. https://dancersgroup.org/2017/05/artistic-ensemble-san-quentin-prison/.

Duke University. n.d. "Dance Program: MFA Curriculum." Accessed September 12, 2019. https://danceprogram.duke.edu/graduate/mfa-curriculum.

Tharp, Twyla. 2013. *The Collaborative Habit: Life Lessons for Working Together*. New York: Simon & Schuster.

University of Rochester. n.d. "Program of Dance and Movement: Undergraduate Program, Interdisciplinary Dance Studies." Accessed September 12, 2019. www.sas.rochester.edu/dan/undergraduate/interdisciplinary.html.

Conclusion

Kingsolver, Barbara. 2003. *High Tide in Tucson: Essays from Now or Never*. New York: Harper Perennial.

Index

About the Author

Courtesy of Ali Duffy.

Ali Duffy, PhD, is a President's Excellence in Teaching professor and associate professor of dance and honors at Texas Tech University. She is the founder and artistic director of Flatlands Dance Theatre, a professional nonprofit dance company in Texas. She holds a PhD from Texas Woman's University, an MFA from University of North Carolina (UNC) Greensboro, a BA from UNC Charlotte, and a professional certificate in online education from the University of Wisconsin at Madison. Dr. Duffy's writing has been published in *Research in Dance Education*, *Journal of Dance Education*, *Dance Education in Practice*, and *Journal of Emerging Dance Scholarship*. Dr. Duffy has been invited for scholarly and artistic presentations and residencies at the University of South Florida, Lindenwood University, Colorado Mesa University, Virginia Tech, University of Detroit, UNC Charlotte, UNC Greensboro, Austin Dance Festival, COCO Dance Festival, and Danca Nova Dance Company. She sits on the National Dance Education Organization's Cultivating Leadership Committee and served on the board of the Dance Critics Association. Prior to her work in academia, Dr. Duffy performed internationally on Holland America cruise ships (RWS Entertainment) and for independent contemporary choreographers on both U.S. coasts. She has also taught and adjudicated for the National Dance Alliance and worked as a dance critic for World Dance Reviews. Her career in dance is endlessly supported by her wonderful family, and she is ever grateful for her brilliant husband, Carlos, and beautiful son, Noah.